DR. RUTH'S GUIDE TO GOOD SEX

DR. RUTH'S GUIDE TO GOOD SEX

DR. RUTH WESTHEIMER

Introduction by Helen Singer Kaplan, M.D., Ph.D.

WARNER BOOKS

A Warner Communications Company

Warner Books, Inc., 666 Fifth Avenue, New York, NY 10103

W A Warner Communications Company

Printed in the United States of America

First printing: April 1983
10 9 8 7 6 5 4 3 2 1

Book design by Jo Bonnell

Library of Congress Cataloging in Publication Data
Westheimer, Ruth K. (Ruth Karola), 1928–
    Dr. Ruth's guide to good sex.

    Bibliography: p.
    Includes index.
    1. Sex instruction.   I. Title.   II. Title: Doctor
Ruth's guide to good sex.
HQ56.W47   1983   613.9′5   82-61878
ISBN 0-446-51260-5

To my husband,
who had to prepare his own dinners
for a long time, and to my daughter,
Miriam, and my son, Joel,
who are the joy of my life.

To my parents and grandparents,
who gave me a set of values,
and instilled in me *joie de vivre*
and a positive outlook on life,
and who did not have the chance
to witness my development.

CONTENTS

Acknowledgments ix
Introduction xiii

1. The Need for Sexual Literacy 1
2. Talking About Sex 12
3. Feeling Good About Sex 29
4. The Importance of Touching 47
5. That First Time 59
6. Touching and Talking 71
7. The Myth of the Fantastic Every-Time Orgasm 83
8. Afterglow 94
9. Perking Up the Sexual Appetite 105
10. Sex and the Elderly 122
11. In Defense of the Quickie 138
12. Beyond the Missionary Position 143
13. Contraception 155
14. Sexually Transmittable Diseases 169

CONTENTS

15. Gay Sex   179
16. Sex and the Disabled   193
17. Relationships   201
18. Parents and Teenagers   222
19. Teenage Concerns   239
20. Think Before Going to Bed   256
21. Am I Normal?   267
22. Would You Marry You?   277
23. Recipe for a
    Sexual Marriage   287
24. Your Sexual I.Q.   297

    Recommended Reading List   323
    Index   325

ACKNOWLEDGMENTS

I wish to thank the many individuals who have had a tremendous influence in my life. If I were to name them all, it would require an additional volume. So this is just a partial list of those who, with their encouragement, friendship, and constructive criticism, have made this endeavor possible:

Jim Anker; Ruth and Howard Bacharach; Martha and Henry Bernstein; Stuart Cattell; Frank Ciarkowski; Lita Cohen; Joy Correge; Georgia Dullea; Adelaide Fitzgerald; Doris Glick; Henry Gordan; David Goslin, Ph.D.; Willy and Else Haudek; Zerline and Rudy Herzberg; Donald Isler; Bernie and Bertie Kahn; Alfred Kaplan; Amy Kassiola and Joel Kassiola, Ph.D.; Else Katz; Dan Kravetz, Evelyn Kravetz, and Nathan Kravetz, Ph.D.; Bill and Marga Kunreuther; Rabbi Robert Lehman; Joanne Lehu; Hope Leichter, Ph.D.; Judy Licht; Lou Lieberman, Ph.D; Philip Nobile; Deborah Offenbacher, Ph.D.; Walter and Edith Oppenheim; Dale Ordes; Dan Rubin, M.D.; Asa Ruskin, M.D.; Francine Ruskin, Ed.D.; Rachel and Max Schramm; Irene and Gerry Shomberg; Fred Silverman; Charles Silverstein, Ph.D.; Walter Simons; Olena Smulka; Matilda and Rudi Steinbach; Hannah Strauss; Eve and Oscar Stroh; Artur and Else Westheimer; Marguerite and Julius Westheimer; Rose and Paul Westheimer; Recha Westheimer. . . .

My friends and colleagues at WYNY-NBC, who gave me the

opportunity to broadcast and taught me all that I know about radio. . . .

Betty Elam, the first person to permit me to talk about sexual literacy on the air. . . .

My producer, Susan Brown, who has made going to work each Sunday night a pleasure to look forward to. . . .

David Chin, my engineer—calm, attentive, alert David, who never misses a cue and who smiles so supportively through the big window. . . .

Jack Forest, M.D., Mildred Hope Witken, Ph.D., and Barbara Hogan, M.D., who shared their knowledge with me and my listeners. . . .

Frank Osborn and Pete Salant, who have guided my radio program with such success. . . .

Roberta Altman, John Behrendt, Dan Daniel, Alex Cimaglia, Diane Dunbar, Michael Eskridge, Dan Griffin, Stan Kaufman, Richard Korman, Al Law, Mitch Lebe, Sid Mark, Marjorie Marks, Janet Mason, Jeff Mazzei, Robert Mounty, Steve O'Brien, Mark Olkowski, Diane Palladino, Richard Penn, Gene Robinson, Don Rollins, Bob Sherman, Elaine Silver, Ellyn Solis, Maurice Turnick, and Daniele Webb. . . .

My colleagues and friends at WNEW-TV Metromedia in New York, who have given me additional opportunity to communicate with an ever-widening audience: Doris Bergman, Rita Coburn, Melissa Keeney, Gerson Nason, Paul Noble, Bob O'Connor, Muriel Reis, Laurie Rich, Norman Ross, Phyllis Seifer, John von Soosten, Kathleen Upton. . . .

My friends at Warner Books, Fredda Isaacson, Howard Kaminsky, Gene Light, Ling Lucas, Debbie Phillips, and Kathy Simmons. . . .

Lee Stevens and Ron Yatter of the William Morris Agency, with my thanks for persuading me to join them. . . .

Rabbi Leonard Kravitz and Rabbi Selig Salkowitz, who freely shared their knowledge with me and co-authored an article with me about sexuality and the Jewish tradition. . . .

Father Finbarr Corr, who taught seminars with me and gave me insight into the beliefs and practices of the Catholic faith. . . .

The German-Jewish Weekly, *Aufbau,* because through them I

found out that I could obtain a scholarship at the New School for Social Research in New York. . . .

The members of the Hebrew Tabernacle Congregation of Washington Heights and all the ''Oscawana friends'' who have given me their support and friendship through the years. . . .

Cantor Frederick C. Herman, who found the recording that provided the theme music for the radio program and suggested the title, *Sexually Speaking*. . . .

Helen Singer Kaplan, M.D., Ph.D., who has given her best in training me as a sex therapist.

Thanks to all my clients, students, viewers, and listeners, who have shared their problems and concerns and who are teaching me constantly how to be a better listener and have given me the satisfaction of offering advice that may be of help. . . .

To Pierre Lehu, for whose wisdom and counsel I am forever grateful. . . .

To Avi Feinglass and Harvey Gardner, who helped me incalculably with my work on this book, heartfelt thanks! . . .

And to Bernard Shir-Cliff, my editor at Warner Books, a true friend who has made doing this book not only possible but a geniune pleasure, more pleasure, more thanks than I can put into words.

INTRODUCTION

Dr. William Masters, the great pioneer of sex therapy, has estimated that fifty percent of all Americans will develop a significant sexual difficulty during their lives. Thus, sexual problems are extremely common, as common as the "common" cold. And yet, the area of sexuality had been so badly neglected by medicine and psychology that, until very recently, there was no adequate understanding of the male or the female sexual response; we were confused about what to teach our children to help them become sexually sound human beings; and the treatment of sexual disorders was so ineffective that innumerable men and women who suffered from what we now know to be simple and curable sexual disorders were doomed to lives of sexual frustration and failure. While science progressed to conquer space and while the rest of medicine entered the nuclear age and conquered one disease after the other, our knowledge about human sexuality had not really advanced beyond what it had been during the Stone Age.

The "sexual revolution" changed all that by liberating our attitudes about sex, removing many of the prejudices that had been an obstacle to progress in this field. At last it became possible for scientists and clinicians to study human sexuality in a scientific manner, just like any other biological process, and finally people began to feel free to admit to and seek help for their sexual difficulties, just as they would for any other health problem.

In the last ten years we have seen a virtual explosion of new scientific information about sex, as well as significant advances in the diagnosis and treatment of sexual disorders. We are now at a point where we understand sexual development and know what it takes to prevent and treat many of the sexual problems that just a few years ago were believed to be beyond help. But these developments are very new, and programs in sexuality are just now being included in the training of physicians and mental-health professionals. It will be many years before the new information is widely available. It is paradoxical that in the midst of the mass of sexually explicit material with which we are assaulted every day, a person with a real problem or question about sex may be hard put to find objective and trustworthy answers.

Dr. Ruth Westheimer has a wonderful talent for translating the new technical and scientific information about sex into practical advice. From her vastly popular radio show, *Sexually Speaking*, she has selected a variety of the typical questions and problems about sex that trouble and puzzle men and women of all ages and stations in life, and to these she gives sound and humane advice.

Ruth's brand of sex education is not dry or boring. Free of jargon, she uses humor and warmth to dispense her practical solutions. She doesn't mince words. She doesn't waste time. She is down-to-earth. She gets to the bottom line while always conveying the message "Sex is a natural human function—enjoy! (but don't hurt anyone and don't get hurt yourself)."

Some people may feel that the kind of explicit sex information contained in this book may create more mischief than good by encouraging immorality and promiscuity and by diminishing the private and intimate aspect of love and sex. While I appreciate these concerns, my own experience has been to the contrary. I have seen only harm come from ignorance: pregnant teenagers, broken marriages, and serious and unnecessary sexual problems are the fruits of misinformation and lack of information about sex. And I have seen great benefits from providing people with the straight, sound, sensible, advice that is contained in the loving, human, funny, encouraging, and wise pages of this book.

Helen Singer Kaplan, M.D., Ph.D.;
Director, The Human Sexuality Teaching Program,
The New York Hospital–Cornell Medical Center

Refraining from licit pleasures
does not make you a saint;
rather, a sinner.

—Based on Rabbinical Explanation
of Numbers 6–11,
Found in the Talmud,
Taanith 11-A

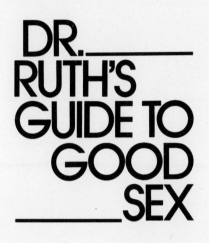

DR.
RUTH'S
GUIDE TO
GOOD
SEX

1
THE NEED
FOR SEXUAL
LITERACY

"Hello, this is Dr. Ruth Westheimer. You're on the air."

"Dr. Ruth, I think you're the greatest, and I hope you can help me with my problem."

"Well, I'll try."

"Okay. It started about a year ago, when I was having some problems with my sexual encounters—you know, in the sack. So I went out and bought some pornographic magazines and looked at them just before and during intercourse. And then my wife started buying these magazines.

"Well, we have an eight-millimeter film projector, and she bought some porno films that she now shows while we're in bed having sex. She turns on the projector and watches movies while we're going through our routine."

"Do you have orgasms?"

"Oh, yeah."

"And she has good orgasms?"

"Yeah."

"Nothing to worry about, then. You've found a way that's right for the two of you. And you both enjoy it. So everything is fine. Bye-bye."

*   *   *

I am the hostess of *Sexually Speaking,* a call-in sex education radio show on WYNY-FM in New York City. Every Sunday at 10:00 P.M. New Yorkers tune in to hear each other's problems—to talk about and listen to the ins and outs of sexual functioning. "Does a normal penis curve?" "Is it okay to use a dildo?" "Am I masturbating too much?"—questions from the curious of every age. The phone lines are constantly busy. Everyone wants to talk about sex.

Sexually Speaking is part of the long-overdue sexual information explosion in this country. Ten years ago Archie Bunker couldn't say "impotent" on TV. Today we can and do, and we are gradually learning to revel in a more mature social acceptance of our sexuality. Communication has become a top priority in this technical, impersonal age of answering machines and computerized supermarkets; yet we are only now feeling the need to share sexuality.

But sharing comes slowly. I am appalled by the media's inattention to explicit sexuality. The airwaves are rife with specialty programs on cars, home repair, personal finance. But sex, an activity that concerns us all so personally, that brings both poetry and pain to our lives, seems too controversial for regular broadcast. What a shame!

It is a shame because people are ready to talk openly about sex. And if more information channels were available, certain problems could be far better treated. For example, unwanted teenage pregnancies now affect hundreds of thousands of girls every year. The epidemic of venereal disease is another tragedy stemming partly from lack of information.

I am probably the first therapist to go on the air with a sex discussion program. I talk about many things, including orgasm, contraception, pregnancy, and impotence. This is extensive sex education. If it's also entertaining, great.

The demand for this kind of information is high. After all, not everybody has the luxury of taking a human sexuality class or paying a sex therapist to answer his or her questions. Often there is no one to consult for advice or understanding, and even if there is a sympathetic ear close by, the subject of sex is so taboo that embarrassment or ignorance may inhibit productive conversation. There

2

are so many moral factors associated with sex that a reliable objective source is all too rare.

Hence the popularity of sex talk on the radio. Anonymity is very conducive to frankness. Even if people have trouble talking about sexual matters, they don't know me, and I'm not here to judge them. They phone in, they talk, I answer, and that's it. And I think people are willing to express their most intimate sexual fears and foibles to me because I don't come across as a voyeur. I am a concerned and authoritative adviser.

I believe in educating people to be sexual gourmets. This is a very simple idea. In everyday life we talk a lot about food and diets. We exchange recipes and introduce one another to different cuisines and culinary techniques. We are happy to share the discoveries we have made in the kitchen. So why shouldn't we feel just as comfortable exchanging recipes for better sexual functioning? Why keep the excitement of exploration to ourselves?

We are the only animals to share our experiences. If we share memories of a wonderful hike or beautiful ski trip, then why not share ideas that might enrich other people's sex lives, too?

The popularity of sex in the mass media, as opposed to sex information, originates in mystery. So I want to make it clear that sex should stay a subject that merits some kind of reverence. But it is still crucially important to be sexually knowledgeable and sexually communicative. Through that knowledge and communication comes greater sexual contentment.

I am constantly surprised by how widespread ignorance is. Misinformation is not restricted to the lower classes or the poorly educated. A college-educated person is as likely as a high school graduate to ask me if a vinegar douche is an effective contraceptive. (It is not.) It seems that everybody needs a beginner's course, or at least a refresher class, in sex education.

I do get a lot of basic questions, such as "Which contraceptive should I use?" or "Where can I find a partner?" But I also get questions that need relatively extensive advice: "I have been married for four years and have never had an orgasm." "I ejaculate as soon as I engage in sexual intercourse." "We do engage in sex, but we don't talk about it, so I can't tell him what pleases me, and he can't tell me what pleases him."

Younger people ask a lot of questions about relationships. For example: "Dr. Ruth, I am a virgin, and my boyfriend doesn't want to wait until we get married. What should I do?" It is hard to answer such questions. My job is to impart facts and common sense. In many cases the callers merely want to hear reinforcement from me. People who are not sexually active like to hear that it is all right to be sexually inactive. Older people often need to hear that it is not wrong to masturbate. The disabled simply need to hear that it's permissible to be sexual.

People who listen to my show come to realize that the grass is not greener on other peoples' lawns—everyone has problems. This relaxes people, making them more comfortable about their own sexual situations.

In addition to the *Sexually Speaking* calls, I receive hundreds of letters, some of them five or six pages long. Once in a while I read them over the air. Most of the letters deal with relationships, and center on issues that people have been carrying around in their psyches for many years and have never dared to pursue.

Here's an example of a typical letter and my response.

Dear Dr. Westheimer:

I have listened to your show for the last few months and I enjoy it very much. I would be embarrassed to call you over the air with my problem, and that's why I'm writing to you. My husband and myself (married for nineteen years) have a fairly good sex life, except that it is boring, despite the fact that I have no problem reaching an orgasm whenever I want to. We always do it the same way. Can you help?

Sincerely,
"Bored"

Dear "Bored":

Thank you for writing to me. Here are some suggestions that you could try, to add some sexual enrichment to your "boring" sex life.

1. Vary the time of intercourse.

2. Vary the place. Do it in the kitchen sometimes, or in the living room. In front of a fireplace. At a motel. (It doesn't have to be expensive.) Under the stars.

3. Try some wine.

4. Fantasize.

5. Experiment with different positions.

6. Buy The Joy of Sex *by Dr. Alex Comfort.*

7. Continue with the list on your own.

Please let me know how you are doing.

Best wishes,

Dr. Ruth

A recipe. When I read a letter of this sort over the air, the entire audience is exposed to the infinite varieties of sex.

One Sunday night at WYNY I took a call that went like this. I opened one of the waiting lines and said, "Hello, you're on the air."

"Uh, hi," a man said. "My girl friend and I just broke up over something stupid. If she eats a crunchy peanut butter sandwich, she gets very horny. But there are certain things I don't think are right. If I go to bed with someone, I don't want to go to bed with her and peanut butter."

"Look, I understand," I said. "If both people would like to go to bed with peanut butter, I would say that if you use contraceptives, that's all right. The moment only one person likes peanut butter and the other doesn't, then you have to take a stand."

In the infinite varieties of sex there are things you will want to do and things you won't. Every human being has boundaries when it comes to sex, and mapping those boundaries with an individual human being can be very complicated. There are things you want to do very much, things you will do to please the other person, and things that—*yech!* Don't be pressured into doing things you really don't want to do. It may only be something you don't want to do right now. In six months or a year you may feel very differently. But don't be pressured. In fact, don't be pressured into having sex at all if you don't want to—not to be in with your crowd, not to show someone that you really do love him or her. You have a right to your boundaries. Stick up for them.

5

What you might not want to do may only involve peanut butter, but if you feel strongly about it, stick up for your individual rights.

If it happens that you do want peanut butter in bed while you're having sex and your partner doesn't, in the long run the thing to do may be to find another partner. There are millions of people out there who won't mind peanut butter at all, may like it a lot, or may even get to like it as much as you do.

People ask me "How did you get to be a sex therapist?" I'll say this: When I was a little girl, I never dreamed of being on the radio and answering people's Sunday night questions about premature ejaculation or failure to orgasm; that I would be the lady with the German accent who surprises people who turn the dial to WYNY from ten to eleven on Sunday night, who talks about penises and vaginas and oral and anal sex and things like that. Sometimes people are shocked by my openness and by my taking such shocking questions in stride. Then I might shock them also by not treating the subject of sex as the most solemn business in life. A man said his girl friend couldn't get enough sex, was wearing him out. "Go to the movies instead," I told him. It only makes sense. You don't have to go crazy to have a sex life.

I am very, very lucky because I love the work I do, and you can't get much luckier than to like your work—really like it. But it was a wandering road that got me here.

I was born into an Orthodox Jewish family, which was a good thing, because now I understand when clients say they can't do this thing or that thing because of their religious backgrounds. An Orthodox Jew, or a devout Catholic, or a strict Baptist, or anybody like that has my respect.

I don't believe that the first thing for them to do is to get rid of religious restrictions.

My Orthodox family lived in Germany. In 1939, just before the outbreak of World War II, they sent me to a children's home in Switzerland, where I would be safe, even if they weren't. After a while my parents disappeared and so did all the other children's parents, and the home turned into an orphanage. I never found out what happened to my parents, but I suppose they died in a concentration camp, like so many other people. When I was sixteen, I went to Israel and worked in a kibbutz. Then I went to the Teachers' Seminary in Jerusalem and learned to be a kindergarten teacher. In 1951 I got a chance to go to Europe to be the director of a kindergarten in Paris. At the same time I studied psychology at the Sorbonne. Then I came to New York and studied sociology at the New School for Social Research. After obtaining my master's degree from The New School, I earned a doctorate from Columbia University's Teachers College in the interdisciplinary study of the family.

From 1967 to 1970 I worked as a project director for Planned Parenthood for three years. Then I taught students at the City University of New York how to teach sex education. The students were future teachers, and I realized they were asking questions that I couldn't answer. I looked around for further training and was accepted at New York Hospital–Cornell Medical Center in the training program headed by Dr. Helen Singer Kaplan, and after two years I was certified as a sex therapist. In my private practice I do work as a psychotherapist, in addition to seeing clients as a sex therapist—and that's the same as a psychosexual therapist, just in case the term comes up.

I also have taught at Teachers College, Columbia University, for a couple of years and at Adelphi University, Mercy College, and Marymount College. Now I am a staff member at New York Hospital in their human sexuality program. I also am a consultant at Bellevue Hospital in the Department of Geriatrics, and I'm invited to lecture at all sorts of places—professional organizations, social gatherings—and, recently, I gave a lecture at Princeton, where my son is a student. Now I'm teaching a course in family life at the United States Military Academy at West Point.

I was invited to speak at a lunch for leaders in the broadcasting industry. By then I didn't mind public speaking. Since I had talked to Orthodox Jewish groups and Catholic groups, I could talk to these broadcasters—sex education is sex education. Then it hit me: I would be talking to the top broadcasting people in the country. I had been mulling over what I would like to tell these people for years! I believe in sex education, in promoting sexual literacy in an age of unprecedented sexual freedom and almost total sexual ignorance. So I told them what I had on my mind. There are programs devoted to growing flowers, cooking quiche and duck à l'orange, interior

7

decorating, upholstery, cabinetmaking, and stamp collecting. Where was there any explicit instruction on *everybody's* hobby, sex?

There *was* sex on the air. The airwaves were charged with it. It was promoted in songs, serials, and commercials for everything from cars and soap to lawn care and sewer-line-clearing services. Children, teenagers, even grandparents, were being bombarded with erotic urgings. But nowhere was there any sensible, reliable information on the air about real-life sex, in an era when unwanted pregnancies and venereal disease and broken homes were all stemming from ignorance about this central fact of life!

I urged the top broadcasting people as a matter of conscience and good sense to get some sex information on the air.

I wasn't worried about my accent. I don't talk like John Gielgud or Laurence Olivier, but I know I can make people understand what I mean. All I cared about was getting my point across to those powerful people. After that, it was up to them.

A few days later a radio executive called me up and wondered if I might be willing to tape a series of fifteen-minute programs to be a filler late at night for taxi drivers, night-shift people, and insomniacs. I jumped at the chance. What they paid me, better not ask. It was very little. That wasn't the point.

Every week I went downtown and taped fifteen minutes. It would have been sensible to tape sixty or ninety minutes at a time, but I preferred to do just fifteen minutes at a time because I wanted each fifteen minutes to be as up-to-the-minute and lively as I could make it.

The tapes were played on WYNY from 12:30 to 12:45 A.M. After a year and a half, I said I wanted to do a live show, and they gave me the 10:00 P.M. slot on Sunday night, answering phone calls from people who were worrying about their sex lives.

It was wonderful from the beginning. Live radio broadcasting is full of the unexpected—that's the charm of it. On these live phone-in shows they have a way of handling nasty callers, called the dump button. There is a six-second lag that lets you get rid of somebody who wants to be disgusting, to say something to bring down the tone of the program just to be nasty. I have never had to use the dump button, although I suppose I'll have to use it at some point.

Sometimes I deal with a question briefly and say "Bye-bye" before the caller expects it, but I have never had to completely cut someone off.

The people at WYNY tell me the show gets three to four thousand calls an hour. I can answer twenty to twenty-five calls in an hour, so hundreds of callers have to be disappointed, for which I am sorry. But it shows how people want to talk about sex and how they want answers to their questions about sex. The callers are very valuable to the show; they make it. All the listeners get their big charge from the fact that the callers are real people, asking sincere questions. The callers give the show its reality; they give it the charm and excitement, these voices in the night, first names only, calling in from the tri-state area around New York City. "Hello, this is Carol from New Rochelle. I love your show, and everyone in New Rochelle thinks you're the greatest." Ridiculous! There is no city anywhere where everybody likes any particular thing. And especially not anything about sex. But it is a ritual, calling in and praising the show and being part of the great unseen Sunday night sexual discussion group, being a supporter. Everyone is very nice and polite, then come the questions about the penis or the sister-in-law or the vagina or the boyfriend's best male friend who seems to be gay. They say "Everybody in Oradell loves your show," and I say "Thank you! I love to hear that!"

People have asked me: Which do I like better, seeing my idea of a sexual information show going so well, or suddenly being a 10:00 P.M. radio star, a media personality? Good question, I like that question, because I can't answer it! All I care to say at this time is that I love having sex education promoted and getting this attention, and I love suddenly being in show biz.

After I went on David Letterman's show and Johnny Carson's show, people really saw how little I am, and that makes it easier to recognize me. They think, the voice and the tiny woman together, it must be Westheimer.

I must say that I have been a small person for some time, but when I saw tapes or replays of those shows, I was startled. Such a tiny woman coming out of the curtain to shake hands with Johnny Carson or David Letterman! They are tall, but I make them look taller!

Yes, I love the whole thing and I keep thinking, Well, that's it—the fun is over now, back to being Dr. Westheimer instead of Dr. Ruth. After the live show had been on two months, I was sure I would see interest in it dying down. After all, there are only so many questions—or problems, as the callers call them—and only so many answers. But it keeps growing because there is a real need for it. People love to hear other people's sex problems. People want a place they can call up to ask questions without committing themselves to a clinic or a sex therapist; without taking the first big step into that world.

I hope this kind of reality—real-life sexual dilemmas and real up-to-date information—this kind of helpful entertainment, has a real foothold in the media now. And my conscience forces me to say, even if it hurts a little, I hope more programs like *Sexually Speaking* will come along. What am I saying? But I mean it.

A last word about my radio show, *Sexually Speaking,* and about this book. Neither pretends to be all the sexual education a person can use—but I do think they both are very helpful and educational for anybody. I know the radio show has been an education for me! Even after years of listening to people in my office and at clinics. Many people find the radio show entertaining, and there is a lot of good-natured laughter to be had from it. Well, I believe education should be entertaining, and I am glad to add to the merriment of life. I know that when people tell me they love my accent, they mean that it amuses them and puts them in good humor, which is a good way to approach sex. My accent is not an affectation. Like millions of refugees and immigrants and adventurers, I speak several languages pretty well, and every one with an accent. But I try to make myself understood when I give advice about sex.

This I want to make clear: A healthy attitude to one's own individual sex life is a happy, sensible, and imaginative attitude, free from peer pressure and free from panic and despair. That is what I want to promote. You should like yourself, the special way you are and that God made you—and remember that while you are alive you are a sexual being with sexual thoughts and feelings.

In the past many well-meaning people have tried to promote a better sexual attitude by making sex dull. Sex is not dirty. Sex is not a sin. Many people have complained that this is taking all the fun out of sex. Well, we are getting away from that boring approach to sex education. I hope so, anyway.

But don't get the idea that I never discourage people from acting recklessly. I have a lot of "don'ts"—basically, I am an overprotective mother. Don't forget it.

I tell people not to drink and then drive. Not to have sex without contraception, unless they want babies and are ready for them. Not to make love to their sisters-in-law. Not to "let it all hang out"—*that* can land you in the police station, or at least make you wish you hadn't! Not to do anything unwillingly, under pressure from anyone; it is your body and your life—and that goes for male virgins as well as female ones, and for anyone who "doesn't like" some kind of sexual activity. Not to offend your family or religion if you can reasonably avoid it—and often you can.

Most of all I tell people "do." Whether you are a grandparent, a young heterosexual single person, gay, or legally married, whatever, do your own thing—but *do* learn all you can about sex because it is part of your life, a part that can make you miserable or make you very, very gloriously happy! And ignorance about sex leads no one into the land of heart's content.

2
TALKING
ABOUT SEX

What fun! Another whole hour of talking about sex on the air. That's what I have come for, to Midtown Manhattan, to the WYNY studio in the NBC Building, 30 Rockefeller Plaza, all the way from Washington Heights.

It is almost 10:00 P.M. on a Sunday night, and I am seated at the table with a microphone in front of me, full of a pleasant excitement. There are ten little lights on the console in front of me, and they are all lit! Callers waiting to talk to me on the radio, to tell me their problems, each one a little story, a human story. What a wonderful feeling of being in touch with real people and their real stories, all around me in the night, stretching for miles around New York City, New Jersey, Long Island, Connecticut, Westchester, and Rockland County—and the thousands of people listening in to the stories people tell me and to me talking to them.

There are the cab drivers with their radios on, high school students listening in groups at friends' houses, college students gathered in dormitories, husbands and wives, all sorts of people listening to these stories of human lives and that great force in life, that universal thread running through every life. Unseen listeners, listening to voices in the night talking about these worrying and fascinating dramas they are caught up in.

What a variety of human sexual experiences out there, and

coming to me and to all the listeners! What a vast interest in talking about sex, hearing talk about it, in this cozy way on a Sunday evening.

I want you to have a sampling of these Sunday night phone calls, each one unique, and special . . . individual, who knows? Maybe having something meaningful for a friend of yours. Or maybe even for you.

So here I am, seated in front of my mike, ready to be Dr. Ruth. From the control room, with its big soundproof glass front, I am told that I look like a creature from *Alice in Wonderland*. All head. I am a child-size woman, and the console cuts me off from the neck down. I have not seen this remarkable sight, but my friend Max says that's what I look like. When I start talking to all those unseen listeners, Max says, it is just a woman's head, "friendly, intent, and animated."

But I don't see that. I can see the people in the control room: David Chin, the engineer; and next to him producer Susan Brown, her pretty brown-haired head bent as she talks to the people on the lines, making notes of the questions they want to ask. She paces the calls, so we don't get several questions in a row about erectile difficulties or choosing the right contraceptive.

I hear the WYNY theme in my headset! The announcer is saying "Next on WYNY is *Sexually Speaking*. This program is a forum for the mature discussion of human sexuality. It deals with discussions of explicit sexual conduct and terminology, which may not be suitable for all listeners." I repeat that warning several times through the sixty minutes of my show.

Then comes my theme, "La Rocha el Fuso," a lovely piece of music found by my cantor friend, Fred Herman.*

I love it. There is a sunny spring day in it, warm and faunlike. It ends and I begin.

"Good evening. What a glorious spring day! It is really fun to talk about sex after a day of seeing trees in bloom. And guess what? I just saw Steve O'Brien on roller skates! Now I know it's spring.

"This is Dr. Ruth Westheimer. We are here on *Sexually*

---

*#1454 *The Mediaeval Sound,* Musical Heritage Society, New Jersey.

Speaking, ninety-seven WYNY-FM radio. I do have a few good friends in the studio listening to me. And I'm going to take your first question."

A light goes on. I pick up the phone.

"Hello, you're on the air."

"Hi. I'm Pete. I'm from Yonkers, just up the river from you."

"Yes."

"My wife's name is Billie. And it's like this. I think she's having an affair."

"Hmmm."

"And it's with our neighbor, Barbie. This Barbie, she's a known lesbian."

"Yes?"

"And they're friends, but they've been close lately, and like, when I have sex with my wife, it's not the same."

"Aha. Okay. I think that if you . . . She doesn't respond to you the same way?"

"That's right. It's like this. Well, when I go to bed with my wife, there's like a little thing that we do. She gets stimulated when we're in bed, and I make noises, like I go 'Hmpp-*nnnnn!*' "

"All right, whatever."

"She gets turned on. I've done this. She's not responding."

"Okay. My advice to you is to have a talk with her. Because if you really suspect, and it's not just a suspicion, but that she really has changed her whole attitude with you, then I would really have an open talk. And then before you make any decisions about separating or not separating, I would suggest that the two of you go and talk to a counselor. Or talk to somebody in the mental health field and put the cards on the table and see what could be done. Sometimes an affair like this—and listen to me carefully, Pete—sometimes an affair like that is just a passing matter. If that's the case, then you two can salvage the marriage. Sometimes it's not. And I would say that by your question, I would say that you are better off knowing the truth. You see, sometimes I say to people, 'You know, forget about it and go on living and see what life brings.' But if you are so worried and concerned about it, I would talk to her."

14

"Okay. One other thing before I go. Is something of this nature, homosexuality, is that normal?"

"You see, normalcy is difficult to define. What I do hear very clearly is, if she does have an affair with another woman, that you would be very upset. And that's what a marriage counselor or somebody who knows about these things really has to discuss with you. Don't let that slide. Okay? Thank you so much for calling."

"I'll do it tomorrow. Thank you very much. God bless you."

"Thank you. Bye-bye."

"You are on the air."

"Hello. I have a problem. About two months ago I was raped, and I've gotten over it, basically—I can deal with myself. But it's my boyfriend. He feels I shouldn't be able to get over it that well and I should be more upset about it. I'd like to know what to do."

"Did you tell him?"

· "I told him that I had to put that behind in my life and just forget about it."

"Right. Let me ask you. Did you talk to somebody besides the boyfriend?"

"My parents brought me to, like, a therapist. I just went a few times, and he didn't say anything that I really didn't know."

"You didn't get pregnant?"

"No."

"Good. But you did discuss it with a therapist."

"Yeah."

"Then what I would say is maybe let some time pass. Maybe your boyfriend . . . Do tell him that it hurts you when he mentions it and that this was a terrible experience for you, that your parents were helpful. Your parents brought you to a therapist. That's exactly what I would do if this were to happen to my daughter. And tell your boyfriend to absolutely stop talking about it. Because constantly bringing it up is not going to make it any better for you. It happened, and let's hope that it will never happen to you again. But tell him to stop, and tell him if he keeps on talking about it, that maybe something bothers him, and maybe . . . You know what you could suggest—that he go and talk to that same therapist that you talked to. Is there a possibility like that?"

15

"Maybe."

"That's what I would do. I would tell him, 'Look, there's something that really bothers you very badly. I know you love me. I know you care for me. I do not want to talk about it anymore. But I would like you very much to go and talk to that same therapist that I talked to' . . . Will you let me know?''

"Uh-huh."

"Okay. Good luck."

"Thanks a lot."

"Thank you for calling."

"You are on the air."

"Hello, Dr. Ruth. I'm from The Bronx and I have a problem. I've been with a woman for about six years—we're not married but we live together. We were both lying down in the bed, and I masturbated. We were both awake. She had her back to me, and I was lying down and I masturbated, and she got upset. So because of that I more or less stopped masturbating when she's around. Do you feel that there's a problem? Should she have gotten upset?''

"Usually, when the two of you are together, is your sexual relationship good?''

"It hasn't been as of late."

"Are you less sexually attracted to her than you used to be?''

"I guess I would have to say yes."

"Because what could very well be is that she felt that—she sensed that. And then by your masturbating with her right next to you, that she felt very rejected. And that she felt that already, somehow sensed that you are less interested in her, and maybe she's worried that you are leaving her. So what I would do is for the two of you, since you have been living together for six years, I would go and see some counselor. It doesn't matter, married or not married— you've been living together. Go and see some counselor before you just split. Because it's not just because of your masturbating. She must sense something about that relationship being less intense or you being less interested. And I would go with her to see somebody. All right?''

"Thank you."

"You're very welcome."

"I love your show."

"Thank you for calling."

"You are on the air."

"Hello, Dr. Ruth. My name is Ellie. I'm twenty-one years old and I've been having sex since I was fourteen. My problem is now I'm starting to have sex on a more regular type of basis ever since then. It was a little harder in the beginning, but now it seems to be getting easier, and I think that's what the problem is. My big question is, How long is the ideal time to wait before having sex with somebody?"

"You mean, once you meet somebody new?"

"Once you meet somebody. You see, the thing is, I met several people that I've been interested in. But right now I'm interested in someone who I really like a lot, and we've been dating for about two months now. And I really don't want to mess this one up."

"All right. I'll tell you what. By your question it seems to me that you ought to wait awhile. Form first the relationship. See what develops. See if that is really the relationship that you want to keep for a while, and wait awhile until this relationship is a little bit cemented. Okay?"

"The thing is, I remember how hard it was for me to get into it—but now the thing is, I don't remember how to say no."

"That you can practice in front of a mirror. Just to say 'I want to see how our relationship is going to develop.' In the meantime, just hug and kiss. Do you feel good when he kisses you?"

"Oh, yeah."

"Great! Do that for a while and then make sure if you do start a sexual relationship that you use contraception. Right?"

"Okay."

"Thanks for calling."

"Thank you."

It's easier to have good sex with practice—and that goes for saying no, too!

I believe in rehearsals. When you have something hard to say to people, think out your line and rehearse it—in front of a mirror. Get used to saying it until it's as easy as "Three tokens, please."

17

This is especially good for inexperienced people. A young person of any sex, approached by an older person of any sex, is sometimes too *embarrassed* to say no.

"You are on the air."

"Hello, Dr. Ruth. I have two problems. The first one is, well, I'm engaged to my girl friend and I love her very much. About three months ago I went over her house, and no one was home, and I had sex with her younger sister. Now what happened after that, I felt bad and everything, but since then her sister uses that against me and has threatened me, to make me be with her."

"Which means the younger sister says that unless you continue that relationship she's going to tell your fiancée?"

"Yes."

"Oh, dear. You do have a problem. Yes. And you cannot live with a threat like that."

"What do I do?"

"You have to take that younger sister aside and you have to say, 'Either you stop it—whatever happened happened. I do love your sister—or I'm going to tell your sister.' I mean, don't tell her if you don't have to. But if the younger sister continues to . . . Let me ask you something. Is she trying to break up the relationship between you and her sister?"

"I don't think so."

"How old is she, the younger sister?"

"Eighteen."

"I would really have a very serious talk with her, but a very firm one. Don't show any fear, because if you show fear about her telling her sister, that's showing some kind of weakness, and she's going to continue like that. Doesn't she have a boyfriend of her own?"

"Yeah."

"She does? Aha! Did you ever threaten her that if she doesn't stop it, then you will tell him?"

"No, he's a little bigger than me."

"But you know what?"

"What?"

"I would threaten her with that. . . . Look, despite the fact that the guy is bigger, I would threaten to tell him. Don't tell him, just threaten.''

"Okay. My second problem . . . it's not really a bad one, but I'm very truthful with my fiancée and—''

"Except for her sister?''

"My ex-girl friend calls me sometimes, and my fiancée gets jealous, and I have to go and get my hair cut by her. . . .''

"By the ex-girl friend?''

"By my ex-girl friend.''

"I understand. If I were your girl friend, I also wouldn't want you to go back to the ex-girl friend. I would want you to choose another barber. I think you will have to do some shopping around, and you will get another barber. All right?''

"Thank you.''

"Good luck to you. Bye-bye.''

I hope he found someone to cut his hair right.

"You are on the air.''

"Hello, Dr. Ruth. I have a little bit of a problem that I think some people might envy. My husband and I have an excellent sex life, and I get orgasms from him that are so good that my movements become so uncontrolled that I end up pushing him out no matter what position we try.''

"Hmmm . . . You mean when he is in the male superior position or also when you are in the female superior position.''

"Right. Even when he enters from behind me.''

"Even from behind. At that time, when you have your orgasm, has he ejaculated already?''

"I don't know. I'm in total oblivion. I don't really know whether he has or not.''

"Okay. I'll tell you something. Can you sometimes hold your body movement, not move so hard?''

"No.''

"Even if he holds you very tight?''

"Even if he holds me tightly.''

"Okay. I would suggest, since you do have good sex, and you do have orgasms, and if you have tried . . . have you tried all of the positions in the book, for example, *The Joy of Sex*?''

"We don't have the book."

"Try that book. That's what I would try first. Try the book, because there might be some positions in there that you haven't tried. If that doesn't work, what I would do is: I would make an appointment at a human sexuality clinic for one session. Sometimes one session with a therapist—if you need some names, send me a letter—sometimes one session clarifies certain things. Thank you so much for calling."

"Okay. Thank you."

"Bye-bye."

"You are on the air."

"Hello, Dr. Ruth. My name is Bob. I have this problem. I'm going away this weekend, supposedly going camping with my friend Richie. What it is, is he is married and he's bringing his girl friend."

"Oh, dear."

"I have to be in the same tent. I don't know whether to say anything—I really don't want to get involved. I'm debating whether I should go or not, but he's going to think that I'm not going because of that reason."

"Shall I tell you the truth?"

"Go ahead."

"*Absolutely* do not go with him. First of all, what is in it for you, to be in the same tent, to be out in the gorgeous nature, and to hear him make love to his girl friend?"

"I don't think he'd do that, because they have separate sleeping bags, but still it's the idea. . . ."

"I understand that, but I honestly would not go along, because you are really being used as a cover. Do you understand? You are being used to cover up his having an affair."

"Let me ask you this: If I bring another friend, if another guy would come along, would it be any better? Then we could be in another tent. What do you think of that idea?"

"I would say that might be a little bit better, but I'll tell you something. If I were you, why can't you go camping with your other friend, and tell your best friend that until he has sorted out his personal affairs, tell him openly that you feel uncomfortable. Don't tell him he is doing right or wrong.''

"Thank you very much.''

"Thank you so much for calling.''

"You are on the air.''

"Hello, Dr. Ruth. I have a problem with my girl friend. It seems like wherever we go she's always putting her hands all over me—not like holding hands or anything like that.''

"On your penis?''

"Last night we went to a play, and she put her hand onto my leg and slowly worked it up to my crotch.''

"In the middle of the play?''

"Yeah.''

"You know what you do?''

"What?''

"You tell her, 'Cut it out!' ''

"I said that, and she told me that I'm a prude or—''

"Never mind a prude. You tell her that Dr. Westheimer said, despite the fact that I speak so openly and sexually explicit, and despite the fact that you do love her, tell her that I said that this is not proper behavior. Because, after all, you don't want to sit in the theater with a full erection. And you don't want to constantly, when you are with her, worry about where she's going to put her hands. You know what you do, tell her that it just makes you nervous, because you never know where she puts her hand next. . . . I have another idea. You start to hold both of her hands in your two hands. Do you understand? Wherever you go, for the next couple of weeks, you take both of her hands and you hold them tight.''

"She does it while I'm driving, too.''

"While you're *driving*?''

"When I have to pull up to a toll booth, then that's what they're looking at.''

"That's really dumb, because you could have an accident. Nobody can really drive with a full erection. I mean, what is she trying to prove—that you can have an erection in the theater and in the car and at the toll booth?''

"You see, we both live with our parents."

"And you don't have a place where you can be together?"

"Yeah."

"Okay. You have a car. Fine. Let me give you an idea. You make a contract with her that every week when you go out, part of the time—either before or after the theater—the two of you will go to a lovers' lane."

"The whole thing is that I kind of like it."

"I know that. But that's okay. For you to like it is all right, but still, it should be done in the appropriate place. You don't want to get arrested for exposure, and then I have to come to the police station to bail you out!"

"That's very nice of you!"

"All right. Thank you so much for calling. I do hope your girl friend is listening in. Bye-bye."

"You are on the air."

"Hello, Dr. Westheimer. . . . This is my problem. I'm a big guy. I'm pretty macho, you'd say, and I don't have any trouble with the chicks or anything."

"Chicks is women?"

"Yeah. With the girls. They're all attracted to me."

"I just wanted to know if chicks is chickens or women."

"Ha ha. All good-looking girls are attracted to me, but the problem is that I just can't . . . I just have a problem relating to them once I get somewhat involved. I've been seeing a psychiatrist, and I've become more aroused by my psychiatrist than I ever have with any girl before."

"The psychiatrist is a man?"

"No, the psychiatrist is a woman, an older woman."

"An older woman. Okay. So the problem is that you . . . How old are you?"

"Twenty."

"Twenty. Did you ever have a sexual relationship with a woman?"

"No, I never did."

"Okay. Relax. You're only twenty. So you do get aroused sexually by thinking about your psychiatrist?"

"Well, I sit there during the sessions and I become uncontrollably aroused."

"Did you discuss it with the psychiatrist?"

" I couldn't. I'd be too embarrassed."

"You'd be too embarrassed. Okay. Does she see that you have an erection, or can you hide it?"

"I try to hide it."

"All right. What I would say is, I think you probably would have to discuss it with the psychiatrist. You know what I would do. Write the psychiatrist a letter, because this way it won't be so embarrassing. Sit down and write her a letter that you do want to tell her something that is difficult for you to discuss, and you write it out."

"Could I go back and see her again?"

"Of course, why not?"

"I mean, if she knows I'm attracted to her, could she talk to me?"

"Of course she could talk to you. She could even be very flattered that a tall, good-looking guy like you of twenty years old is attracted to her."

"Okay. Well, what do I do if she doesn't want to fool around with me?"

"Of course she's not going to fool around with you! You just write her a letter so that you and she can discuss it. She is *not* going to fool around with you. No therapist—no sex therapist, no counselor, no psychiatrist—ever, ever has anything to do sexually with a client. Never, absolutely never. What's in your fantasy is something else. But do write to her and then let me know what happens. Okay?"

"Thank you very much, Dr. Ruth Westheimer."

"You are welcome. Good luck to you."

"Thank you."

"You are on the air."

"Hello, Dr. Ruth. I have a problem. I'm about twenty-five. I've been going out with someone for over a year, and since then we've broken up, but I feel I've done her a lot of wrong. I misled her. I never really loved her. She loved me. Toward the end of the relationship we did *not* have sexual intercourse, but we both did gratify each other in physical ways. Now, being a deeply religious person, I feel it affects me in future relationships. Do you know what I mean?''

"Yes. What will affect you in future relationships is that you misled her? Or that you mutually gratified each other?''

"That we mutually gratified each other. It's very important for me to marry a virgin, and even though I am a virgin I feel that I'm not one hundred percent like that.''

"Yes, I understand that very well. Which religion do you belong to?''

"I'm a Jew.''

"Okay. If I were you, what I would do, and I understand very well what you are saying. I understand both counts. And in terms of misleading and in terms of sexually gratifying, I would suggest that maybe you do talk to a rabbi. A rabbi that you feel comfortable with.''

"Let me ask you. I'm going to find it very difficult—I always do—to face this girl or friends of hers.''

"Yes, what I would do, in your case, is to find some Orthodox Jewish group that is not familiar with that past, just so that you can start with a new slate. But let me also make a suggestion. The next young lady that you will find and that you will take out, do not discuss it with her. This is something . . .''

"I feel that selling myself as an honest product is what I should do, but not until the relationship is very solid.''

"That's fine. I think that sounds terrific, and very mature. So I would say to you, first of all, I would hope that that young lady keeps her mouth shut.''

"I think she is mature enough now to do that.''

"Good. Then I would say to you, look, put it behind you. It happened, it happened. There's nothing to be gained by your making yourself miserable, but keep that virginity until the day you get married.''

"Absolutely.''

"All right?''

"Thank you very much, Dr. Ruth.''

"Good luck to you. Bye-bye.''

It's a fact that there are many, many young people of that sort, with similar ethical and religious feelings. It just doesn't get the publicity.

"You are on the air."

"Hi, Dr. Ruth. This is the first time I've listened to your program and I'm really enjoying it. I'm learning a lot."

"Thank you."

"I hope you can help me. Right now I'm seeing a man who used to be a gigolo, and he still sort of carries on that way. I don't enjoy knowing he's been with other women."

"When you say 'gigolo,' that means that he was with other women, or was he paid?"

"He's paid by other women."

"Okay. And he still continues . . ."

"He doesn't feel that it's affecting our relationship."

"Is he doing it still right now?"

"Yes."

"And he wants to continue doing it while having a relationship with you?"

"Right."

"Hmmm. That's a difficult problem."

"Frankly, I don't know what to do."

"I'll tell you. If you would tell me it doesn't bother you, then I would say 'Have fun, I hope you use contraception.' But if it bothers you, which I do hear very clearly, I think you might have to tell him, 'Hey, honey, it's either having sex for money with the other women or having sex with me with no money, just for love.' I don't think that you should just go along with that. Why does he do it? Does he need the money?"

"Sometimes."

"Does he have a job?"

"Yes."

"And he makes enough money?"

"It keeps him in rent and food, so I guess he makes enough money."

"I think you have to do some very serious talking with this man. Whatever happened in the past, happened in the past. That's

25

different. But right now, for you to have to share doesn't seem fair to me.''

''I don't feel like I want to end the relationship because of it, though.''

''But then you have to take a stand. Maybe he is willing to give up the sex for money if he feels that you really mind it and you really don't like it. Will you try to talk to him?''

''Sure.''

''Okay. Bye-bye.''

''You are on the air.''

''Hello, Dr. Ruth. My name is Janie. I've had this problem with my husband. I've been married for about a year and I became pregnant recently, and he is very upset because he didn't want me to be pregnant, and it upsets me greatly. We had a very good sexual relationship before our marriage, and once we got married it just seemed to dwindle into nothing, and he accuses me of having affairs with people.''

''You don't have affairs?''

''No, I don't. There is a man I work with who I am very interested in, and he's very nice as a friend, but do you feel I should maybe just leave my husband? I mean, this man is willing to marry me. My husband seems to feel that I should have an abortion, and I don't feel it's right. I would love to have this child.''

''Okay, Janie. Let me tell you. This is not something that I can advise you over the air like that. This is much too serious. You absolutely must—before you make any decision, either on an abortion, or on leaving your husband, or on the other man—you *first* have to go and get some counseling. Absolutely. This is a very, very serious decision. And I could never in my wildest dreams just give you advice like that over the air, without knowing you, the circumstances, your husband. . . .''

''I would just like to ask you one other thing. I never really had a . . . I feel funny saying it.''

''An orgasm?''

''An orgasm. I don't understand why that would happen. Was I apprehensive or . . . ?''

''That might have many reasons. Now, one of the things that I would suggest to you is absolutely tomorrow to find a counselor. That's number one for the first question. For the second question, this happens to thirty percent of American women, so don't worry about it.''

"I thought I was out of the ordinary.''

"No, you are not. And the one book that I usually suggest is a book that is by Lonnie Barbach. It's called *For Yourself*. It does teach women how to give themselves an orgasm first and how then to transfer the ability of orgasm, to have an orgasm with their partners.''

"Right. Because I feel that he gets more pleasure out of our sex than I do.''

"You absolutely have to learn to have an orgasm. There is no question. But you first can learn it by yourself. And then teach your husband how to give you an orgasm. But for the other question, you absolutely need either to go to your priest . . . Do you belong to a church?''

"Yes, I do.''

"Absolutely tomorrow make an appointment with the counselor at your church.''

"Yes. I listen to you all the time and I trust your word, and I feel you're very honest.''

"Thank you so much for calling.''

"Thank you very much.''

"You are on the air.''

"Hello, Dr. Ruth. I'm having this problem with my current boyfriend. It seems every time we're having sex he has this idea that I'm holding back—I'm not really opening up to him. I keep telling him it's not anything that he's not doing. I feel it's me, and it's causing problems between us.''

"Does he mean holding back with sexual pleasure, or holding back by talking to him, or holding back because you don't have an orgasm?''

"No, it just seems like I'm not really giving myself to him.''

"Do you know exactly what he means? Does he mean that you are looking at other men?''

"No.''

"Is he jealous?"

"No, he's not jealous or anything. It happened in the past with my past boyfriend—they all accuse me of, you know, holding back on them."

"But I think that the current boyfriend—forget about the other ones before—but the current one, ask him specifically what does he mean. Are you not smiling when you see him? Are you not jumping up and down for joy when you meet? Are you not calling him often enough? Are you not buying him a birthday gift? Ask him exactly what does he mean."

"What he means is, like, while we're in bed."

"He means that while you are in bed you are not warm enough? Not responsive enough?"

"Right. It seems I'm not opening up to him. It seems I'm holding everything back."

"Okay. Why don't you ask him to actually be more specific. To ask him, does he want you to move more? Does he want you to move like some of these movie stars that he sees in films? You really have to ask him. You just saying 'holding back' doesn't tell us enough of what he means. Do ask him and call me back. Okay?"

"Okay."

"Thank you so much for calling."

"Thank you."

The other day I left my office and caught a cab to WYNY. The driver knew my voice from the radio. Nice man—Irving. (First names only!) He was a part-time stagehand with a rival network. He asked me, "Are those phone calls real?"

Yes, Irving, they are real. I may tell people to rehearse in therapy, but we never rehearse *Sexually Speaking*! Real calls from real people.

3
FEELING GOOD ABOUT SEX

"You are on the air."

"Good evening, Dr. Ruth. I want to get on your good side by saying that I do use contraceptives, and I approve of it."

"I love when people say that! If that message gets across the country, that for those people who are sexually active to use contraception, then all this work has been worthwhile. And your question, now that you are on my good side already?"

"This is a complicated problem. I'm presently married. This past weekend I went over to my sister-in-law's house for dinner with my wife. I notice more and more that I'm getting stimulated by my sister-in-law, and what gets very embarrassing is when I have an erection at the dinner table, and I can't leave the dinner table for at least fifteen minutes until after the people left. Then they ask me, why am I staying here. Then I start eating very slowly."

"Let me tell you something. First of all, don't get fat, staying at the dinner table. All right?"

"Okay."

"But the other thing is, as long as you just get erect under the table and nobody else knows it, that's one thing. But don't encourage it, because no good can come of it."

"She's very sexy, you know."

"No good can come from it, so do tell your sister-in-law that you do love your wife."

"No, I don't think she's coming on to me, but the way she dresses—low-cut blouses."

"Well, that you can't help. You can just do something else. You can just say to yourself, 'Hey, hold it!' because your brain has certain controls over your penis."

"I've tried that, and it doesn't."

"Try it out, but in any case, keep it without telling anybody. That's the most important thing."

"Is there anything I could think of?"

"You can start thinking of some problems with your boss, or some money problems, or, you know, you could think of something. But, I'll tell you something, if you ignore it a little more, it would be better than to force yourself to think of some other things. All right? Try it."

"All right. I'll give it a shot and I'll let you know how it turns out."

"And thank you for using contraceptives. Bye-bye."

Embarrassment over something natural like an erection—which comes of its own accord, without regard to polite behavior or where the guy is when he has it—that's as natural as the erection itself.

Men learn tricks to overcome an inconvenient erection. One man thinks of a pitcher of ice water poured on his penis. Another thinks of something else that he knows really turns him off—driving on a sheet of ice, for instance. Or he learns to "go blank" mentally for a moment or two.

The erection itself should be reassuring. It shows you are sexually healthy—nothing more.

A bad attitude toward erections is to think they point the way you have to go or you will explode or become sexually impaired in some way. If an inappropriate woman causes your erection, don't blame yourself. And don't wreck your life pursuing the woman.

We sex therapists and sex educators have to lead people toward better sexual attitudes. Not that we invented healthy sex, or have a patent on it. But that is our job.

SEEING A SEX THERAPIST

Very often I tell people who call in to *Sexually Speaking* that they ought to see a physician—a gynecologist, a urologist, an internist. Or I suggest going to a sex therapist. The people who listen to the radio show have all heard of sex therapists, but many don't know what going to a sex therapist will really get them into.

If you go to one recommended by a clinic or hospital, the person will be a responsible professional. You don't have to be afraid of getting into something "far out." And you don't have to go broke. You can go once and get the picture, and talk about charges and what kind of treatment you can expect. Sometimes one visit helps your problem.

Sex therapy often is a much shorter course of treatment. That is because the sex therapist frequently does not deal with deep-seated psychic problems but specifically with sexual difficulties. Sometimes people come to me for treatment and get into a more relaxed feeling about life before going on with psychotherapy. Sometimes it's the other way around. Sometimes sex therapy seems to be all that is needed.

A sex therapist can't do the impossible—but within the realm of the possible we can do a great deal.

Here's a sample of what is impossible. A man wants to marry a woman thirty years younger. He thinks by coming to me he can regain his youth—have the energy he had thirty years earlier. That I can't do for him. But I can give him a picture of a possible sex life with such a young woman, supposing that she will accept certain limitations, like his giving her a great deal of sexual gratification without always having an erection or an ejaculation himself. Or I can lead him to a sensible view of giving up marrying the woman if that won't satisfy her. I mean, I can lead him to that sensible point of view *in some cases*—not every older man is that reasonable!

But let's talk about healthy sexual attitudes.

People often tell me they are worried by what I know are natural sexual urges, urges they should recognize for what they are— healthy signs of being alive.

Having sexual urges is a sign of being in good health; good health physically and good health emotionally. An erection in a

31

man, or vaginal lubrication in a woman, is nothing more—and nothing less—than a healthy response to sexual stimuli and should be welcomed, in the same way that an appetite for food is welcomed, as a sign of good health. And if your mouth waters when you see and smell a rare steak or a gorgeous cheesecake, you don't have to satisfy that appetite immediately. Especially if it is someone else's cheesecake!

RANDOM ERECTIONS

Healthy men, young ones especially, can get erections that make no sense, for no reason. But the penis doesn't need a "reason."

Pressure on the penis can make it start to harden, but a healthy man doesn't always need that. In his mid-forties a client of mine began to have problems with erections. When trying to have sex with his wife, he would start an erection, but it wouldn't last long enough. Naturally this troubled him.

While this was going on he had other seemingly contradictory problems. He frequently experienced erections at random moments during the day, without any sexual stimulation. He would be driving his car, shopping in a department store, or talking on the phone when, suddenly and unaccountably, he would have a big, strong, lasting erection.

He began to have the idea that he was "sick," that he might be some kind of "pervert." This worry worsened the tension with his wife.

I told him that his random erections were not abnormal, that they showed a strong sexual drive. He didn't believe me right away. But then he began to believe me, and after that his random erections encouraged him, as they should any man. And knowing that he was really strong sexually helped him solve the erectile troubles he was having while making love to his wife.

SEXUALITY IS FOR LIFE

We must understand, if we want to have healthy sexual feelings ourselves, and pass them on to our children, that sexuality is part of being alive. *Acting on* sexual impulses must, of course, be kept within reasonable limits.

Human beings are born with sexual feelings. A male baby is often born with an erection, or a baby girl with vaginal lubrication and even an erect clitoris! The sexual urge continues throughout childhood, adolescence, and maturity and on into the sixties, seventies, and beyond. Sexual desire may slow down with age, but it never goes away entirely.

ERECTIONS AND AGING

Sexual desire undergoes certain changes with age, however. The most common change for men is the loss of the psychogenic erection, an erection that comes without any direct physical stimulation like rubbing. Simply looking at a woman may be enough to stimulate a younger man to erection. Or thinking of some sexual scene. With age, however, this ability is frequently lost; an older man may need physical contact to his penis in order to obtain an erection.

"Dr. Ruth, I'm ashamed to ask my wife to do that."

"Dr. Ruth, my husband wants me to touch his penis to make it hard. I never had to, I can't get used to it. I don't think he loves me anymore."

You know, this kind of shame and shyness really happens between older married couples. And if they knew what was happening, that it is natural and ordinary, much unhappiness would be avoided.

You would think an older couple would be on good enough terms to trade little favors—you touch me, I'll get it up for you. A little good humor and playfulness would help. Besides, "touching" has so many variations, a friendly couple can find ways to press and move the penis—their common property, as it were—to put it in a jolly upright stance.

But shame comes in. The older man is afraid he's impotent and he's afraid to show he's afraid. The woman thinks her prince has turned into a dirty old man with kinky old-man wishes. These are unhealthy sexual attitudes that cause misery, poison a relationship—and they come simply of ignorance.

Many an older lover can get it up, with a little loving cooperation. And you know what? He can often keep his penis hard longer than when he was younger, for much more prolonged intercourse.

MYTHS ABOUT MASTURBATION

There are many long-established myths that get in the way of healthy sexual attitudes. Masturbation myths are most common. They may sound funny, but they have done great harm.

You don't hear these lies about masturbation so much these days, but you still hear them—as jokes if nothing else. If a boy masturbates he will: go blind; break out in pimples; grow hair on the palm of his hand; become sterile. His penis will fall off. He will go insane. Fortunately, boys are less often prey to these fears today, but there is still one very harmful myth that is widespread: masturbation is shameful because you ought to be having sex with girls. This has contributed to the rise of teenage V.D. and unwanted pregnancies.

Until he is ready to take up a responsible sex life with a partner, a boy is better off masturbating. And while he should do it in private, he should not be made to feel ashamed of this natural behavior. His privacy should be respected.

The same goes for girls. For both sexes masturbation is not only healthy but an important part of learning about sex.

"You are on the air."

"Hello, Dr. Ruth. I'm calling about my daughter. She's three years old. I'm wondering if there is anything to be concerned about. She is putting herself to sleep with the blanket, like, between her legs, and she's really rocking on it hard, and it seems as though she's really pleasing herself."

"Right. Let me tell you something. This is something that three-year-olds do very often. And actually what happens is, she actually has an orgasm. It's really an orgasm, because children are sexual beings, and she has luckily found how to stimulate herself and how to give herself pleasure. But let me ask you, is the rocking for a long time in the evenings, or is it just a little while and then she falls asleep?"

"I never looked really at the watch. I put her down to sleep, and then she is sleeping."

"I would leave it alone. I would just ignore it. I would let her have that blanket. I would make believe as if I didn't see it. I wouldn't stand there and say, 'Bravo! You are having an orgasm!' ''

"I try to ignore it the whole time. I tried in the beginning to give her a doll, to try to switch her attention to something else, but it seems that she's really into it.''

"I'll tell you what. Don't try that. Because you know what will happen, after a while . . .''

"Is it natural or not?''

"Yes, it is natural. Absolutely, and it's part of growing up. It's part of becoming a sexual being, and this type of girl very often, later on, will not have any problems having an orgasm. You see, if you ignore it, it is absolutely normal. And after a while, she herself might get interested in other things and might not be interested in doing it. But by you putting so much attention—by trying to give her a doll to put there . . .''

"I was afraid of making an issue. But I thought I might be able to quietly divert her attention to something else. Also, sometimes it's for a long time—it can be twenty minutes. Is it too long?''

"It's nothing like too long. It's just, when I asked how long, I thought if she has any problems sleeping—if it's for hours and hours—that she might have some nightmares. But if it's just for, like, twenty minutes, don't worry about it. I do thank you for calling.''

"Thank you very much.''

"You're very welcome. Bye-bye.''

Even enlightened parents who want to give their children a healthy sexual attitude sometimes find themselves embarrassed.

Children naturally touch and explore their own genitals. If the child is made to feel that this is "dirty,'' quite often the child will develop negative feelings about his or her own body. On the other hand, if the child is given to understand that touching the genitals is perfectly natural and acceptable and no more wrong or dirty than touching a wrist or an elbow, the child may engage in genital manipulation in public, to the embarrassment of the parents.

You can explain to the child, once the child reaches the age when he or she can understand, that there is nothing wrong with touching the genitals, but it is one of these things that other people do not particularly like to watch, like picking one's nose; an action that is not "wrong," but is rude to do in public.

GROWN-UP MASTURBATION
In researching their classic work *Human Sexual Response,* Masters and Johnson found that many people reported experiencing stronger, more intense orgasms during masturbation than during sexual intercourse. This is not uncommon.

One of the characters in Harold Robbins's popular novel *Dreams Die First* is an internationally acclaimed stud who ultimately gives up both heterosexual and homosexual sex in favor of masturbation, saying, "Nobody does me as well as me."

While the sheer intensity of orgasm may well be strongest during masturbation, the point of sex is not, of course, exclusively orgasm. One of the main benefits of a good sexual encounter is the warm intimacy that only human beings can have.

MYTHS ABOUT MENSTRUATION
Menstruation myths abound, too. If a menstruating woman bakes a cake, the cake will fall; if she washes and sets her hair, the set will not hold; if she eats fruit, she will fall ill. She must stay in bed during menstruation. A girl should not study at this time because mental effort will damage her brain and/or make her sterile. If a man has sex with a woman during her period, he will become impotent or sterile.

I hope you are smiling, because a smile is all these ideas are worth.

MYTHS ABOUT NOT GETTING PREGNANT
There are some sex myths that are alive and doing much harm today. Here are some wrong ideas I get frequently from patients.

It is still a common belief that a girl cannot become pregnant during her first sexual experience or if she has intercourse while standing up. This myth has contributed to the high rate of teenage pregnancies in America, a rate that is the highest in all of the western world.

Another related myth is that a girl can't get pregnant if the man practices coitus interruptus—withdraws his penis just before ejaculation. This is in fact a good way to get pregnant, since that drop of sperm that is emitted before ejaculation contains thousands of sperm cells. And it takes only one of these to fertilize an egg cell.

THE MYTH THAT WOMEN DON'T NEED AN ORGASM

Perhaps the most damaging of all the myths that are current today— yes, it is, in spite of the sex information explosion—is that women do not need to experience orgasm. That it is quite acceptable for a man to arouse his partner and then not bring her to orgasm, because a woman does not need sexual release in the same way that a man does. Of course we know much better today.

In my clinical practice I keep learning and relearning that it is very difficult for a man to understand how a woman feels about sex and her own sexual satisfaction.

Obviously women *should* have orgasms. While only thirty percent of the women in America today experience orgasm during intercourse, that number is growing with the increasing sexual knowledge of the younger generation. Fully ninety-five percent of all women are capable of experiencing orgasm in some way—if not during intercourse, then by manual or oral stimulation. It may not always be necessary for a woman to have an orgasm, but by the same logic it should be equally acceptable for a man to bring his partner to orgasm without ejaculating himself.

THE PERILS OF FAKING IT

In recent years a new myth has gained ground. It too has resulted in much unhappiness for both men and women. This is the myth that in order to please her partner, a woman should pretend to have an orgasm simultaneously with his in order to make him think he is a good lover. This often leads to a very bad sexual relationship.

A typical case: The lady had never experienced an orgasm, but in many films she had been impressed by the women thrashing about in the throes of ecstasy. She felt that in order to please her mate, she should make him feel like a stud. She was a good actress, because he never had an inkling that she was faking it.

Whenever they had sex, she made sure that as he ejaculated she too was "apparently" reaching her climax. Whenever they had sex

37

she reassured him so well that right afterward he would kiss her blissfully and roll over and fall asleep, leaving her "throbbing with desire."

Over the eight years of their marriage she had eventually come to avoid sex. This baffled him, since he had always assumed that he was pleasing her as much as she was pleasing him. In reality she deeply resented him, and their marriage was in trouble.

At last she went to a sex therapist. Now this will not cure all the world's ills, but it helped her and her mate wonderfully. It opened up communications, started a dialogue. During her therapy sessions this client finally revealed the truth and admitted that she had never experienced an orgasm.

The treatment for the problem (developed by Dr. Helen Singer Kaplan) was both simple and successful. First, she learned to masturbate alone, discovering for herself the best ways to apply pressure, where not to apply pressure, the most effective movements, and the best rate of manipulation. Once she knew the techniques that worked for her, she was able to teach them to her husband. By putting her hand over his, she was able to guide him, and for the first time in their marriage he truly brought her to orgasm.

PARENTS, CHILDREN, AND SEX

Sex is a sensitive subject between parents and children. It is good and necessary for parents to acquaint their children with knowledge of sex rather than letting them pick it up on the streets. Once a child reaches the age of adolescence, it is natural for him or her to be curious about Mom and Dad's sex life. As a rule, it is not a good idea for parents to share intimate details of their sex lives with their children. Nor, once their children become responsible adults, to probe too deeply into the sex lives of their children. Sex is a very private matter to be shared with a loving partner or, if a mutual bond has been established, with a trusted friend. It is neither necessary nor helpful to tell all to one's child. In some cases telling all the sexual details can have a very disruptive effect on both the child and the parent.

An example of the importance of excluding children from Mom and Dad's sex life—a humorous one. Mom and Dad were a young couple in their late twenties who came to see me with a complaint that their sex life had become boring. They attributed the fact to Mom's loss of passion in bed.

It was not until the second session that they told me their three-year-old son slept in the bedroom with them. They were very surprised when I pointed out that the boy's presence was very probably keeping Mom from giving herself up wholly to somewhat noisy lovemaking. Despite their protests, I told them that I would have no further sessions with them until the child was moved out of the room. When they said that he would cry if his crib was moved out of the room, I agreed he probably *would* cry for the first night, and they should feel free to go to him to comfort him and assure him that all was well. But they were to remain firm in keeping him out of the room during the night.

As they predicted, their son did cry, and they got very little sleep that first night. And, as I predicted, on the second night the child slept quite soundly. Mom soon regained her sexual "voice," and their sex life resumed with the old vigor and passion.

FEELING BAD ABOUT HEALTHY FEELINGS

A young woman of nineteen came to see me, deeply troubled by recent events. She was from a very sheltered and religious home and had gone through a traumatic sexual encounter.

Studying late one night, she found herself alone in the school library with a boy she had come to feel very close to. She knew her parents would never approve of this young man, who was from a different background. During a study break, as was their habit, they talked together. One thing led to another and soon they were kissing and petting. Our heroine returned home in a highly emotional state.

Flustered by what had happened, she told her mother. Though the boy had gone no further than to touch her breast, her mother flew into a rage. She screamed at the girl that she was now "tainted," that she had as good as lost her virginity, and that soon everyone would know what a terrible whore she was. Her mother threatened to withdraw her from the college.

By the time this young woman came to see me she was emotionally crushed. And she was quite taken aback when I asked her the simple question "Did you enjoy it when the boy touched your breast?"

39

No one had bothered to ask this young woman how she had felt about that. Her mother was concerned with how *she* felt about it, and very much concerned with what the neighborhood would think. The girl had broken a very definite set of moral and religious rules. She felt that she fully deserved all the misery she was going through.

After thinking about it for a moment, she admitted that when the boy had touched her breast, she *had* enjoyed it. The sensation had been very pleasurable, her nipples had been erect, and she had felt "very warm and soft inside." She revealed all of this with some hesitancy.

"Good," I told her. "Now at least we know that when you get married, you will probably not have to worry too much about your own sexuality. You should be glad that you learned something positive from the experience."

Because this girl's background was of a very strict kind, I advised her not to allow herself to be in a situation where she was alone with a young man in such tempting circumstances again. Any studying she had to do in the school library, especially late at night, was to be done only in a library wing where there were many people present. It was easy advice to give and easy to follow, and she had no further difficulties.

SEXUAL PUBLICITY

A much sadder incident brought a young woman of fifteen to my office. She had been dating a boy of seventeen who had repeatedly told her that he loved her deeply. He had asked her to have sex with him, and since she was a virgin, she had at first refused. He kept up the pressure. He said she did not really love him; if she did, she would give in. The girl saw that it was very important to the boy. So, to prove she really did love him, she finally consented.

They had intercourse in the backseat of his car, and it was an awkward, painful, and generally unpleasant experience. But she was convinced that she had done the right thing by showing the boy how much he really meant to her. The next day she was in for a shock.

When she arrived at school, she discovered that the boy had bragged to all his friends that he had "had" her the night before.

And he had described the experience in the minutest details. As she walked through the corridors going from class to class, she was aware of the other students staring at her. Smirks, giggles, and wolf whistles followed her throughout the day.

When she confronted the boy and asked how he could have been so heartless about their deeply personal and meaningful act of love, he laughed in her face and turned his back on her.

Her romantic dreams crumbled into dust, and she became, at fifteen, a very hurt and bitter young woman.

She returned home at the end of the day in tears, swearing never to go back to that school again. She confided in her mother, who was very sympathetic and supportive and convinced her that she ought to try to forget the incident and return to school, which she did. But she had acquired a deep mistrust of people and an especially profound distrust of men. This distrust has persisted to the present day, and the scars will probably never heal completely.

The young woman is twenty-six years old now and single. She finds it very difficult to trust men on any level. Though she has had subsequent sexual encounters since that first unfortunate experience, she has generally found them disappointing and unsatisfying. She is afraid she may never meet a man she can both love and trust. But there is still some hope that, with help, she will find the necessary courage to risk making an emotional commitment, with all the self-exposure and vulnerability that it entails, once again.

The idea that sex is a game, with points scored for each virgin deflowered, is one of the cruelest and most damaging examples of an *unhealthy* sexual attitude. In this case the victim was not the boy who had these negative attitudes but the unfortunate girl.

MORE MISPLACED FEELINGS OF GUILT

One fifteen-year-old client of mine was sexually aroused when her father happened accidentally to brush his arm across her breast. That night she lay awake in bed, tortured by feelings of guilt. She was sure there was something terribly abnormal about her. As is common in such cases, she "buried" the incident until, as a young woman, she recalled it during a therapy session.

For many years she had labored under the delusion that there was something basically wrong with her sexuality. Whenever she began to become sexually aroused, she would apply an emotional "brake" and stop herself from flowing with her sexual response, which was mixed up in her own mind with guilt feelings about her "incestuous lust" for her father.

She finally came to realize and accept the fact that, like all people, she had a sexual component in her nature that was entirely natural and nothing to be ashamed of. Once she was past that, she began to make progress.

CONTROLLING THE SEXUAL ON/OFF SWITCH

Sex begins in the mind, not between the legs. A person's mental attitude toward sex is all-important. A common sexual problem involves the inability to control sexual desire.

One housewife in her mid-forties described her problem, which I have encountered many times in my practice. She said she had "a mental on/off switch" for sexual desire which tended to "lock into the 'off' position at the wrong times." Frequently she spent an entire day in a high state of sexual arousal. On those days she made it a point to take a long bubble bath and to arrange her hair carefully, all the time imagining all kinds of sexual fantasies revolving around her husband. As the time for him to return from work approached, she would put on an attractive dress or pretty housecoat in anticipation of an evening of passionate lovemaking with him. Upon his arrival home, however, she often found negative thoughts intruding into her plans. Thoughts like He's gotten awfully bald lately, or He does have a pot belly. Thoughts like these destroyed all her sexual desire for him.

And a man may spend the day fantasizing about getting his wife into bed at night only to lose all desire at the sight of her in hair rollers.

It is important to recognize such responses and to learn how to control them.

When such thoughts do begin to arise, a useful strategy is to think about something else, anything else, that will turn the mind to better channels. Remembering a particularly warm, emotional moment with your partner may be enough to forestall the effects of momentary negative reactions.

COUPLES WITH NO SEX LIFE

Increasingly in my clinical practice I encounter married couples who tell me they have not engaged in any sex at all for a number of years. Perhaps it is not a sign that more people are having this problem, but that more people are talking about it. Nowadays people feel freer than they ever have before to confront their sexual difficulties and seek ways to resolve them, and they go to sex therapists for help.

The source of the problem lies sometimes with the woman, sometimes with the man. In most cases it is a basic failure, not of an individual, but rather of the function of basic sexual desire. Lack of sexual desire is often fatal to a relationship.

One troubled couple were in their late twenties when they came to see me. They had been married for seven years and at the time had not had any sexual relations for four years, since the birth of their second child. It had been a very difficult and painful delivery for the wife, and her fear of pregnancy had a lot to do with her lack of sexual desire, since the couple's religious principles forbade the use of contraceptives. But it became clear during the therapy sessions that the wife had absolutely no sexual desire for her husband. He was not, and never had been, sexually appealing to her. She confessed that she had not wanted to marry him in the first place and had done so only because, as a promising attorney with a brilliant future ahead of him, he was what her mother called a "good catch." She had been raised to believe that when it came to marriage, the only thing that really mattered was that the man should be a good provider of the material things in life.

He had found her very attractive sexually when they were first married, and still did. To relieve his sexual tension he frequently masturbated, often fantasizing about her as he did so. But he felt very guilty about it, because as a boy he had been taught that it was wrong. She did not masturbate and so had no sexual outlet at all. They both were, and still are, desperately unhappy. Unfortunately, there is no easy solution to their problem.

Sex therapists are not magicians. We can help most people but not everyone who comes to us.

In another case it was the husband who had no sexual desire for his wife. He lost interest soon after their son was born, and when they came to see me, they had not had sex for more than five years.

When the problem first arose, the wife had attempted to initiate their sexual relations. But his continual rejections, and the fear of further rejections, finally forced her to stop. This couple too were deeply unhappy. They both masturbated, and for the wife masturbation was accompanied by feelings of deep resentment toward the husband.

What emerged in our sessions was that he had very little sexual drive and had married because that was what a man of his age and background was supposed to do. This same passionless conformity to convention holds many people locked together in misery, refusing even to consider the option of divorce.

It is impossible to implant sexual desire in people. Where sexual desire is present, it can be stimulated and channeled in positive directions. But where there is an absence of sexual desire, the outlook is decidedly grim. For couples with difficulties rooted in a basic lack of sexual desire, the problem extends beyond the realm of sex therapy into the area of marriage therapy.

KNOW AND LOVE YOUR VAGINA!

There are harmful negative attitudes involved in the image many people have of their own bodies. Women frequently suffer from the delusion that the vagina is ugly, dirty, and smelly. This is simply not true. If the vagina is reasonably clean, it does not have a bad odor, and many men find the smell of a clean vagina very stimulating. (Unfortunately, there are some men too who have a bad picture of a woman's vagina and need to be enlightened.) The belief that the vagina, the region "down there," is a swamp, a Black Hole of Calcutta, can be very damaging. We all need a healthy appreciation of the natural beauty of the human body. And the vagina is interesting, important in the life process, and to many people beautiful.

Because both the urinary and sexual functions of the female body involve the vagina, many women have a fear of letting themselves relax during sex for fear that they may leak urine. While a drop or two of urine may actually be discharged, this should not be considered a catastrophe. If a woman is truly concerned, she can always place a towel underneath her to absorb any random drops.

The younger generation seems to be less subject to negative perceptions of the vagina. The increasing popularity of contraceptive creams and jellies manufactured in a variety of colors and flavors would seem to indicate a shift to a healthier outlook, an outlook very much to be welcomed.

One woman told this story to a friend of mine, an actor. The woman was an actress and very sensitive to beauty in natural and humanly created things. She went to an exhibit of exquisite constructions, little objects of art. One was a shell-like object into which she peered, and hanging down was a lovely pearl on a delicate link. The piece was mounted so that any vibration in the area made the pearl tremble. To the actress the work of art was a vagina and the pearl was the clitoris, charmingly idealized.

The man who told me this was not the woman's lover; they were friends on such terms that they could tell each other things like that. I like her appreciative feeling for the vagina and also her feeling that she could talk about it politely to a sensitive man. Both the feeling and her expressing it do her credit.

I do *not* say that every woman has to talk to male friends in this way. It is an individual matter.

KNOW AND LOVE YOUR PENIS!

Many men have negative attitudes about their own penises. A man cannot see how his penis looks to others unless he stands in front of a mirror, and perhaps it is ignorance about what that organ looks like that prompts all the worry men have about the size and shape of their own penises.

I often hear complaints from men who bemoan the fact that the penis is too short, or too small, or too thin, or too thick, or hanging to the left side, or hanging to the right side—a hodgepodge of totally unimportant concerns.

As studies in human sexual behavior have clearly shown, the size of a man's penis has nothing to do with his ability to perform sexually and to bring his partner to sexual satisfaction. It is the stimulation of the clitoris by the root of the penis and by the pubic bone that brings a woman to orgasm. Despite the fact that such studies have been well publicized and are easily accessible, many men continue to be troubled by doubts concerning the effectiveness of their "tool."

And men also are frequently worried about the fact that the penis is involved in both urination and sex. It is, however, physiologically impossible for any urine to seep out of a penis once the man has an erection.

There is a technique many experienced women have used to arouse men. As part of sex play the woman can use a mirror to show her partner what his penis looks like to her. She can also diplomatically praise his penis and let him know how it arouses her; how she likes it, loves it, finds it noble, handsome, darling, a charming toy, etc. This has a remarkable effect on the penis—it can make it engorge and become erect!

It is as if the penis has a life of its own and can hear the nice things being said about it.

In fact, a very nice thing is for the woman to pretend she is talking *to the penis,* and both partners can watch with joy as it responds!

Practically any man will like having his penis praised and talked to in this way. It can improve the health of his sexual feelings immensely. It can lead him into thinking appreciatively of that other wonderful thing, his lady's vagina.

4
THE IMPORTANCE OF TOUCHING

Everyone knows the telephone commercial. ''Reach out, reach out and touch someone'' they sing, joining in from coast to coast. But not everyone knows the real, deep, noncommercial value of touching in a love relationship—reaching out and touching each other.

The deepest touching is bringing someone to that moment of total release we call orgasm. But a real relationship calls for lots of touching of every kind—hugging, kissing, patting, stroking, feathery touching, and joking little hip-bumps. Loving, friendly, reassuring touching. Not just the kind of touching we call foreplay and afterplay.

You don't expect to get touched back every time. Not when your partner walks by with a basket of wash from the machine, and you give a nice pat. But both partners are generous with touching in a tender and valuable relationship.

Touching is a language. And it takes two to keep up a conversation.

I get hundreds of letters addressed to Dr. Ruth at WYNY. So many people can't get through to me on the phone because there are callers ahead of them, and some people would rather discuss their special problems by mail. Here is a typical letter that fits in nicely here.

Dear Dr. Ruth:

My husband and I love your program. It has become part of our Sunday nights. The funny thing is, something in our own marriage is bothering me and I don't know how to tell him. . . . We have been married eight months and I see him losing interest. We still have lots of sex but I miss the way he used to be all over me all the time. He couldn't keep his hands off me, and now it's got to be bedtime sex or nothing. How can I tell him, or should I?

Ann

Sometimes it takes time to catch up on this mail, but many get answered in the end.

Dear Ann:

It often happens that a husband begins to forget to show enthusiasm. He gets used to the comfort and regularity of marriage. That's good, but if you want his hands on you, it may be up to you. You want to be touched, but how much do you touch him? If you give him a pat on the behind as he goes by you, it will remind him that he likes to pat you, too. Or give him a little hip-bump. Rub your breasts on his back while he's washing his hands when he gets home. This is a nice way of saying "Hey, how about a little touching?" If you try doing this regularly, in a nice affectionately sexy way, you may never have to say anything about it in words. Write and tell me how this works out.

Thanks for writing and good luck!

Dr. Ruth

YOU MUST HAVE BEEN A BEAUTIFUL BABY

Babies love to be touched. When a baby is bathed, it coos with delight. When its genitals are caressed, that cooing intensifies, and the baby beams with pleasure. Often when a baby boy's penis is washed, he will have an erection, and a baby girl's clitoris frequently becomes erect when her genitals are washed. And they don't care if you notice.

Much of grown-up sex is like that. People let go, they laugh and squeal with delight, unabashed with their companions in love.

In many ways sex is a return to infantile pleasure. And that means lots of touching.

It is a simple fact of nature that babies enjoy being touched. And all of us started out in life as babies.

Babies enjoy touching themselves, exploring their bodies—playing with their fingers, sucking their toes. While self-touching—and especially toe sucking—tends to lose much of its charm after infancy, the sensually aware adult finds touching and being touched to be very basic pleasures.

It is also a fact that some of us lose the pleasure of touching—some more than others. And to these people a large part of the language of love is lost. But it can be relearned, and learning it again can improve one's sexual partnership marvelously.

Of the five senses that human beings are born with, the sense of touch is the least localized. Indeed, the skin of the entire body has nerve endings that are sensitive to the touch. Anyone who has watched a child snuggle with a soft blanket or a plush animal knows how important that sense of touch is in fostering a sense of comfort and security. The feeling of security provided by a favorite cuddly toy animal sometimes lasts long beyond the years of actual childhood. We never outgrow our need for the pleasure and security we get from hugging something cuddly. Ideally, of course, the cuddly thing should be one's sexual partner!

While some children enjoy being hugged and kissed more than others, it is important for *all* children to be touched and hugged and cuddled sometimes by their parents.

Too much hugging can cause a child to feel smothered, and too little may cause a child to cling to its parents, demanding more. How do we judge what's "too much" and "too little"? Try to learn how the child feels about it, remembering that even the most stand-offish and independent child can use a hug at times but may be shy about demanding it.

"IT'S JUST SEX"
The basic need to be touched is not confined to infants and young children. Many adults complain that they are unhappy because their husbands or wives never seem to just reach out and touch them anymore.

49

One of my patients, a woman in her early forties, told me that after twenty years of marriage, her husband seemed to have forgotten *how* to touch her.

"When it comes to sex," she said, "it's always one kiss on the cheek, one kiss on the mouth, one touch on the left breast, one touch on the right breast, and then his penis is on its way into my vagina."

When he heard this description of their sex life, her husband was shocked and hurt.

"But we *always* do it that way!" he said. Because she never asked for more than this perfunctory foreplay, he had persisted in it. For him it had become a ritual, because they "always" did it that way. But for all the shock to his ego, they were both fortunate that she had finally spoken up. A lot more misery could have resulted if she had remained silent and endured the situation.

Sexual frustration was not the issue. She was able to reach orgasm even with her husband's very limited repertoire of foreplay. What *was* at issue, what mattered so terribly to Linda, was the lack of any sense of intimacy and tenderness in their lovemaking. "It isn't lovemaking at all," she said. "It's just sex. And even though I come, it just isn't enough."

There are a lot of grown people starving for affection today. Why?

It may be a holdover from Victorian attitudes. Unlike many other countries and cultures, in America there is a pretty strict inhibition regarding body contact during the day. When we are forced to touch others, on a crowded bus or packed into an elevator, we become uncomfortable. In many other countries crowding is not disturbing. This inhibition to touching can be very difficult to overcome when touching and intimacy *are* called for. It may be expecting a lot of a person that after spending all day carefully avoiding body contact with others, he should suddenly be able to drop all the barriers and indulge in physical contact with loved ones. It may be a lot to ask, but it must be asked nonetheless.

We *need* to touch those we care about. We need to make physical contact with them, to reassure them that we are there for them, that we care about them, that they are secure in our love.

WHAT WENT WRONG?

What happens between infancy, when one enjoys the physical sensation of being touched, and adulthood, when the pleasure of touching is so often lost or buried? Part of the answer is that in the years between infancy and adulthood new meanings are learned for the act of touching.

Dear Doctor Ruth:

I would have tried to ask you this on the air, but my daughter listens to you at her friend's house and she would know my voice. This is my problem with her. Awhile back she asked my husband and me to stop hugging and kissing her in front of her friends. This hurt my husband, but he respects her wishes.

Recently my husband said, ''She doesn't want her father to kiss her, but I see other people can.'' He had noticed something with her and a boyfriend. I know this troubles him. What should I do about this?

Francine

Dear Francine:

At a certain age children ask their parents not to kiss them or hug them in front of their friends. This is because being hugged by parents means that they are babies, and they want to be grown-up. They are very serious about it, and they don't worry much about hurting Mom and Dad's feelings. Mom and Dad are still giants as far as they are concerned!

Tell your husband to be patient and that it's just part of growing up. And so is her kissing boys. Now is a time for both your husband and your daughter to get used to some new things. Tell him the best thing now is to be very kind and understanding with her, do some grown-up things with her, buy her a necklace or a dress that shows he knows she is growing up but that he is still her daddy. And you have a talk with her about the responsibilities of being grown-up and deserving Daddy's trust. Let me know how this works out.

Good luck!

Dr. Ruth

When children ask their parents not to hug or kiss them in public, adolescence is on its way. And then suddenly they are interested in contact with people outside the family circle, a new kind of touching. That's growing up, and it's why the human race has not become extinct. This is an important time for parents to keep the confidence and trust of their children, and keep them talking easily to their parents about all kinds of things.

The new kind of touching creates a wonderful new world for the youngster, but all too often, in our competitive society, every touch has a price tag on it. The young people beginning to touch each other are learning in many ways that unless they get something for it, any effort is wasted. Children study for good grades, engage in sports to win recognition and prizes, and work at part-time jobs to earn the money to buy the things they want. "You don't get something for nothing" leads logically to "You shouldn't do something for nothing." It is a principle that people learn well in our society, and when it comes to touching, it can result in a highly destructive attitude.

Young men may acquire the notion that touching and hugging and kissing their girl friends is fine—up to a point. But if it doesn't lead to the ultimate prize, to "going all the way," it is an effort expended pointlessly. Many young women accept this philosophy and may begin to bargain—so many kisses and touches, so many degrees of warmth and intimacy—for clear rewards: a victory over other girls, a conquest of the chosen boy, an invitation to the prom, status among their friends.

Young men and women often come to view touching as a medium of exchange in a kind of barter system. It is lost to them as a pleasure in itself, a way of showing affection.

"COST-EFFECTIVE" TOUCHING

When a couple has been married for several years, familiarity may take the edge off their wanting to fondle and touch. They may all but give it up. This has killed more marriages than anything else I know.

Many people become "cost-effective" about touching—touching their partners just enough to satisfy their minimum sexual needs. While being cost-effective may be a fine way to manufacture automobiles, it is a bad way to keep love alive.

When one wife complained about her husband's lovemaking style, he asked why she needed more touching. "If she has an orgasm, isn't it enough?" he asked.

The answer was no. Reaching orgasm was *not* enough. What his wife needed was the intimacy of regular touching and hugging and kissing—out of bed, as well as in.

Some people feel threatened when touched by another person. Touching *can* be a form of aggression, an invasion of the person, when the toucher has no "right" to touch. Some people find it hard to grant the right to others, even to mates or relatives, because they have learned too well to protect themselves from aggression, invasion, disrespect, and crass possessiveness. They have learned to shrink back from any physical contact that is not absolutely essential. While some people actually *are* extremely uncomfortable being touched—and no one should be forced to be touched if she or he simply can't stand it—love partners usually do *need* to touch each other as much as possible. A light touch on the hair, a stroke on the arm, a pat on the rear end, whatever mode of touching seems natural for both partners, should be encouraged. This habitual intimacy can go a long way toward the enrichment of all aspects of a relationship. Simply put, touching is good for you.

BROOKE SHIELDS, BURT REYNOLDS, AND REALITY

People are often troubled by poor self-images. You can learn a lot of good things by going to the movies, but sometimes watching the beautiful people on the screen making love can make us feel we are too thin, too short, too fat, too flat, etc. As a result we may flinch from being touched. We need to get away from the idea that if we aren't like Brooke Shields or Burt Reynolds, we aren't fun to touch. The following letter is typical:

Dear Dr. Ruth: . . . She has this idea that her bottom is too fat, sticks out too far. I think it's just what I want, but she pulls away when I make a fuss over it. . . .

That can lead to trouble. Some men like that kind of bottom, but the lady is sure he hates it and won't let him touch her there. Constantly trying to prove how much he loves her bottom may only make things worse. Well, if one thing doesn't work, try another approach. This feeling about her bottom is one of her lovable little quirks, and she has to be wooed out of it. I told this lover to leave her bottom alone for a while! Kiss and fondle what she thinks are her good features, and give her lots of those touches that aren't strictly sexual. Hold her hand, kiss her brow, circle her waist with your arm at times when there is no question of immediate sex. Let her know you love her all over until she feels well loved, and when her confidence is built up, she will probably let you kiss her bottom, and insist that if you love it, then it must be lovable!

And you ladies! Men have loved every conceivable kind of female form. If you have that kind of bottom, go someday to a museum and look at all that lovely African sculpture. Your bad self-image is keeping your lover from showing you why you are a queen of beauty to him, and keeping you from being loved as much as you should be.

Frequent mutual touching teaches partners that they are loved and lovable, desired and desirable.

All over the world people love touching and being touched, but some of us have to learn how to touch and respond to touching, things we have lost since our touch-loving babyhood.

Many a woman flinches from her husband's touching because it only means he wants sex. He never touches her any other time. That leads to the complaint you hear so often: "He only wants to use me to relieve his erections." Sex should always be preceded by touching, but not every touch should say, "Come on, honey, I have an erection."

LEARNING HOW AND WHEN TO TOUCH

There are very few mind readers in the world. Your partner has no way of knowing exactly where you like to be touched, or how, or how often, unless you speak up. How could he? This takes exploration, the willingness to please, and a lot of self-knowledge. "I love to have my feet stroked," one lover tells the other. And the other may wonder how he or she found out. Both lovers have to realize that this kind of self-knowledge is helpful, whether it was gained by self-caressing, from parental tickling, or from a prior lover.

"God, I love to have my back massaged," a young woman told me. "But he will only play with my tits. And you know, for all the good that does me, he might as well play with my running shoes in the other room."

She had been in love before, with a man who had a way of rubbing her back that drove her wild. Whenever she asked her new lover to do this, he complied very briefly, then turned her over and had at her breasts again. She told him she loved having her back rubbed and begged him to do it some more.

"I don't just want to be an imitation of some other guy," he complained. "Besides, most women *love* having their breasts fondled."

She gave in to him on this and her back remained unrubbed, and she knew she was not being brought to her peak of sexual desire. And after a while he realized it too, and he resented it. No one was the winner.

Finally she spoke out about it. She was *not* trying to recapture her earlier love. She just had this thing about having her back rubbed. He finally saw the light and he decided to give her such great back rubs that she would forget any others but his. He got a book on massage and mastered the art. She reveled in his attentions and learned how to massage him in return.

In the end everybody won. But it didn't happen by itself. She had to face up to the problem and tell him just what she needed.

I often recommend that couples learn massage, either by taking a course or by buying a book and studying it.

"MAYBE I'M WEIRD"

There's a lot of far-out, inventive touching going on around the world. Clever scratching, rubbing, tickling, using the tongue, the nose, the big toe. Using fur or feathers, velvet, silk. Or vibrators.

George discovered by accident one night when his wife playfully licked at his nipples that it made him feel "like I'd died and gone to heaven!" But he hesitated to ask her to do it again. But after that, whenever they made love, he found himself wishing she would lick his nipples.

55

Finally George overcame his embarrassment and told her. She willingly put it into their repertoire. This admission on his part made it easier for her to tell him about some funny little things she liked but had been too shy to ask for.

"I didn't think our sex life could get any more fantastic than it already was," George told me later. "But it did."

TOO TIRED TO TOUCH?

Touching your partner establishes an emotional intimacy between you. It fosters a sense of trust and caring. The message conveyed by a touch is, "You're a good person. I value you. I care for you." And you mustn't forget to do it.

Dear Dr. Ruth:

I love your radio show. I heard it one Sunday night driving home from Philadelphia and I thought it was a gas. I love the way you talk. But not just for laughs, I think you give great advice. I'm hooked on it now and listen every Sunday. I wonder if you could tell me how to explain something to my roommate, a great woman but sometimes almost too great.

Sometimes when I get back home I'm too knocked out to do anything but flake out in front of the TV. I don't feel like physical contact of any kind. Hardly like talking. Just feel like watching the tube and letting it put me to sleep.

I try to tell her this doesn't mean I don't love her, but she doesn't get it. How can I explain?

Mike

Dear Mike:

We all get tired, but even when we are tired there are some things we must regard as sacred duties. How did you get knocked out, doing big important things more important than showing her you love her? Look, when a parent is wakened in the night by a sick child, the child has to be looked after and comforted, even if the parent is tired! The same for your lady. You don't have to swing from the chandelier or dance the kazatsky to show her you care, but you can give a big tired hug and kiss. And when you flop on the sofa to watch Johnny Car-

son, get her to sit next to you and do it together. Maybe she could sip some of your beer. Maybe after a while one of the dog food commercials will arouse you and something wonderful will happen on the couch! Some of the best loving in the world has been done by men who thought they were too tired. But even if you don't do that, you will show her that everything is better with her close to you, even Ed McMahon.

Dr. Ruth

I have no patience with people who tell me they are too tired to touch their partners. Let them know "You're very special to me. You matter a lot in my life, no matter how tired I am. I don't take you or what we have together for granted."

Tired or not, people have to work at a relationship. What's so terrible about feeling tired, anyway? If you slept twenty-four hours a day you might *never* be tired—just very, very bored.

A COURSE IN TOUCHING

Touching plays a vital role in a technique I use in sexual behavior therapy. The sensate focus exercise, first developed by Masters and Johnson and later modified by Helen Singer Kaplan, teaches people *how* to touch each other and how to use touch as part of a sexual language.

Recently I prescribed this for a young couple. The husband was having difficulty maintaining an erection.

On several occasions when he and his wife were making love his "failure" had preyed on his mind to the point where he was so concerned with "Will I have an erection?" that his anxiety kept him from having one at all. I prescribed the sensate focus exercise.

During the first week of the exercise I told them to forget about having sex altogether. Instead, they were to just touch each other. From head to toe and all stops in between—except the genitals—they were to stroke and caress and pet, to take showers together, to rediscover the art of touching. They were to get to know each other's bodies, but they were absolutely *not* to have intercourse. The purpose of this was to get them, and especially the husband, away from the idea that touching *had* to lead to sex.

After the first week, they returned to tell me what happened and reported that the touching had, indeed, felt very good. They had forgotten how much they liked each other's bodies. He joked about her little round "pot." She referred to the thick hair on his chest as his "rug."

I told them to continue with the exercise for another two weeks, only now they could touch each other's genitals. But no intercourse! They could use their tongues. He was to allow her to "pleasure him" to orgasm but with no action from him. Even if he got an erection, as he reported he had begun to do in the earlier stages of the exercise, he was not to attempt intercourse. The purpose of this was to instill in him a comfortable sense that his erections could come and go, and to remove the anxiety associated with them.

This second stage proved to be very difficult for the man. "I almost couldn't do it," he said. "After two minutes of her stroking me, I felt I had to caress her in return. That's the way I was raised. After all, I'm a man, not a woman who just lies there passively. I have to be active."

Not since he had been a baby had he been permitted to lie back and enjoy being touched. He constantly wondered if his wife was getting tired or bored. He worried that she might think he was strange or perhaps a homosexual.

In the next stage of the exercise I told them to take turns: one night of her pleasing him while he lay back passively, one night of his pleasing her. He was allowed to bring her to orgasm as often as he liked but was still not allowed to have intercourse, though by this time he was reporting that he did maintain his erections regularly.

Eventually he overcame his problem and he and his wife later told me that their sex life had been immeasurably enhanced by what they had taught each other about their bodies. And he had even come to enjoy lying back and being pleasured occasionally, saying he felt "like a sheik with a harem of one."

5
THAT
FIRST TIME

"Hi," says a young woman caller. "I'd like to know if it's very painful for a girl when she makes love with a man for the first time and if they're contemplating it, how should they go about doing it?"

"Right. Number one, it does not have to be painful if the man is gentle. It doesn't matter if he has had experience or not. The important thing is to be in a place where you cannot be interrupted, to be at ease, to have made up your mind, and to use for the first time a lubricant. Even if the woman is lubricating—even if she is very wet in her vagina—it is a good idea to use a lubricant for the first time in order to make penetration smoother. And the important thing is to use a contraceptive, because I do see too many people who come and say, 'I thought that sex, for the first time, that you can't get pregnant.' You *can* get pregnant. Now, if it is the first time for the woman and if she doesn't have a diaphragm fitted for her, then the best contraceptive is to use a condom. But the most important thing is to do it very slowly—to do a lot of foreplay and to really let the fellow insert the penis in a very slow way—and very often what helps the woman is to put her behind on a pillow. This way the intromission is a little bit easier. Thank you so much for calling. Bye-bye."

Virgins worry a lot about the first time. It ought to be lovely. And for lots of people it is. It is *hardly ever* the deepest sexual enjoyment of a lifetime—that would hardly be fair, would it? One great moment of lovemaking, then all downhill after that!

But all first sexual encounters are memorable, even if somewhat disappointing. All too often I see people in my private practice, people who come to me because they have sexual problems, who tell me that their first sexual encounter was not a good one. And frequently they say it was quite bad.

If the first sexual encounter is poor, the memory may be engraved on a person's mind and heart for some time. But it doesn't have to be a poor experience if the virgin (female or male) approaches it with some knowledge—especially knowing that however things go, they will eventually go much better.

WHY FIRST TIMES CAN BE BAD

In most bad first times the couple are simply not prepared. It has not been planned. They find themselves caught up and can't stop. It happens in the backseat of a car, a darkened room at a party, a secluded part of a public beach, or the home of one of the couple's parents. They are afraid that someone may catch them in the act, so they try to get it over with quickly. Their anxiety is high, there is little time for foreplay and touching and hugging and kissing, so it is difficult, if not impossible, for the woman to feel relaxed enough and aroused enough to lubricate properly. There is little chance that she will be able to experience an orgasm. So, from the outset, this kind of first time has little going for it.

IGNORANCE IS NOT BLISS

In these circumstances a young man who is highly aroused often becomes so excited that he ejaculates before he can complete actual penetration. And few young men realize that if they relaxed and waited for fifteen minutes or half an hour, they could try again. Most are too embarrassed to think of anything but how foolish they feel.

Rather than torturing himself, of course, the young man should simply relax for a while, perhaps take a shower, perhaps do some of the things mentioned in the previous chapter on touching, and then start again.

All of this takes time and a lack of pressure.

Another problem a man commonly has in his first sexual encounter: he can't obtain or maintain an erection. He is too nervous. This can cause him to doubt his virility and his sexual identity. He may wonder if he is going to be impotent for life or if he is a latent homosexual. The sad thing is that sexual ignorance is responsible for most of these baseless worries. And these worries may lead to a self-fulfilling prophecy, so that in future sexual encounters the man worries so much about his erection that he can't have one.

Farmers know that if a young bull does not have successful mating experiences the first few times, the animal may become effectively impotent, so farmers take care to ensure that the first few times are successful. This makes a stud animal luckier in one way than the average young man, who gets no expert supervision his first time.

To be truly good, as it should be the first time, sex should ideally take place with a person one feels affection for and with plenty of time and privacy to establish intimacy.

We are taught to expect a great deal from the first time. Movies, television, books, and magazines all present to us images of handsome, virile men and beautiful, sensual women writhing in ecstasy as they engage in sex, moving together like a pair of perfectly trained dancers. Sex *can* be like that. But seldom the first time.

The key to success in a first sexual encounter lies in planning and setting the scene for it, as you would for any other important event in your life. The most important thing is to ease as much as possible the pressure to perform.

A WEDDING NIGHT

A young woman asked me for advice about what to do on her wedding night. Neither she nor her fiancé had had any sexual experience at all.

"Are you going to have a big party?" I asked her.

"Yes. Between his family and my family, five hundred people are coming."

Knowing how exhausted they would both almost certainly be after a large party, following the emotionally draining business of a large wedding, I urged her not to let herself and her future husband worry throughout the party about how things would go in bed later on.

"You'll have enough on your mind," I told her. "So just relax and enjoy the party. Getting married is the biggest thing that has ever happened to either of you in your lives, and you don't need more on your minds than you'll already have.

"Afterward, when you're alone together in your room, don't worry about rushing to consummate the marriage. If you're tired, go to bed together and do a lot of touching and kissing and hugging, but don't try to have sex. Just go to sleep. There is no hurry, no rush. You've got the rest of your lives together. If you like, set the alarm clock so you get a few hours sleep and then have sex when you wake up. Or wait until you wake up the next day. Neither of you has to be out to prove anything."

I suggested that she have some vaginal lubricant handy in case the tenseness of the moment prevented her from lubricating sufficiently. I also advised her to place a pillow under her buttocks. That would raise her vagina a bit and make the angle of penetration somewhat easier.

They were both Orthodox Jews and, according to strict Jewish law, would have to abstain from sexual intercourse for seven days after the initial consummation of their marriage. After their first time, they would have to wait a week before trying to improve things. Rather than spending that week remembering an unpleasant experience, and worrying that the rest of their lives would be a repetition of it, it was important that the first time be as pleasant as possible.

In some countries it was the custom for the wedding guests to wait outside the bridal chamber until the marriage had been consummated and the bedsheet displayed for all to see the telltale spot of blood from the bride's ruptured hymen. The bride's mother would wave the sheet around proudly.

I have wondered how any couple could perform sexually at all under conditions like that. I suspect that wise mothers sent their daughters into that bridal chamber with a vial of chicken blood.

FAKING IT

Women commonly do not experience orgasm during their first sexual encounter. For a woman it takes more than genital friction to reach orgasm. Her clitoris needs to be stimulated in a regular rhythm either indirectly through intercourse or directly through manual or oral manipulation. It takes awhile for her partner to learn her rhythm, and while most couples can eventually develop successful lovemaking techniques, in the beginning it is much like dancing with a new partner. The first few times around the floor may be somewhat lacking in grace.

UPTIGHT

It is common for a woman's vaginal muscles to tighten up with the tenseness that accompanies the first sexual encounter, making intercourse uncomfortable. If her anxiety about sexual intercourse is not allayed through pleasant experience, and the gentle ministrations of a considerate partner, that problem may persist.

Extreme cases of this, in which the vagina tightens up so much that penetration is impossible—a condition called vaginismus—are relatively rare.

DON'T LET YOURSELF BE DISAPPOINTED

First times with inexperienced lovers should be approached in an understanding mood, with the idea that, naturally, sex gets better as you go along together. Even an experienced lover may not know just how to please you, may have some sexual stage fright. Experienced actors have rough first nights in plays, and experienced lovers do have some poor first nights in bed.

It used to be thought that the man should be experienced in order to deflower a virgin nicely. In Europe there was the idea that a young man should have lessons from an older woman before he was up to initiating a virgin. Sometimes that worked, sometimes it didn't.

I like to think of two young people exploring sex together, gently and understandingly, bringing knowledge, if not experience, to their early attempts. And they should think of them as attempts. People have to get to know each other gradually—and that goes for knowing each other in the biblical sense of having sex together.

63

The young couple should know that the woman might not have an orgasm through intercourse in the beginning and should be ready for a lesson in how she can be pleased. She can masturbate with his hand over hers.

If they have had sex other than penetration with the penis, they can do that again now, before or after the trial intercourse.

A young man should understand that a woman who has knowledge of her own capacity for pleasure is a fascinating creature, a mystery to be studied and excited by. That is a very helpful attitude.

If the bridegroom is too insecure to like having his bride pleasure herself, she had better do it by herself. But it will be a nicer experience for her to do this lying comforted in his arms than to do it surrounded by cold bathroom tiles.

In any case, it is far better for a woman to masturbate than to remain tense and lie there thinking, That stupid guy, he doesn't know anything. And to be worried that the rest of their sex life together will be unsatisfying for her.

TALKING ABOUT IT

Before the first sexual encounter, talk things over with your partner. You're crossing a threshold into a whole new period of your life, and the experience—good, bad, or indifferent—is one you will remember always. Set the scene as well as you can. Arrange to have the privacy and the time and the kind of peace and quiet that fosters a sense of intimacy with your partner. The experience, and your reaction to it, will color your feelings about your own sexuality for a long time to come, so you owe it to yourself, and to your partner, to talk about it in advance.

For starters, admit that it is your first sexual encounter and that you may be a bit awkward the first time out. Contrary to popular myth, talking about sex beforehand doesn't take away any of its romance. You can still have the candlelight and music—it doesn't have to be a matter of mute grunting and groping in the dark.

Sex *can* be all that it's cracked up to be, delightful and beautiful, a reaffirmation of humanity, and all the rest. But try to realize that not every sexual encounter, especially the first one, is going to make the earth move for you. And don't use the first sexual encounter as a standard of measurement for all your future sexual encounters. This holds equally true for the first sexual encounter of your lifetime and for the first sexual encounter with a new partner.

ON A SCALE OF ONE TO TEN . . .

Especially in the first sexual encounter, a woman may be wondering to herself if she is performing the way she saw Bo Derek perform in a movie. Is she doing it *right*? Is she pleasing her partner? Is she as exciting in bed as she hoped she'd be? Or is she a total sexual wash-out?

It may help to know that such thoughts cross most peoples' minds the first time around and have a tendency to linger long after that. Both men and women worry about their performance, but comparing sexual performance with an unreal model can do no good. Feelings of anxiety during the first sexual encounter are something you already have enough of. Anyway, even movie stars have off days. And nights.

At the beginning of a new sexual relationship one frequently wonders how one stacks up. "Am I as good as his last girl friend?" or "Do I perform as well as that guy she told me about up at the lake last summer?"

In the high-pressure world of today's single's scene this kind of competition can intensify. People worry that if they don't deliver a good sexual performance, "He won't call again" or "She won't go out with me again."

The best advice I can give is "Try not to worry." First sexual encounters should not be approached as a kind of audition. Caring and tenderness are the things that matter in a relationship, in bed and out, not a high X-rating bestowed on performance. Sex is not an area in which to strive for awards. No one is handing out Oscars.

"HURRY UP, PLEASE, IT'S TIME"

Women often tell me, "I didn't really care for him much, but I felt it was time to lose my virginity." These usually strike me as very sad words. The attitude that if you don't lose your virginity at a particular time you're going to be stuck with it forever can be very harmful. In the case of a woman of thirty who decides to do away with her virginity and find out what all her friends have been talking about over the years, such an attitude is probably harmless enough. She's an adult, and as long as she takes proper contraceptive precautions and enters into things with her eyes open, chances are little harm will be done.

It's a more serious matter with the younger girls, teenagers and even preteenagers, who don't really want to have sex yet but feel they must bow to peer pressure; feel that they must go along because their friends are already sexually active and because their boyfriends are pestering them to have sex.

"What should I do?" a girl of fifteen asked me recently. "Everyone's doing it, but I don't really feel ready."

The answer was simple. "If you're not ready, you're not ready. It isn't a race, and no one is standing by you with a stop-watch."

"Yes, you are on the air."

"This is probably a strange question from a girl from The Bronx, but I was wondering . . . My boyfriend is pressuring me into going to bed with him, and I was wondering if there was any way I can avoid doing it. I mean, I don't need the pressure and I don't want to go to bed with a guy until I have a ring on my finger. I mean, just in case something happens . . . if we break up, or . . ."

"Listen to me very carefully. Under no circumstances let him pressure you into having sex. You tell him that the moment you have that wedding band you are going to be the hottest thing in bed. You are going to be the best lover that this world has ever borne, but that you have decided to wait until you have that wedding ring, and there is nothing wrong with that."

"Okay. What happens if he decides to leave me? Then what do I do?"

"You know what—seriously speaking, not just sexually speaking, very seriously speaking—if he leaves you just because you want to stick to your belief that you want to wait until marriage, then you know what, let him run, and you find yourself someone else."

"Thank you very much."

"Thank you very much for calling."

* * *

The extra danger in sexual activity at this early age is demonstrated by the increasing number—one and a half million—of teenage pregnancies in this country each year. Everyone should use proper contraception. It is absolute folly not to, but so often youngsters rely on hope, hoping that they won't get pregnant, as their only contraceptive. It is a particularly ineffective device, and a terrible toll in human suffering results.

Many young women are anxious to have their first sex because they see it as a magic ritual that will turn them into a different person—an adult. They are in for a disappointment. A girl needs to know that after her first sex she will *not* be a different person. She will still be very much the person she was before she had sex. And she is going to go on being that same person for many years to come. There is no overnight substitute for the long process of growing up.

Boys shouldn't let themselves be rushed, either. And they are feeling the pressure too, believe me.

"You are on the air."

"Dr. Ruth, I have a friend whose name is Randy, and his girl friend wants to go all the way and he doesn't."

"His girl friend wants to go all the way and he doesn't. Tell your friend Randy that Dr. Westheimer said not to do it. You know what, what happens very often is that a girl who is assertive and who says, 'Ah, that means that you are not a man,' and 'That means that you can't have an erection,' and all these things that we hear—this is not really a good relationship. If he doesn't want to go all the way, he should stand up, be counted, and say, 'No, honey, I decided not to.' If she then still insists, then maybe she just doesn't have any respect for his wishes, not only for sexual desire, but for his wishes in general, and they really should reevaluate that relationship. Okay?"

WHEN IT IS GOOD, IT IS VERY, VERY GOOD . . .

If the relationship is a good one, the first sexual encounter stands the best chance of being a good one. It is not very important how long a couple have known each other. It is very important that they care for each other, that they both want to have sex, that they are both in the mood and in a conducive setting.

When things are right, though some anxiety may be present, the first time can be truly wonderful. And since people do carry the memory with them for many years to come, it is only fitting that it be as truly wonderful as possible.

BUT WHEN IT IS BAD, IT IS HORRID

One couple that came to me for help had been married for only a few months. Things had gone from terrible on their wedding night to much worse by the time they came to see me.

The wedding night was the first experience for both of them. He ejaculated before he could penetrate. At first she blamed herself, feeling that there must somehow be something wrong with her to cause the problem. She didn't have an orgasm that night, nor in the succeeding months of their marriage. It took them two weeks to consummate their marriage, and by that time she had stopped blaming herself and had turned to blaming him. He in turn blamed her. But neither talked about it. Instead they allowed their hostility toward each other to grow and fester, effectively destroying their marital relationship before it had had a chance to begin.

Neither of them was to blame. The real culprit was sexual ignorance. And by not talking about it they only made it worse. It took a lot of therapy, and a lot of painful self-examination, before they were able to take the first steps toward undoing the damage that their early ignorance had caused.

"Hello, Dr. Ruth. My name is Liz."

"Yes, Liz?"

"I'd like to ask you . . . I am eighteen years old and I am still a virgin, and I have never masturbated before and I'd like to know, is the reason because I am a virgin that I never have?"

"No. I will tell you what. Number one, if you are a virgin, don't worry about it. There will be a guy in your life either after you are married or before, and just stay a virgin—don't worry about it— don't let anybody pressure you into it."

"I won't let anybody pressure me into it. It's just that I was wondering . . ."

"Let me tell you something about masturbating. It has nothing to do with being a virgin or not. Some people do masturbate and some don't. Just don't worry about it. Are you in school?"

"I'm going into college."

"Terrific. Don't worry about it. It will just come by itself. It has nothing to do with being a virgin. Some people being virgins do masturbate and some people not being virgins don't masturbate. Somehow you might at some time or other get sexually aroused and think of some great guy that you are in love with and you might find yourself touching yourself down there, and touching the clitoris, and bringing yourself to orgasm, and that is okay, but don't force it. If right now you haven't masturbated, don't worry about it, and leave it alone. Okay?"

"Also, I'd like to ask . . . is an orgasm the same as coming?"

"Yes."

"Okay. Thank you."

And some people say there is too much public information about sex! Liz's questions are typical of the questions in the minds of young people in the 1980s. And we see what comes of ignorance about sex. A young person like Liz needs someone to go to with all sorts of questions—someone she can trust.

THE POWER OF THE IMAGINATION

The only sure aphrodisiac is the one between your ears—your mind. Our imaginations and our fantasies and moods can transform the sexual encounter into something sublime. But this imaginative ability can be a two-edged sword. It can lead to bitter disappointments. When a young woman has convinced herself that her partner has all the charm of a Robert Redford, she can be in for a rude awakening when they make love. If all she can think of is how heavy he is lying with all his weight on top of her, and that he is suffocating her because he doesn't know how to kiss and has positioned his face so that it has sealed off her nose and her mouth, rather than experiencing ecstasy, she may instead be convinced that she is shortly going

69

to die. And though she may not complain, because she doesn't want to hurt his feelings, the experience can be keenly disappointing. In this case imagination won't be enough. She will have to tell him frankly how she feels. Or risk an early death by suffocation!

DON'T BE AFRAID TO STUMBLE

If the first sexual encounter is less than ideal, take heart. Look at it in terms of a child first learning how to walk.

When a child sets off on its first steps, there is usually quite a bit of stumbling along the way. Sometimes a child makes it across the room on the first try but, more often than not, some time will pass before it gets past the stumbling stage. But, eventually, that child *will* make it across the room. You may be one of the lucky ones who gets it right the first time. But just because you do stumble the first time or two doesn't mean you won't ultimately cross the room just as well as the kid who zipped across the first time out. Or even better.

Just as most children do eventually learn to walk across the room, most people can eventually learn how to have good sex.

6
TOUCHING
AND TALKING

One of the most frequent complaints I get from women is that their husbands' lovemaking lacks foreplay. Men *sometimes* voice this complaint about their wives, but women raise the issue more often.

> *Dear Dr. Ruth:*
>
> *Before we were married there was so much petting and kissing it was like he couldn't get enough of it. We'd drive to a lovers' lane and spend hours "making out." We never had intercourse but we would get tremendously excited with all the fumbling over and under our clothes and all the hot and heavy kissing. . . . Maybe it was frustrating but it was so exciting. . . . But in the two years since we got married it has all become so mechanical. A kiss or two and then we're having sex, and then we're falling asleep. We both orgasm, but something is missing. It's like we had all the foreplay before we got married and now all we have is the sex. . . .*

There *is* something missing. Foreplay provides more than a means for a man and a woman to stimulate each other to the point where they can engage in sexual intercourse. Foreplay is a form of communication between two partners in a relationship. It elevates the sex act into the art of making love.

71

Foreplay should not be viewed as just a prelude to orgasm. Even women who have orgasms easily say that they crave it. They want the message of reassurance it carries that their partners love them and care about them and take pleasure in kissing and caressing their bodies.

Often a man feels that as long as he provides enough foreplay so that the woman lubricates enough to have intercourse and experience an orgasm, it is enough. Many men view foreplay as the price they have to pay for having sex. But this bartering attitude can be highly destructive to a relationship. And once the pattern has set in, it is difficult to overcome.

Foreplay is not merely a matter of mechanical expertise. It is part of the entire lovemaking experience. If a couple are well tuned-in to each other, it will be a natural part of the flow of their love-making. Both partners will want to touch and hug and kiss each other and revel in the joy of giving and receiving pleasure from each other's bodies. A continuing sense of romance and love and human contact is kept alive through regular foreplay, and the bond of caring that marks a good relationship is strengthened each time a couple make love to each other.

Men often complain that after a hard day's work they simply don't have the energy for extended foreplay. And now that women have entered the job market in significant numbers, I hear that from women as well. All they want, they say, is sexual release. While sometimes a quickie may be perfect for the occasion, the relationship risks becoming dull and boring if quickies take over entirely. Too many quickies point to a relationship in which the people really have very little to say to each other. If they have little communication of any kind, sex may become merely ''getting their rocks off'' so they can go to sleep.

PERILS OF THE ELEVEN O'CLOCK NEWS

Johnny Carson sometimes jokes about his show being the American substitute for foreplay, or the biggest modern threat to it. I often think that the eleven o'clock news is worse, because the news can be so depressing. It can put you off sex at night entirely.

Regular TV watching every night of the week is bad for a couple's sex life. By the time the eleven o'clock news comes on they are so numb from staring at the tube that they go on watching the news, with its depressing effect. Let the late news go; you can catch it in the morning! Spoiling your love life won't have any improving effect on world events in any case.

Or try leaving the set off the whole evening. Spend the evening together. Have some wine, go for a walk together, turn on the radio or the stereo. Have a nosh together. Or if you don't live in New York and don't know how to nosh, have a snack! Doing things together through the evening is in itself part of foreplay.

Very often, after a year or two of marriage, the foreplay seems to simply end. But foreplay should not end when the novelty of a relationship has worn off. That is just the time when it becomes more important than ever. Extended foreplay has to be cultivated. It is a large part of what keeps a sexual relationship alive and exciting over the years.

SPORTS WEEKENDS
During the fall and winter many wives complain of becoming football widows.

> *Dear Dr. Ruth:*
> *After a whole weekend watching games on TV he suddenly remembers he hasn't got laid. This happens about 11:30 Sunday night, when he has caught the news of all the sports events he missed. Then it's time to fit me in, or rather to fit it into me. . . . After forty-eight hours of nothing but grunts and "Hey, fix me a sandwich?" he tries to make up with about ten minutes of foreplay. I'm glad we don't have a gun in the house because I might shoot him. . . . I try to watch some games with him, but I'm just never going to be a sports freak. A five-yard gain just doesn't turn me on. . . .*

But she does have another option, and that is simply to talk to him. She can ask him to sacrifice one game out of the whole mishmash of games and events featured each week to spend time with her. While he might react with astonishment at the outlandish nature

73

of the request, the woman needs to be firm enough to resist her husband's protests. She must make him understand that if he wants her to be there when the season is finished, he had best pay some attention to her.

It really is unrealistic to expect a woman to want to make love to a man who has totally ignored her over an entire weekend. During the weekend, she has to go on taking care of him and of the house and the kids while he has enjoyed himself. If a man simply can't deprive himself of his sports, he should make an effort to spend some time with his wife before or after the games. But maintaining contact over the long sports weekend is vital if he would like to be able to approach her as something other than a stranger when the weekend is over. And then he had best be prepared for a long and devoted stint of foreplay. She deserves it.

TELL ME YOU LOVE ME

It has been said that men fall in love with their eyes; women fall in love with their ears. Women, more than men, take pleasure in words and phrases calculated to arouse their ardor. The old cliché about whispering sweet nothings in her shell-like ear refers to a world in which a man spoke the words of love and the woman then gave him her heart—and perhaps something more. Has the world changed? A once-popular song lyric announced that words of love were no longer enough to win a girl's heart. I doubt that. Anyway, they certainly don't hurt.

Talking to your partner, whatever the subject matter, brings you closer together. Sharing the events of the day with each other, opening up your lives, sharing your plans and dreams, reviewing all the trivia that makes up a day, are all a kind of foreplay, because they all contribute to intimacy between you.

DR. JEKYLL AND MR. HYDE

Those of us who go out to work and come home at night are often expected to be at least two different people each day. Perhaps your job calls for you to be aggressive, manipulative, ruthless, cost-effective, all day. When you get back to your dear ones, these are not the traits that are called for. A loving person is expected in the home. For some people the change is like a movie monster transformation, not easy to make and, in fact, there are times when you are more apt to become a monster *after* the day's toil and the rush hour are behind you. You have held in your frustration and anxiety at work, and the hurly-burly of family life makes Mr. Cool of the office turn into a snarling beast with fangs, unless you have a little wind-down time. Or at least a quiet doze alone before dinner. Some men find it hard to make their wives understand the need for this. Alone all day at home or with the childrens' prattle and demands, a woman is looking for a bit of lively adult chatter.

Or these days, where the wife works and has the more demanding kind of job, the situation may be reversed. Or it may be that both partners work and one is just temperamentally more likely to fray toward the end of the day.

This is a time when people have to understand each other's needs and be ready to listen to requests for individual privacy. Partners in a marriage or relationship must have a way of getting and giving what is needed.

TALKING LEADS TO TOUCHING

Foreplay isn't just pushing all those buttons and twiddling those dials of your partner's body to show your expertise, like somebody in an old 1950s space opera. It is words, thoughts, fantasies, and games just you two share. And you can't get into all that unless you talk to each other about it.

My observation is that the talking couples are the great foreplayers. The things they get into!

There's making love with some of your clothes on, for instance. That requires a struggle with the clothes, and breathing heavily.

"It's that feeling of doing something illicit," a man told me. "Something premarital, sneaky, *bad*! My wife and I have this thing. We act sometimes the way we did before we were married. We always had to fight our way through and around buttons and straps and snaps and buckles, doing it with some of our clothes on. . . . It sort of underlines the fact that you both *mean* to do it, in spite of obstacles. Now sometimes I'll undress her down to her bra and panties, and she undresses me to my underwear, and we hit the

75

bed like we can't wait. These sessions get pretty passionate! Sometimes I go crazy and rip her panties to get at her.''

It was all good raunchy fun, though. The wife told me she would put on underwear she felt was expendable, ready to throw away. And he'd pretend remorse and buy her nice new things, very sexy.

YOU SCRATCH MY BACK . . .

Different strokes for different folks indeed! The things I hear that people like, that either arouse them wildly or that they can take by the hour, slowly working up . . .

Back scratching, stroking the insides of the thighs, feather-dusting the erogenous zones, massaging the toes and feet . . .

One client had been in a relationship for years with a woman who loved him to play with her nipples a long, long time. When they broke up and he acquired a new lady, he went on with this routine because by now he was good at it and, of course, he liked it. You know what? After they had been together awhile, the new lady confided that she didn't mind it if it turned him on, but she had other preferences, one in particular. He took this very good-humoredly, and in time he asked what her particular pleasure might be. She didn't speak but guided his hand to her anus and moved his finger lightly around the outside. That was what she liked. Later she did the same thing to him, and the results were electrifying!

And sometimes it's worth reversing roles, the woman being the aggressor, the skilled love technician, the caressing, tickling, just-barely-scratching, I-know-just-where-and-how-you-like-it turner-on, while the man lies back and takes it until he's moaning with desire.

There are men who can't let this be done to them. Perhaps they are still little boys inside, who think cowboys kiss only their horses. Well, a lot of men just literally don't know what they're missing by not allowing themselves to lie back and enjoy being pleasured!

Making love and being made love to reinforces a sense of being cherished, and both men and women *need* to feel they are cherished by their partners. Foreplay, verbal and nonverbal alike, sends the message "I cherish you, you are very dear to me." There are few more important messages a person can deliver. Or receive.

A LITTLE LOUDER, PLEASE

When two people don't talk to each other about sex, there is often a deathly silence in the love chamber, too. A lively love chamber should not sound like a tomb. What are the sounds of love?

Listen!

Wet, sucking, smacking sounds mingled with inarticulate high-pitched squeals and guttural grunts. Pigs eating slops from a trough? Not likely, in the pitch dark. Pigs are fed by daylight. Not pigs eating, no—two human beings making love in the dark on a hot night, no air conditioning.

This is not the sound track of a movie. It is real life.

In the movies the beautiful couple make graceful love in gentle light and soft focus, as a symphony orchestra plays somewhere out of sight. This is the image of lovemaking many people prefer, and that is why stereo or radio music is played in many bedrooms, to drown out the grunts and bumps and squishes.

Some people *like* the barnyard or suction-pump sounds of sex and find them very exciting.

Some like unmuffled wet sounds one week and Brahms's lullaby the next.

A record player is best if you want total control of music selection. You can ask your partner to help choose the record. You can suit your mutual mood—Debussy one night, the "Anvil Chorus" another, when you both want music to thrust by!

Lots of people prefer the radio because, tuned in to an all-music station, you don't have to get up at the wrong moment to turn the record. But avoid all-news programs. They can be distracting. One couple told me they were doing mutual oral sex (sixty-nine) when a story came on the news about an alligator rampaging through a small southern town and chewing up the residents. This put a halt to the proceedings, at least for a time.

But whether you like those earthy, uncouth natural noises or prefer to fill the love chamber with baroque sounds or rock 'n' roll, you are better off than the people who make cautious, inhibited love in a stifled and stifling silence.

Dear Dr. Ruth:
I feel certain that I have an unusually large vagina, and

when we have sex it makes these unromantic slurping noises. I try to move less, which I realize is counter-productive. He does not complain but once he began to laugh, then stopped when he realized I wasn't laughing with him. I felt myself blush in the dark. I wish at least that I didn't blush. A cow has a vagina this big but at least she doesn't have to blush. What can be done about this? . . .

My Dear:

One is lucky to have a vagina; it can be such a pleasure, and it gives such pleasure. And never gets caught in a zipper! Your lover sounds like a nice man. He has a sense of humor, and also is considerate—he stopped laughing when he sensed it was inappropriate. Perhaps when you get to know him better and trust him you will be able to laugh at something funny with him. Laughter is not entirely out of place in the bedroom. In a tomb, perhaps. Meanwhile, play the radio. If you are embarrassed to suggest this innovation in your lovemaking, tell a little fib. Many people find music erotic. Tell him you are one of these. He may guess your real reason, but he will think you are a clever woman to think up such a tactful way of dealing with this problem. Anyway, if either partner finds the earthy sounds of real copulation upsetting, music is called for. It is better than trying to suppress these sounds by reluctant lovemaking.

When you are ashamed of something, you do it as stealthily as you can. Making love is nothing to be ashamed of.

As a sex therapist I am distressed when I hear about sexual silence. There are two kinds of sexual silence—one produced by no noises in the bedroom where people are coupling, one produced by people never talking about sexual matters with their spouses, lovers, constant companions, partners, or whatever you care to call them.

Neither kind leads to real sexual happiness.

THE STRONG, SILENT TYPE

I frequently hear women complain that their husbands never make any sound during lovemaking. Aside from a grunt at the moment of ejaculation, many men make love, as one woman put it, "Like he's a burglar who's afraid he'll be arrested."

Many men raised to be "the strong, silent type" and taught not to express their emotions have difficulty voicing their emotions during sexual intercourse.

But women want the awareness of what the man is feeling. After all, if a woman makes her partner moan and cry out with delight, it is a tribute to her own sexuality.

BE A LADY AT ALL TIMES

Many women, from the time they were little girls, were taught always to behave like ladies, with dignity and self-restraint. Obviously, a lady doesn't shout in bed and she doesn't screech. What would the neighbors think? Let alone the children in the next room. But there are times when you can be too much of a lady.

WHAT *WILL* THE CHILDREN THINK?

While I certainly don't recommend that parents invite the children into their bedroom to witness their sexual encounters, if children do occasionally hear some noise coming from their parents' bedroom—so what? Sexual activity does not have to take place in graveyard silence. If young children ask the following morning what all the noise was about, they can always be told that Mommy and Daddy were joking with each other or that Daddy was tickling Mommy. If the kids know that Mommy and Daddy have fun together when they're in the bedroom, no harm is done.

Suppose a child does hear or see something and is upset?

"You are on the air."

"Hello, Dr. Ruth. My problem is that my five-year-old daughter walked in on my husband and I while we were having sex, and I wanted to know how to deal with this. What should I say to her?"

"Okay. Did she say anything? Did she ask any questions?"

"She was very scared. She was crying. She thought he was hurting me."

"You know, I'm glad you are asking me that, because this is something that happens to many, many parents of small children.

Now, the first thing for the future is, please do close your bedroom door. Just so *you* don't have to worry."

"Right."

"Okay. Now, the next thing is, I would take her aside when you are alone with her—maybe with an ice-cream cone—and I would say to her, 'Honey, the other day when you came in, Daddy didn't hurt Mommy. Daddy and Mommy made love, and it feels good. The only reason that you might have thought that he hurt me was because of moaning and groaning'—You know, use the terms that she can understand. And you can pick up a book, like *How Babies Are Born,* and tell her this is exactly how Mommy and Daddy hugged and kissed and made love. Use that term, and tell her it feels good. If there is some moaning and groaning, it's just because it feels good."

"Right."

"And when you grow up you are going to have a husband of your own and you are going to make love, too."

"Okay, I will. Thank you very much."

BREAKING THE SILENCE BARRIER

If you are afraid to make any noise in the bedroom, your lovemaking will be inhibited, and if you are afraid to express your feelings, you won't want to say "Press harder here!" or "Keep on going there!"

If you feel free to talk about sex out of the bedroom, it will be easier to ask for something *in* the bedroom. Sexual silence is a bad habit and hard to break, but take the chance—break it.

A good time to tell about your special sexual preferences is during that delicious time when you are lying there after sex, waiting perhaps for the next wave of desire. And this is a way to break that silence barrier. Say what was nice about what just happened between you. "Honey, that was great!" There's a good way to start. But don't add "Why can't it always be that good?" Watch those little jokes and so-called gentle criticisms! On this subject, everyone is hypersensitive. One little negative comment at the wrong time and you seem to have attacked your whole sex life with this partner.

Now, it may be that you just have to speak up about something in your sex life that is not good. But don't talk about it in the bedroom! That is the love place, and the good mood there is sacred, never to be spoiled. Talk about upcoming bills and visits from your , sister-in-law and bad aspects of your sex life in the kitchen, over a nice cup of coffee, some time long after or before your coming together sexually.

There is the place to explain that "kitchee-kitchee-coo" baby talk during sex is just what you can't stand! In the kitchen, not the bedroom.

Tell your pleasures, your wants, your fantasies, in the bedroom. Keep the bad news for elsewhere, at another time.

THE SIGH THAT MADE ALL THE DIFFERENCE

"It's not that our sex life is bad or anything," the wife said. "It just lacks something. We want more, I don't know, *zest*."

The husband and wife were in my office. The wife did the talking. She had plenty of zest! The husband was silent. I made a guess—that the lack of zest was from his side of the bed! He was uncommunicative. I picked this up while talking with them—I mean talking with *her*.

I learned that theirs was a silent bedroom. Even if she made some noise, he could drown it in his silence, which extended out of the bedroom into the whole apartment. He was a good provider of income—an accountant—and an even better provider of silence. He wasn't ill-natured or uncooperative, and in one-word sentences he agreed that he was not contributing a joyous sound to their marriage. I asked him to try to express some emotion at home, as an exercise. Not to overdo it, just try a little at a time. He said he would try, but he didn't know how he would do it.

A few nights later he was lying on the sofa with her, his head on her shoulder, trying to let out emotion. What emotion? The idea was foreign, it had him stymied. He let out a sigh.

She stroked his hair.

Was this it? Communicating? Expressing?

He sighed again. She stroked his hair, and made a little tender sound, and he sighed. Then he moaned a little. His wife decided they had something going here.

In bed that night she encouraged him to snuggle and sigh some more, and he did. He sighed and moaned and after a while they had sex. And guess what the sex had! Zest!

After that this strong, silent accountant would come home and lean on his wife and moan on a regular basis, and she loved it! She was getting something out of him at last! All these wonderful soulful moans and sighs, after all that silence!

That first sigh, in response to my suggestion that he should express something, made all the difference in their marriage.

7
THE MYTH OF
THE FANTASTIC
EVERY-TIME
ORGASM

"You are on the air."

"Hello, Dr. Ruth. My name is Fred. I have a little problem. I had a question asked of me, and of course I refer to you. My girl friend and I have an intimate relationship."

"With contraception?"

"Yes."

"Good."

"Very much so."

"What is the question?"

"We're getting married in about two years. Okay. But she asked me . . . How can I explain to her when she had an orgasm?"

"How can you explain . . . ?"

"She asked me what is the feeling, and I couldn't explain it to her."

"I tell you something. She wants to know how it feels when *you* have an orgasm?"

"When *she* has one. She doesn't know the feeling . . ."

"Aha!"

"That if she had one or not. She's not sure."

"Okay. Now I understand. You can't explain that to her, because the only person—that's an interesting question—the only person that can say if she had an orgasm is herself. No way can you tell her if she had an orgasm or not. And if she tells you that she doesn't know if she had one or not, I would suggest . . . Remember the book that I suggest very often, *For Yourself,* by Lonnie Barbach, because it sounds to me, I'm not sure, of course, but it sounds to me that she probably does not have an orgasm. Otherwise, she would not ask such questions. She would know that she had an orgasm.''

''Right. To me it seems like she has one because she'll start shaking. . . .''

''Right. But there is something in the sexual therapy literature that's called a missed orgasm. There are some women who do have an orgasm, who have all the physiological feelings of an orgasm, but it doesn't register as a pleasurable experience, as an orgasm. If that's the case, then a sex therapist could help her.''

''Right.''

''So what I would do is, you have a good relationship, you're using contraception. I would suggest to her that if she doesn't really know if she has had one, to read the book, *For Yourself,* and if that doesn't give her the answer, to make an appointment. You know, sometimes it's enough to talk with a counselor, with a sex therapist, for one session, just to get some education.''

''Right.''

''But don't let it slide. You sound like a concerned guy, so don't let it slide. Okay?''

''Okay.''

''Thank you so much for calling.''

Many women are wondering what an orgasm is like, or if they have ever had one, or if they'll ever have one. And many women I see in my private practice are in search of the fantastic orgasm that never fails.

Orgasms provide a wonderful feeling of release after the build-up of tension during a sexual encounter. But one orgasm may not necessarily resemble another. Orgasms are really very much like sneezes—sometimes big and sometimes small!

CLITORAL VERSUS VAGINAL ORGASMS
Sigmund Freud taught that there are two kinds of orgasms. He distinguished between clitoral orgasms, in which the clitoris is directly

stimulated—rubbed, massaged, moved—until the woman reaches orgasm; and vaginal orgasms, in which the woman reaches orgasm without stimulation of the clitoris. Without going into a whole physiological treatise here, it is enough to say that this is not what we believe today.

This is important because Freud went on to say that whereas vaginal orgasms were experienced by women who were "mature," clitoral orgasms were experienced only by "immature" women. Until relatively recent research, pioneered by Masters and Johnson and others, many people believed in Freud's division of orgasms. Many people today, men and women alike, still live with the mistaken belief that if a woman does not have an orgasm during intercourse, that if the sensation of a penis inside her vagina does not bring her to orgasm without stimulation of the clitoris, she is not a mature woman.

It is important for people to understand that in one way or another, through direct or indirect stimulation, the clitoris is *always* involved in female orgasm.

THE NUMBERS GAME

Research has shown that today approximately thirty percent of women in America experience orgasm during sexual intercourse. Fortunately, this percentage appears to be growing as people become more sexually literate. But, even for this thirty percent who experience orgasm with the penis inside the vagina, stimulation of the clitoris is involved. The clitoris sits at the upper tip of the vagina's inner lips. During intercourse the hood of skin that covers it moves back and forth over the "erect" clitoris, providing indirect friction.

Approximately another thirty percent of women in this country do need direct manual or other (oral, or with a dildo or a vibrator, etc.) stimulation of the clitoris in order to have an orgasm. Some of these women can be taught to have orgasms during intercourse. Many factors are involved, one major factor being the intensity of their own desire for that experience.

Another thirty percent do not experience orgasm at all. Most of these women can be taught to have an orgasm through direct stimulation of the clitoris, and some of them can then be further taught to have orgasms during sexual intercourse, again providing that they want to. In any case, every woman who *wants* to have an orgasm should learn how it is done or to be attempted.

The remaining ten percent of women are divided roughly in half on each side of the curve. Five percent are quite easily orgasmic—have orgasms easily. Such women can sit in a boring lecture, at the beach reading a book, or in a movie, and they can tighten the muscles of their thighs, providing indirect friction to their clitoris, while they think erotic thoughts, and thus bring themselves to orgasm.

One elderly woman told me how it was in the sweatshops in New York City, where she worked as a young woman, back in the days when sewing machines were operated by foot pedals. When she first started working in the shops she noticed that some of the other women from time to time would grow very red in the face and begin pumping away faster and faster at their foot pedals until they suddenly relaxed and sighed and, with a little secretive smile, went back to pumping at a more normal speed. After a while this woman, who happened to be highly orgasmic, chanced upon the discovery that by using a certain rhythm on the foot pedal and sitting at the right angle, she could bring herself to orgasm. It was then that she understood what those other women were smiling about!

The remaining five percent of women on the curve of orgasmic response are those women who simply cannot have an orgasm. As a rule these are women with deep-seated psychological problems, such as acute depression, or women who suffer from serious physical ailments. Other reasons for a total lack of orgasmic response include alcoholism and certain drug-related disorders.

No woman should conclude on her own that she is in this last five percent. If she suspects this, and desires orgasm, she should seek medical help. And she should not accept the word of the first physician that she is in this percentage, nor the second, nor the third. Even for women in this category there is hope, with in-depth therapy.

AN ORGASM IS AN ORGASM IS AN ORGASM

A common myth about orgasms is that every single time a woman experiences one, the earth has to shake and the stars have to twinkle. It simply isn't like that. Often an orgasm will be more a mild feeling of pleasurable release than an earthquake. But if a woman does not understand this, she is liable to be terribly disappointed both in herself and in her partner. She might tell her partner that he is not a good lover because other men have brought her to heights of ecstasy, while he has only given her a little orgasm. If instead of blaming him, or herself, she understood that at some times her orgasms will just be greater than at other times, much unhappiness could be avoided.

There is also a phenomenon in psychosexual therapy called a missed orgasm, mentioned in the beginning of this chapter. This is an orgasm that does occur but is so vague that it doesn't register with the woman as pleasurable. She may simply find that her sexual tension has been somewhat released. Again, an awareness of the phenomenon can prevent a lot of disappointment.

QUALITY NOT QUANTITY

"You are on the air."

"Hello, Dr. Ruth. How are you?"

"I am fine."

"Okay. My problem is, I have an extremely small penis. I feel, you know, I have to get it enlarged some way. I was wondering if any of these items work."

"Let me ask you a question. Did any woman that you have had sexual intercourse with ever complain? Or is it in your mind that you have such a small penis?"

"I don't think they ever complained, but . . . I think it's mostly in my mind. Well, let me tell you this. When we go to the beach with some of the other guys, this friend of mine, he usually makes fun of me, you know."

"First of all, how come he sees your penis?"

"How come? Well, you know, we go skinny-dipping sometimes."

"All right. First of all, then, he's not a good friend. Let's start with this. Because a penis, even a small penis, does get erect, and gets erect proportionately more than a larger penis. And if you've never had a woman complain, then I would do two things. I would not think about a device. I would, first of all, go to a physician (to either a urologist or an internist) and find out if your idea of that small penis is really true, or if it is small but within the norm. Then you tell your friend to cut it out, because that's not very funny to make fun. That would be like somebody making fun about somebody who is a little bit heavy or somebody who's very short, and that's not very funny. What I would tell your friend . . . is cut it out if he wants to stay your friend. For you, I would go and see a physician. Also what I would do, next time you masturbate, I have an idea.''

"Right.''

"You take a measuring—you know—like a ruler.''

"Right.''

"And I want you to measure your penis.''

"Right.''

"And once you have measured it, I want you to write me a little note and tell me how big it is when it is fully erect, before ejaculation. Can you do that?''

"Sure.''

"You masturbate, and just before ejaculation, you take the ruler—have that ruler next to you—and measure it, and then send me the measurement.''

"What is a normal size? Can I ask you that?''

"There is no normal size. But I just want to see if even that kind of measuring doesn't do something to give you a little bit more confidence.''

"That's what I need—encouragement!''

"That's right. And you tell that guy to cut it out. Okay?''

"Okay. Will do. And have a nice day.''

"Thank you for calling. Bye-bye.''

Yet another myth! The larger the penis, the more satisfying the orgasm. The truth of the matter is that the size of the penis does not matter. Even a small penis can provide the indirect friction to the clitoris that results in orgasm. It is the man's skill and patience and understanding as a lover, not the size of his penis, that will bring his partner to orgasm.

But, in fact, a woman's orgasm has less to do with the skill of her partner than with her own willingness to let go and give herself up to the sexual pleasure that leads to orgasm. The greatest lover in the world cannot give a woman an orgasm unless she allows herself to have one.

HOW TO HAVE AN ORGASM

Women who have difficulty having an orgasm and want to learn how, should first learn to masturbate. Dr. Helen Singer Kaplan has developed a method that works for most women. They must learn how to have an orgasm by themselves and, very importantly, they must learn how to give themselves *permission* to have an orgasm. Very often, because of their upbringing, women have a strong unwillingness against expressing good sexual feelings. The best way for a woman to overcome a reluctance to give herself up to sexual pleasure and to learn how to have an orgasm is to explore her genitalia.

A good way to begin is by lying on a bed, putting her legs up, and using a mirror to take a really good look at her own vagina. She should explore the inner lips and the outer lips and take the time to caress herself. It is also helpful if she caresses herself in a bubble bath or in the shower. The important thing is to take the time to explore and discover the amount of pressure she needs on her clitoris and the rhythm and the speed which are most effective in bringing her to orgasm.

She can also insert a finger, or something smooth and hard, like the handle of a hairbrush, or a dildo, into her vagina in order to approximate the feeling of a penis, while she strokes her clitoris and fills her head with sexual thoughts. It is important that she relax and give herself up to her sexual fantasies in order that she not be a spectator to her own sexual response. If a woman is anxiously thinking Am I excited? Am I more excited now? Am I feeling any pleasure when I do this? she is unlikely to be able to give herself up entirely to the sensations of sexual pleasure. And this surrender to her own sensuality is crucial.

Often, when trying to teach themselves how to have an orgasm, women don't give themselves enough time. If they do not experience sexual arousal and orgasm within ten minutes, they may get impatient and think, Who needs it? and get very upset. If this reaction is anticipated, it may be easier for a woman to be patient, to overcome whatever awkwardness she may feel, and persist in exploring her own sexual response. If she simply cannot let herself go, it is a problem that counseling can usually solve relatively easily.

A woman has to understand that there is nothing wrong with taking the time and going step by step, slowly and very patiently, to learn about her body as she teaches herself how to have an orgasm. It is important that while she's doing all of this she has privacy and a sense of security that she will not be interrupted. I usually advise the women I see to take the phone off the hook and be sure they have at least an hour to themselves when no one will interrupt them. Often I advise that they put on some music, perhaps have a glass of wine, and generally do anything they can to distract themselves from other things.

Teaching yourself to have an orgasm should not be looked upon as a chore. If it doesn't work the first time, don't lose heart. Wait a few days and then try again. Most women are able, eventually, to teach themselves how to have an orgasm.

Once a woman has learned how to give herself an orgasm, she can teach her partner how to give her one. As they lie in bed together she should place his hand on top of hers as she stimulates her clitoris and brings herself to orgasm. Later she can put her hand over his and guide him through the necessary motions. All of this can be awkward and embarrassing, but with a loving and patient man who is concerned that his partner experience sexual pleasure, most women can eventually learn to share a truly fulfilling sexual relationship.

GOOD VIBRATIONS
"You are on the air."

"Hello, Dr. Ruth. My name is Doug. Me and my fiancée, we had great sex for six months, and now all of a sudden I can't seem to please her anymore."

"Did you talk to her about it?"

"Yes. It seems we get to the point of the climax, and it never gets over it."

"But that is something that might be on her mind. It might have nothing to do with you."

"A lot of times we'll have sex, and I'll ejaculate just before she's ready, and it bothers her."

"Yes, but are you ejaculating very fast?"

"No, because I love to caress her. . . ."

"If it's a question of premature ejaculation, then that is easily curable if you go and see a sex therapist or a sex clinic."

"Okay."

"But if it is something that she has on her mind, then even if you could hold the erection and would not ejaculate for a long time, it wouldn't help. So, it's not clear if it is something that's on her mind, because, after all, before this problem came up, it worked well."

"It worked fantastic."

"Then there must be something that's on her mind."

"All right."

"And maybe what you ought to do is to talk to her."

"Okay."

"All right."

"Can I ask you another question?"

"Yes?"

"What do you think about using a vibrator?"

"I think it is great, except that I want to warn women not to get used to having an orgasm only with a vibrator, because the vibrations are so strong that sometimes afterwards neither the penis nor a man's hand can duplicate that strong vibration. But as a sexual enrichment and as having additional fun, I think it's great."

"You think it's good to have?"

"Yes. Absolutely okay."

"Okay."

"Okay."

If a woman has trouble bringing herself to orgasm, a vibrator can be of great help. Because the vibrations produced around the clitoris by a vibrator are so strong, most of the time, unless there is a massive psychological reluctance on the woman's part, the vibrator will bring her to orgasm.

The problem with a vibrator is that a woman may get hooked on it. No penis and no hand—not hers and not his—can duplicate the strength of the vibrations. But if she does get "hooked," she can always wean herself away from it.

Some couples enjoy sharing a vibrator. A woman can ask her partner to use it with her, but she has to be careful. Some men may feel threatened, they may feel that the vibrator is a replacement for them. She needs to make it clear, both to herself and to her partner, that no vibrator, however effective, can replace the warmth and fulfillment that comes from the relationship between two people who love and care for each other. A vibrator is simply an added variation to the lovemaking, both for women who have difficulty having orgasms and for women who don't have any trouble at all.

Most men do not enjoy the sensation of a vibrator on the penis. However, many men enjoy the stimulation of a vibrator at their anus or used for massage on their back muscles and the rest of their body. As in everything else, if a couple have a basic love and trust between them, they should have no trouble exploring their likes and dislikes, sharing their discoveries, and finding ways to give each other pleasure.

There is no right way or wrong way to use a vibrator. Whatever feels good to you, feels good to you. If you should decide to try a vibrator, there are several places you can get one. Many of the slick magazines for men, and for women, offer them by mail order. Many cities have stores that sell sexual aides. Large pharmacies often carry vibrators in a variety of shapes and sizes. If you are going to buy a vibrator at a pharmacy, however, it's a good idea not to buy it at a place where you regularly do business. One thing you don't need is a clerk giving you a knowing smirk every time you walk in to buy a tube of toothpaste or a box of Band-Aids!

MIRROR, MIRROR

I said earlier that to learn to have an orgasm a woman can begin by studying her genitals in a mirror. Many women have never seen their own private parts, in which they ought to take an interest for many reasons, and which they have every right to study. As little girls they have been taught—less often, of late—not to touch themselves there, that "down there" is dirty. Every woman should overcome this negative idea about her own body.

Little boys have more familiarity with their penises than little girls do with their vaginas, because they see their penises every time they urinate. But many men have never seen their erect penises from the perspective a woman sees it from. Just as a woman should examine her vagina in a mirror, a man should look at his erect penis in a mirror to get an idea of what it looks like to his partner.

SUMMING UP

The majority of women can learn to have fulfilling orgasms regularly and fantastic orgasms sometimes.

A woman must first give herself permission to have that luxurious feeling of sensuality that allows her to experience sexual arousal and fulfillment. She must learn to be aware of her sense of touch so that she can enjoy the differences in texture between, say, the skin around the pubic area, on the inside of the thigh, and on the smooth muscles of the back.

A woman must give herself the time, and make her partner understand how important it is to have that time, to have an orgasm.

Attitude is equally important. Healthy sexuality requires a positive and natural attitude in order to overcome whatever taboos have been ingrained about the genitals and sexual relations being "dirty." Women owe it to themselves to have fulfilling orgasms. A woman must educate herself and her partner in how to give her pleasure. If she is shy and uncomfortable talking about such things, it is understandable and natural, but it is in her own interest, and in her partner's interest as well, that she have good orgasms. Good sexual functioning will give her a feeling of fulfillment and her partner a sense of being an accomplished lover.

It is important to remember that orgasms really *are* like sneezes. Some will be small and some will be big, and they will not always be the same. This is just as well, since if everything was always the same with sexual relations, it would all get very boring.

Most women can have good orgasms if they just have the patience to teach themselves about their own bodies. And all women owe that much to themselves.

8

AFTERGLOW

"I live with a man who does what he does very well," a woman wrote me.

> *He has a good technical job and he plays tennis very well. He is intelligent and strong. I appreciate this, but at the same time it is threatening. . . . When we have sex he goes at it like a master of the art and we both orgasm, but I feel like I'm being played like a violin. I want it, but when he goes to sleep afterward I feel that I am left alone and I can't sleep. He seems to live in another world I am kept out of. I lie there all alone next to him and I want to cry or scream or break something. . . .*

Everyone knows the word foreplay—they hear Johnny Carson use it in his monologue!

Afterplay is a word too, and it belongs in everyone's vocabulary.

I have seen many people in my private practice who have got into the very bad habit of turning over and going to sleep immediately after they have sex.

There is a common myth that only men do this, that after they have "spent it all," they are so exhausted, they just can't stay awake. But women do this too, lots of them. One man told me that after an orgasm his wife "passes out like she's been hit with a sledgehammer."

Falling asleep immediately after having sex is just a bad habit, and like all bad habits, it can be broken. And should be. Afterplay continues the closeness between the lovers. It is mutually comforting and promising.

Afterplay also serves as a prelude to the foreplay of the next sexual encounter, whether that next encounter is later on that night (or day) or takes place a week later.

TRY A LITTLE TENDERNESS
Afterplay doesn't mean passionate embraces and fiery kisses. A gentle hug and a tender kiss on the forehead are fine. The important thing is to convey the message "I love you."

This message is very important and yet, so often, women complain to me that after sex there is no kissing and hugging at all. Even if they have had an orgasm, they feel used. Without that afterplay they feel that they're not needed, not appreciated, that they've been cast away like a used paper cup.

One woman described her husband's after-sex behavior and her reaction to it with strong resentment. "He uses me the way I use my vacuum cleaner. I take it out to fulfill a specific function, and when I'm finished using it, I stuff it back in the closet and forget about it until I need it the next time."

There is an old joke about a couple that slept in twin beds. The man kept murmuring endearing invitations until she woke up; then he kept it up until she got up and came across to him, stubbing a toe on the way.

"Ah, diddums stubbums little toe?" he crooned.

After they had finished, she got up and went back to her bed, again stubbing that same toe. Of course it hurt worse this time.

"Pick up your goddamn feet," he growled.

That is the opposite of afterplay.

Afterplay is not just something two people do while they're waiting for the sensations of sexual gratification to fade. Afterplay reinforces all the spoken and unspoken statements of love and caring that two people exchange during foreplay and sexual intercourse—things like "I love you. You're a good person. You're a warm person. You're a sensual person."

The message "I love you" cannot be conveyed too often. But though you can't walk around all day repeating over and over "I love you, I love you," you *can* show it in other ways.

AS THE TIDE GOES OUT

There is a definite physical release after the sexual climax. The blood that has flowed to the man's penis to make it erect flows back into the rest of the body. The pressure of the blood in the engorged lips of the woman's vagina lessens.

"It's as though," one woman told me, "we were lying on a beach together, just at the edge, feeling the waves slowly recede as the tide goes out." A man described that aftermath as "resting together on a raft, gently bobbing up and down as we watch a sunset."

However that sensation is described, most partners in a good relationship do feel a wonderful, sensual calm after intercourse— and it is something they experience *together*.

For too many people, however, afterplay doesn't happen often enough. People have to be educated toward an appreciation of the fact that sex does not end with ejaculation and orgasm.

Sometimes sex can be made part of an evening's activity, allowing time for a good sexual encounter to be followed by a leisurely period of afterplay and then another of activity. This works well for couples who have sex before they go out to dinner, so that the time spent over their meal is an extension of the afterplay of the first sexual encounter and a start of the foreplay of the next.

PIZZA, COOKIES, AND CONVERSATION

What is important to afterplay is reinforcing the intimacy two people feel as a result of having made love to each other. How afterplay is done doesn't matter very much. It can include getting up and ordering a pizza to be shared in front of late-night television, or fixing a midnight snack, or having a drink, or making some hot chocolate. Or just talking.

When people reflect on their sexual encounters over the years, the ones they remember most fondly are those in which they did something together *afterward* rather than just falling asleep. They may not remember the sexual encounter itself, but they will remember those shared moments of special intimacy.

But obviously none of that is possible if a couple gets stuck in a rut. Always having sex late, after the eleven o'clock news and then immediately drifting off to sleep afterward, is a catastrophe to good sexual functioning.

MULTIORGASMIC WOMEN

For a woman who is multiorgasmic and requires more than one orgasm to be sexually satisfied, the afterplay following her first orgasm becomes the foreplay for the next. While her partner may think he is putting her to sleep, he may actually be gearing her up for the next round. If he should then fall asleep while she is still sexually aroused, she is going to be disappointed. She can, of course, masturbate to give herself successive orgasms, but she would do better to tell her partner what she wants. A man who is a good and considerate lover, and who cares about her, will soon learn to recognize whether what they are engaged in is afterplay or foreplay or a combination of both.

ABUSING AFTERPLAY

Afterplay is so very nice there has to be a way to spoil it.

Suppose a couple begins to look for afterplay, plans some afternoon sex on a day off so there is plenty of energy for a stroll. Window shopping is lovely. But one thing can lead to another, and presently the couple find that after every afternoon session there is a big stack of bills coming in, and the budget is shot to pieces! One or the other of that couple—the careful one is more apt to be the wife, as a matter of fact—will see that afternoon sex is a luxury they can't afford. The thing is to just look, not buy everything, rather than to give up the lovemaking, but with a big impulse buyer in the relationship that may be hard.

Even if money is no object, one partner can come to resent that misuse of afterplay. A wife dragged her husband to my office because she said there wasn't enough afterplay in their life. She had come to love it, but little by little he had cut it off, falling asleep right after they had climaxed. He was not interested in the gentle talk and companionship after sex, it seemed. Only she really liked it.

It turned out that she had a way of getting at him after sex, while he was in a nice, agreeable mood. Her mother had told her that this was the time to ask him for things, so she would ask for a new coat, for new linoleum for the kitchen, or to be taken on his next business trip.

He had the money, and he wasn't stingy, but very naturally he got the idea that every good time in bed had a price tag on it. She did not love their lovemaking for itself, or just because it was with big, wonderful him! So, after sex, he got into the habit of going to sleep, ducking out before the bill came.

His cynicism grew and grew, and he came to realize that certain things cost more than others. If she offered oral sex, he knew she wanted something very big. Thinking this, he was less inclined to feel close and trusting with her after the big treat.

There is enough in life that makes us feel that we always pay for what we get. Sex shouldn't be like that.

This husband not only avoided sharing the afterglow with his wife, but after a while got into the habit of just putting enough into the actual lovemaking to reach his orgasm, and then going to sleep. He was using sex as a sleeping pill.

Why shouldn't he use it anyway he liked? He was paying for it.

But the wife took my advice and learned to present her shopping list at other times, not in the bedroom. He was touched by her making this effort and slowly got over the idea that she was granting favors, bartering sex for more important goodies.

No bad situation is made better without somebody trying.

THE ART OF TOE TOUCHING

Afterplay takes many forms. Snuggling together in each other's arms after sex can be a greater intimacy than the sex itself. Some people are too hot and sweaty to be comfortable with their arms wrapped around each other, but they like to lie together with just toes touching.

If you need to go to the bathroom or to get a drink of water, there is nothing wrong with breaking off the afterplay for a while.

And afterplay doesn't have to take place after *every* sexual encounter. Sometimes it is nice just to fall asleep together. It is important to vary the menu. But afterplay should be enjoyed as part of sexual relations because it is such a good way to maintain the harmony between two people.

Some people like to talk together after sex. This can be a good time to discuss your future plans and hopes and dreams. It can also be a good time to discuss painting the garage, or to get involved in a philosophical discussion, or to talk about whatever else seems right to both of you.

If you've had good sex, it seems that you've climbed a mountain together and are standing on the top, looking down on all your everyday cares. Sometimes you can see things in a different perspective. Problems don't go away, but they do seem smaller and to matter less.

KEEPING YOUR HEAD IN THE AFTERGLOW

That same intimacy is a warm and secret place for you and your lover. A small place, without room for certain unwelcome things in it. Sometimes during this time of mutual confidence people tell each other things that should not be told.

Your lover will know if you have been married before, if you have had an earlier lover, but doesn't need to know everything about that earlier intimacy. For some crazy reason nowadays people have the idea that they must tell each other everything, every detail of their past, every thought in their heads.

In your search for a happier life you may think of trying something called sensitivity training. Some schools of sensitivity training urge everyone to tell everything, even to strangers. This is not good sense, and it isn't even very sensitive about other people's feelings. Your lover doesn't *want* to know some things you know about yourself.

And if you tell everybody everything, you will be sorry.

I had a client who was an executive. He spent a weekend at a company retreat where everybody was urged to reveal his or her most private fantasies. When my client's turn came, he stood up and said, "I'll tell you something I've never told anyone, not even my wife. I get sexually aroused when I see a cow."

Everyone present was sworn to secrecy, remember.

That Monday, when he went to work, what was the first thing this trusting fellow heard?

"Moo! Moo!"

All the department heads, even his own secretary, thought it was a great joke to "turn him on."

He lived it down, but he had learned a lesson about "sensitivity."

At another sensitivity training session the leader told everyone to turn to the person next to him or her and ask, "What turns you on in bed?"

That's good knowledge to share with a lover, but even there you should use good sense. You don't tell everything to anybody, not even a best friend, not even a lover.

Within the intimacy you have with a partner there is room to realize that each has his and her private territory. We are all of us unique beings, no two alike in every need or desire or capacity.

FILET MIGNON OR A CHEF'S SALAD

Quite often I see partnerships in which the woman has more desire for sex than her partner. Sometimes she comes to believe that her partner has lost interest in her or that he is having an affair or is "giving at the office." I also see many men who complain that their wives don't share their interest in sex.

At one time the popular myth was that a man's sex drive was greater than a woman's. This myth has been dispelled to a large extent. Women today are more assertive and more willing to recognize their needs and set about fulfilling them. As one woman I know quipped, "Today we're more willing to lie down for our rights."

It is important for people to understand that sexual appetites may *not* always coincide. I have advised many women who say that their sexual appetite is often aroused when their partner's is not that it is perfectly all right to say to him, "I'm in the mood." And it is perfectly all right for him to hold her in his arms and give her an orgasm, or two or three orgasms, without having an erection himself. It can be a sexual time for *her* alone. And there is nothing wrong with a woman bringing a man to ejaculation when she is not in the mood for sex herself. It can be simply a time for *him* alone.

A woman who asks her partner for sex, whether in words or by touching, does have to be prepared to take the risk of being rejected. She has to be prepared for him to say, "Not tonight, dear, I have a headache." But understanding partners should be willing to pleasure each other, even when they're not in the mood themselves.

This may sound like a throwback to the age of "wifely duties." Perhaps the best way of looking at it is *mutual* responsibility for sexual fulfillment. All of us do things everyday that we are not really in the mood to do—at work, around the home, with the children. We owe our partners, and ourselves, no less.

It is perfectly all right for the man to hold the woman in his arms while she gives *herself* an orgasm. Or for her to hold *him* while he masturbates. In some cases I even advise that they leave the television on so that the unaroused partner will have something to occupy him or her so as not to be bored and fall asleep.

I have counseled some couples to whom the idea of the man giving his wife an orgasm without his having an erection was absolutely appalling. But if the relationship is good and the two people care for each other and can talk out their sexual needs and differences, this technique can be a very good way to meet the different needs of partners in a relationship.

MR. (MRS.) RIGHT DOESN'T LIVE HERE ANYMORE

There is an old story I like very much. A man set off on a quest, telling his friends that he was going to search the whole world to find the perfect woman. When he returned alone, many years later, his friends asked, "What happened? Didn't you find the perfect woman?" "Oh, I found her, all right," he replied, "but she was looking for the perfect man."

No one person can fulfill someone else's every need in life. Even the best partner in the world for you is going to have likes and dislikes that differ from yours.

In selecting a sexual partner you should, of course, look for someone who can fulfill your sexual needs. If there are some differences between you in that area, the best thing to do is to talk them over together.

SIGNIFICANT OTHERS

The sociological term "significant other" refers to people who figure significantly in a person's life. A significant other can be a parent, a friend, a child, or a partner, someone who fulfills some of your important needs.

One woman I know had a very good nonsexual friendship with a man that had lasted over many years. At one point they discussed having an affair and decided that it would almost certainly be short-lived, and that afterward they would find it difficult to remain friends. Since they both valued the continuance of their long friendship more than a short affair, they decided not to have sex together. They remained friends, significant others in each other's lives, fulfilling definite, nonsexual, needs for each other.

BORED TO TEARS

We all know couples who are simply bored to tears with each other. The only things he wants to talk about are his job and sports and office politics and all she wants to talk about are the kids and her friends.

While intimate talks between two partners should deal with aspects of a couple's sex life together, sex does not have to be the *only* topic. Such talks are a time for two people to share something of each other's lives, to talk about the mortgage and the front lawn and the vacations they plan to take.

The purpose of getting together to talk is just that. Whatever the topic of conversation, the act of talking together is usually beneficial to a relationship.

But many people find they have very little to talk about that their partners are at all interested in. Why? Television. Many couples spend far too much time sitting in the same room, not communicating, and only staring at the little screen. Ideally people should read—books, magazines, newspapers, whatever they choose—and ideally not the same things, so that they will have things to discuss and share with each other when they talk.

Taking up hobbies, enrolling in classes, finding other interests, either together or separately, can be a way to put new interest into a relationship.

Talking together does not have to be a summit conference or a contract negotiation; it doesn't have to be a forum to resolve every single problem in your lives. Rather it provides an opportunity to touch base with each other and get to know each other's lives.

THE ART OF LISTENING

"Sometimes I'll be talking to him," one woman complained to me, "and I *know* he hasn't heard a word I've said." Or, as another woman put it, "I listen to him when *he* talks, I know everything he's involved in at work—all the names of the people at the office and everything else. But he doesn't even know what I do all day long."

For some reason women generally seem to be better listeners than men. Or perhaps they are only better at giving the *impression* that they are listening and interested in what they are hearing. But both men and women do need to listen attentively when their partners talk to them.

One clue to being a good listener is to make a mental note of something the other person says and then ask a question about it later, to show that you have been paying attention and *are* listening. *Showing* that you are listening eventually becomes the habit of *really* listening.

Another common fault of bad listeners is that what they are really doing is just waiting for the other person to stop talking so it will be their turn. When they do talk, it is clear they haven't heard anything the other person has said. This is not having a conversation, it is only mutual lecturing.

Another clue to being a good listener is to learn the names of the people your partner regularly talks about. Most people have no trouble remembering the names of many fictional characters from books and television. With a little effort anyone can learn the names of the people in his or her partner's life. And that can be a start to really listening to what the partner has to say.

There are natural listeners and listeners who have learned to listen. Listening is an ability of a disciplined mind, sometimes more than of a naturally sympathetic one.

LEISURELY CONVERSATION

In Europe the art of leisurely conversation is highly valued. One of the highest compliments a German can bestow on his or her partner is to acknowledge that he or she is an equal in the dialogue, a good *Gesprächs* partner. The French have always valued highly a good storyteller, a raconteur, who can hold his audience spellbound with a tale about absolutely anything. In Mediterranean countries dinnertime often lasts for hours with the conversation as much an element in the dinner as the food.

From time to time a leisurely dinner at a good restaurant with your partner can be a very good idea. Even if the cost of the meal is a little higher, the time to talk is well worth it.

Some people may feel that having a leisurely dinner together is a waste of time, time that could be better spent at the movies or at a party or in bed. But time spent with your partner is time invested in the partner and in your relationship. Just as in anything else, time and effort invested in your partner usually pay off.

9
PERKING UP
THE SEXUAL
APPETITE

"You are on the air."

"Dr. Ruth, my name is Connie. . . . My problem is I have been married nine months now. Our sex life was very good at the beginning, but I notice now as the months are going on it has been going down and down. I mean, we're both not really into it anymore. I thought maybe you could give me some tips on how to bring it back up."

"Okay. Now, tell me a little bit. What happens in your life? Are you both working very hard?"

"Yes, we are. We both have jobs and we come home very tired."

"What time do you come home?"

"I come home at five, and he is already home."

"Aha. And what do you do then, when you get home?"

"I cook dinner. We eat. I do the dishes. He goes on the couch and goes to sleep. And that's it."

"Oh, my gosh . . . I have an idea. When you get home, for example, tomorrow . . . When the two of you do have sex, is it good?"

"Yes, it is."

"And you have sexual satisfaction?"

"Yes."

"Okay. It's not just the timing. It seems to me it's a question of interest."

"Right."

"Do you usually have sex in the same position?"

"Yes, we do. It is the same position all the time."

"Is it the missionary position—the man on top?"

"Right."

"Aha! Okay. One suggestion that I would have is that you do get the book *The Joy of Sex* by Dr. Alex Comfort, because he does describe, and he has very beautiful illustrations about, different positions. The other thing I would do, if I were you, is I would turn around a little bit, and when you get home, since he's already home, why don't the two of you have sex first and then make dinner? Have a little snack, close the door, take the telephone off the hook. You can lower the shade and have sex right then and there. Don't wait until dinner is cooked and until you do the dishes and until you clean up. Have sex right then and there. And do make sure that you vary the position. Will you try that?"

"I will."

"I'll tell you something. I see my engineer, David, and Susan and Rory, and Howard from Princeton, and Walter and Edith and Sandy—I see them all nodding. They all think that that's what you ought to do. Okay?"

"Okay. Thank you very much, Dr. Ruth."

"Okay. Bye-bye."

There is nothing new under the sun, but things don't always have to be the same. Not *exactly* the same. Too much of one thing, even a good thing, gets to be boring. That is why people have invented sex fantasies and sex games since before the beginning of recorded time. Peasants used to pretend to be kings and queens when they made love, and kings and queens pretended to be shepherds and shepherdesses. And very respectable members of the school board pretend with their wives that they are having sex in a bordello, a whorehouse! If both go along with it, no one is forced, and the harmless pretense spices up the sex menu.

People come to sex therapists like me, and very often I tell them to try doing it a different way. Do different things. Sixty-nine may not be everybody's dish, but once in a while, why not? So naughty and French! (The French did *not* invent this. *Escargots à la Bourgogne,* snails in the Burgundian style, perhaps. But not oral sex. It's as old as the pharaohs—and older.) I tell them to try various positions. But I don't tell people to do things like that until they come to me complaining that sex, that central and important part of life, which can improve everyone's waking and sleeping hours, has become *boring!*

Sex, boring! Try to imagine a worse emotional disaster.

But the truth is that except for certain people with an enormous and unfailing sexual appetite, sex can become stale.

It is seldom boring for the newlyweds. But when they get used to seeing each other naked, and to having a license to lock themselves up and have it whenever they please, the edge can dull.

There may be too much talk about how marriage or long relationships get dull. I want to explain that it isn't the nature of the thing to be boring. Long sexual partnerships offer pleasures you can't get any other way. Making love with a partner you have had for twenty years, who knows you better than anyone else, who has shared life's ups and downs with you, is a royal pleasure.

But people get into a routine of hard work and being together only when they are tired, and the wonderful thing of novelty goes away. They need little variations to perk up their appetites: a weekend that is really "off," not all catching up on homework and housework; having people over on a weekday evening; going to a cabaret and dancing, the way they did before they got married; or a week away somewhere.

They need things like that. Not just switching from the "mish posish" to "doggy" fashion, or something like that. Don't get me wrong. Lots and lots of people who never would have allowed themselves to try other sex positions, until I made the indecent suggestion, have found this has cheered them up wonderfully! But it isn't the only thing, not at all.

Stimulating the sexual appetite, I repeat, does require some thought and variety. And maintaining it requires imagination and surprises. Couples must beware of monotony, of always having sex in the same way, at the same time, and in the same setting.

"But we *like* it that way. The way we do it every time has become a self-enriching ritual," someone once said.

Sure—whatever turns you on. But most people find that monotony promotes loss of appetite.

THE ONLY APHRODISIAC

Aphrodisiacs are substances you ingest to make you horny. It's a funny thing, but when people lose their sexual appetites, they don't just go off and play pinochle or take up stamp collecting. They want those bothersome erections back!

Since nothing they ever ate or drank really seemed to do the trick, people go to witch doctors and the corner drugstore and the mail-order columns of magazines looking for aphrodisiacs. They have eaten powdered rhinoceros horn, pearls powdered and stirred into women's milk, ground-up beetles, vitamins, and heaven knows what. Sometimes these edibles seem to do a little something, but the truth is that their good effect is ninety-nine percent psychological. Maybe one hundred percent.

A little wine is good. That may relax both of you, and being relaxed is helpful.

But there is not one real aphrodisiac I know of that helps you with your sexual appetite except the aphrodisiac between your ears—in your brain. Whatever "turns you on," whatever stimulates sexual appetite and excitement, functions as an aphrodisiac.

Some men, for example, find certain perfumes very stimulating. Some women find that the strong muscles and tendons in a man's hands arouse them. Other women do not react to hands but have a thing for broad shoulders or curly hair. All of us react sexually to stimuli that trigger some sexual association for us. There is no universal formula that works on everyone all the time.

The magical way a sight, smell, or thought makes the penis engorge or the vagina get wet and expectant cannot always be taken for granted. Nearly all of us come to a moment when the wonderful trick seems to fail us. You may have to use your brain to help yourself get sexually aroused, by concentrating on a sexual image or remembering a sexual experience that excited you. One client of mine found that after his wife passed the age of sixty, it became harder for him to get hard. He solved the problem by concentrating on memories of how she looked when they were first married and on thoughts of the sexual experiences they had had together in the past. When he asked me whether he should tell her what he was doing, I advised him not to.

CUPID'S ARROW

When Cupid shot his arrow into a man, that man fell into passionate love with the next woman he saw. When Cupid shot an arrow into a woman, she immediately fell head over heels in love with the next man she met. Love at first sight still seems to happen, but what we have to put more thought into is sustaining a lasting relationship. Nine out of ten people *need* a lasting relationship and *want* to keep it alive—that's what this chapter is all about.

Techniques to stimulate sexual appetite vary from person to person. Sometimes just a playful wink is enough. Other subtle sexual hints, such as lightly touching a person's arm or stroking their hair, or a gentle suggestion that it would be nice to cuddle, can do the trick. Many a young woman has told a young man she is cold to get him to put his arm around her. And many a young man has taken his girl friend to a scary movie or on a scary ride at an amusement park to make her frightened and want to press against him. Those are little tricks of the trade—very primary but cunning. There are more advanced tricks!

One couple I counseled found a direct approach that worked. As they sat together in their living room he would begin telling her how he wanted to slowly undress her and make love to her, describing the procedure in great detail, all the time just holding her hand. After nine years of marriage, she found this very unsubtle approach highly arousing!

Sometimes he would ask her to take off her clothing, one piece at a time, while he watched. She found this so exciting that she tried a variation on him. When she wanted to make love, she would start undressing for him as she described what she wanted him to do to her and what she was going to do to him in return. He loved that!

While this technique worked very well for these two, it is not for everybody! If you try something that doesn't work, try something else.

Other couples find that when they spend an afternoon together reading or listening to music in their living room, the subtle movements of their bodies and the nearness make them want to reach out and stroke and caress each other. That often leads to a sexual encounter.

THINK POSITIVE

It helps to feel sure that you are going to arouse your partner one way or another, not to get grounded because the first move you make doesn't work. If the first subtle hint doesn't get a rise, don't think right away That idiot! Can't he tell I'm horny? or Isn't she *ever* in the mood when I am? or Is the sex dying down in this great love affair? That's negative thinking.

Try something more obvious. Put an arm around your partner, volunteer a little neck and shoulder massage, lay a hand lightly on his or her thigh or lap. Women can use moves like this as well as men.

Man or woman, you can press on if the first signal seems somehow to have been missed. In the past a certain way of sitting still and sending ESP messages may have worked. But tonight suddenly your partner isn't psychic! Press on! A little bold show of interest may be just what your partner needs.

Traditionally men run the risks. They chance having their subtle, less subtle, bolder, then more blatant, moves rejected by their ladylove. Women should learn to take the same risks, always understanding that if they don't work this time, the world isn't lost, the relationship hasn't ended. Your man, like you, may be too tired or not in the mood. A glass of sherry may change his outlook—maybe not! In that case, taking the turndown nicely will be appreciated. Nothing ventured, nothing gained. But for the man or for the woman, it can't hurt to ask.

WILL FLATTERY GET YOU EVERYWHERE?

Almost. Flattery, especially when it comes as part of a sexual advance or invitation from an accepted lover, is very pleasing, and once the flatteree is in a nice mood, it can be *arousing*. But don't be ridiculous! Build your flattery on reality.

Exaggerated flattery, that the flatteree doesn't believe for a moment—that just says you want to have sex—may be stimulating.

But really good flattering means selecting something truly attractive and finding a way to say it. Telling a woman who knows she relies on her style, her disposition, on making the most of some good feature, that she is the most gorgeous dish in the entire world might put her off. It reminds her of what she *isn't,* not of what she is, and she thinks you are a klutz not to realize that. And a guy who knows he isn't a movie star or football star prefers flattery that says that *what he really is* can be very intriguing.

Flatter a woman who counts on her hair or on her nice skin, or a man who is sure of one thing—his receding temples are distinguished and skinny means sexy—on some real point that can be exploited. Or else your compliment will say only that what you really like is another type of person entirely.

A good compliment has an element of sincerity. People will usually sense when all you're doing is trying to con them. An honest, positive observation about a person is far more effective.

The same holds true for compliments about a person's intelligence or sensitivity or sense of humor. Getting a believable compliment makes us feel very good about ourselves and also about the person making it.

The art of flattery demands that you pay attention to the other person's appearance and actions and personality. Your attentiveness shows your interest in the other person. That is *really* flattering!

However, if the man or woman to whom you are giving the compliment doesn't respond, you should not go into a deep depression for the next ten years. Attempts to stimulate sexual appetite in another person always carry some element of risk. But if you care about the other person, that risk is worth taking.

"I'M GONNA WASH THAT MAN [WOMAN] RIGHT OUTA MY HAIR"

If you try to arouse another person's sexual appetite and you do not succeed, it doesn't have to mean that there's anything wrong with you or with your partner. It just means that different things turn you on.

The song from the 1949 musical *South Pacific,* "I'm Gonna Wash That Man Right Outa My Hair," is usually thought of as a bitter farewell to a man who was no good. But the lyrics actually talk about a situation that is very common when people are in the beginning stages of a relationship, a situation in which two people aren't on the same wavelength and just don't click with each other. When that happens, try not to prolong the inevitable parting. Go on to find someone else, someone who shares your sexual appetites more closely and with whom you can have a good relationship.

DESIGNER JEANS AND THE RIGHT TOOTHPASTE

The advertising energies of Madison Avenue are devoted to telling you that if you use the right toothpaste, drive the right car, and wear the right kind of designer jeans, you'll attract the right partner. There is something to that. The first glance a man casts on a woman's well-rounded rear end packed in tight designer jeans, or a woman's reaction to a man wearing a sexy designer shirt, can strike a spark that later becomes a fire. But clothes only set off the self-image a person projects. Walking down any street, you can see people who are clearly sending the message that they are happy about themselves. It shows in the way they walk and carry themselves that they like being who they are. And other people respond to that.

It is equally easy to spot people who do not like themselves. Depressed people tend to be indifferent to their own appearance, to walk hunched over, staying close to the walls of buildings rather than out in the middle of the sidewalk.

If you feel good about yourself, and dress to show your positive outlook, others will notice it.

Interestingly, while many men do not care much about what they wear, women usually find it impossible to *believe* that men do not care. If a man is dressed badly, women will take it as a sign—not that clothes don't matter to him, but that the poor fellow doesn't know how to dress. So if you don't care about how you dress, maybe you should start caring.

SEXUAL BOREDOM

Sexual boredom is a real problem to a lot of people. I see it in my private practice very often. There is a cure, of course: variety, the spice of boudoir life.

I had a very successful couple as clients. He was an engineer, she was a lawyer, and both were doing well. They had been married twelve years and had three nice children. They enjoyed each other's company, they did things together, they had lots of friends. So what was bringing them to a sex therapist? Nothing better to worry about?

The trouble was that she got the idea that he was avoiding sex with her—because he was. Now she was bored with it too, and she was, in fact, more relieved than anything else when he began saying good night and going to bed and to sleep before she did. But then this got to be a regular thing—"Good night, hon, I think I'll turn in." *Every* night. That had to mean something, and she decided it was serious. Maybe their sex life was *kaputt*. Maybe their marriage was in danger. She was a lawyer; she had seen a lot of that in other marriages.

The more she worried, the worse things got. And instead of being glad the sex was getting less important, she was feeling old, doomed, and rejected because their sex life had really become nonexistent.

Avoidance is very common when sexual boredom sets in. A lot of marriages become all custom, all living partnership, and no sex. And once the pattern sets in, it is hard to get sexual activity going again.

But in this marriage the pattern was still new when they decided something had to be done about it. I gave them some advice, and they set about following it.

Sexual boredom and avoidance happens with many kinds of couples, but in this case perhaps the businesslike, efficient way they went about it, in the same way they dealt with so many things in their successful lives, had killed the magic of it. Early in their marriage they settled into a sex routine: three nights a week, using the three basic positions they started out with, which had seemed a wild and satisfying variety when they were first married.

When they began trying to liven their act up, it was summer and the kids were at camp. They had the apartment to themselves. So one night in the living room she sat in his lap, before he had got tired and ready to do his "Night, hon," act. She loosened his tie. He was startled, then he remembered that they were supposed to start a new chapter in their marriage, so he just sat there with a funny look on his face while she took off the tie and tossed it away, then began to undo his shirt buttons. . . .

113

Doing it on the living room couch seemed to be more fun than the old "Well, it's Tuesday, let's get it over with" routine in the bedroom.

A night or so later he picked her up, laid her down on the rug, and made love to her there.

It got to be a game, startling each other that way. And the game began to provoke the urge to play it more often. While the kids were away they made love in all the rooms, on most of the furniture, and at all kinds of odd times.

After the kids came back, they had to stick to the bedroom. But they did it on his big desk there and they took bubble baths together, and they began having "illicit" sessions at noon in hotels and "shack-up" weekends at motels.

She bought some of that sex-farce underwear and appeared in front of him in that old favorite: black stockings, garter belt, and (wow!) nothing else. The funny thing was he found that very sexy, some kind of teenage fantasy hidden away there. She had felt a little like a fool when she first put on her tart's getup, but his reaction encouraged her.

Once they started, nothing could stop them. They tried all those positions in the sex manuals, and they tried really naughty things. Oral and, *you know*. They would think things up and whisper requests in each other's ears. For an engineer and a lawyer they got to be quite a couple of cutups.

Not everything they tried was a real success, but it was entertaining to give it a try.

Sometimes one of them would dream something up and the other would reject it. No hard feelings. Well, *once*. . . .

He thought a fantasy up that she didn't go for when he suggested that a third party to their partying would be fun. It shows how uninhibited he had become. She just said "No, thanks" very nicely. But shortly after she bought one of those inflatable life-size rubber women in a sex shop and brought it home and put it in the bed when he was in the bathroom. It was an amusing idea, but after one try the doll ended up in the back of the closet. She was only a passing fancy, it seemed.

The wife found herself thinking about this new love life a great deal, and her imagination became colored by it. Having to choose a birthday present for a woman friend one day, she dropped by a sex shop and brought the friend a garter belt and stockings. The friend thought it was funny and wore it for her husband. Soon these two women were trading ideas for spicing up their sex lives, like two women swapping cake recipes.

This way *two* marriages benefited by my counseling, though the second couple never paid me a fee! I can't think of any way to collect.

Thinking about amusing little ways to brighten their sex lives developed their erotic imaginations. The only potent aphrodisiac is in the imagination.

CAN YOU FORGIVE HIM? OR HER?

The problem of sexual avoidance is surprisingly common. Many couples go on for years living in sexless marriages. One couple came to me after twenty years!

Somewhere in the second or third year of their marriage she got mad at him for something he did. Neither of them remembered exactly when, or what it was he had done, but way back then she decided to withhold sex from him. Eventually this became a pattern. Occasionally the pattern would be broken, and they would have a more or less regular sexual relationship for a month or two, but then she would find another reason to be angry at him. Over the years their sex life was halted more than it was active; eventually it stopped altogether.

In therapy it became clear that the real reason for their dead sex life was not the things he did that made her mad. It was because she found sex with him so dull. And he was as bored as she. Their unvarying routine was a kiss, a hug, and then penetration, the whole business lasting six or seven minutes.

They both felt that divorce was out of the question because of their children. And they both liked the social life they had with the other married couples in the neighborhood.

When they came to see me, the first question I had to ask was whether they could forgive each other for all the years of frustration and anger.

It can be very difficult for two partners to pull themselves out of a pattern that has been built up over many years. It requires a great deal of determination and a tremendous amount of psychic energy to climb out of that rut. Not everyone can do it.

In the end this couple could not. Too many years had gone by, and they had become too set in their pattern of avoidance. And, most importantly, they were unable to forgive the unhappiness they had caused each other. After a lot of painful soul-searching they decided to stay together without having sex until the children were grown. Then they would probably divorce.

Ironically, this decision relieved much of the tension between them and improved their relationship. They had confronted a problem together and found a way to resolve it. If they do, in the end, divorce, they may be able to work out better relationships with new partners in the future.

A LITTLE IMAGINATION: LET'S PLAY RAPE

In pornography the word *bizarre* means "kinky." Some clients get into very bizarre sex games with each other. In most cases I advise that as long as no one gets hurt, and both people enjoy them, whatever sex games they come up with are fine.

One pair of partners enjoyed exchanging fantasies. One night he would tell one of his fantasies to her, and they would act it out. The next night she would tell him hers, and they would play *that* one out. One of his favorites was "playing rape," in which she pretended that he was a stranger, and he made love to her while she "resisted." She never resisted too hard. Occasionally they found themselves giggling so hard, they couldn't go through with it. At other times they would carry things to the extreme that he tied her hands behind her back and "forced" her to have sex with him. His fantasy triggered one of hers, which was to rape *him*, and so she tied his hands behind his back and "forced" him to have sex with *her*. He said he didn't know which role he enjoyed playing more, the rapist or the rape victim. She said it depended on her mood.

SEXUALLY EXPLICIT MOVIES

Dear Dr. Ruth:
We have been married four years and I think our sex life has been pretty good. I do orgasm very often and I find sex enjoy-

able even if I don't achieve an orgasm every time. My problem now is that recently my husband has begun to ask for things I don't think I can handle. A few months ago my husband suggested that we go to a porno movie together. I said I'd hate to and to my surprise he was very upset and accused me of being unaffectionate and unresponsive to his needs. I found out that he has been going to porno "flicks" alone since we have been married. My impression had been that it was something he did a couple of times out of curiosity and partly for laughs when he was a bachelor. I have gotten over my shock at his seeing them still and no longer think that it means he is sexually unsatisfied or abnormal but I do not want to go into one of those movie houses. I feel sure someone would see me and for some reason this is something that would make me feel ashamed. It would be like getting caught masturbating. And I am afraid of what I will see on the screen. But I want to work out this misunderstanding with my husband. After I refused to go to a porno movie with him he began suggesting that we rent a film or a videodisc. I don't want to have that before sex with my husband. How can I deal with this?

Della

Dear Della:

First of all, I think you are blaming yourself for being unloving and unwilling to go along with your husband, and you should put that out of your mind. That is not true and the problem, which you are trying to solve, lies in another area.

If you don't want to see porno movies (which I prefer to call sexually explicit movies) there is no reason why you should—and very good reason why you should not. On the other hand, don't form the idea that there is something wrong with your husband seeing them, or that it means he doesn't really love you anymore or finds you not stimulating enough. These films, except for some made for "special tastes," with pain or physical injury or children in them, are harmless. They are harmless and they serve a good purpose—they enrich people's sex fantasies and improve their sex lives. So if your husband goes, don't worry.

117

But you don't have to go and you don't have to watch them at home before you have sex. If you did want to do that before sex, there would be no harm. But you don't; it is outside your own private sexual fantasies. So don't do it if you feel that way—and don't do anything else in your sex life that you really feel very strongly against. Try not to be too rigid, try to be willing to follow his lead in other matters in your mutual sex life, or to initiate something sometimes. Try to keep your sex life lively and imaginative, amusing, varied. But don't do what you don't want to do.

Your husband probably feels a little rejected and disappointed and maybe that you look down on him. Just tell him it is something you don't feel like doing but that he can. I think I know a good suggestion you can make to him. Ask him why doesn't he go to a sex movie sometime and then meet you after at a hotel. Or come straight home and you will be waiting for him, waiting to have a good two-person orgy with him. In a sheer negligee or sexy underwear!

Tell him that you have your own fantasies and that seeing a "blue movie" would spoil them for you and you don't want to spoil your sex with him.

Sometimes there is something we don't want to do now and in a few years we won't mind it at all. We are different people at different times in life. I want you to think about that. And this: you can go along with your husband sometimes even if you don't really enjoy it, because it makes him happy to have your company. A wife will go to a ball game with her husband, and he may return the favor and go to a concert or ballet with her. Some wives do go to sexually explicit movies with their husbands in the same spirit. But don't do it, now or any time, if it really goes against the grain.

Good luck.

Dr. Ruth

COSTUME DRAMAS

A client of mine told his wife that he had always wanted to make love to a woman who had no pubic hair, so she shaved it off. She then complained that *his* pubic hair scratched, so he shaved off his.

Later she confided that she had a thing about tattoos. He bought a package of gag tattoos that washed off with water and they spent an evening "tattooing" each other. Their games may have been silly, but they were harmless and enjoyable.

Another husband always slept in pajamas. When he and his wife made love, he kept his pajamas on and only unbuttoned his fly. For years this practice had bothered his wife. (I should think so!) So she asked him to come to bed naked. Just once, as a favor. He was uncomfortable, but he agreed. While undressing he suddenly felt silly with no clothes on and he paused a moment at the closet before coming to bed. When his wife saw him, she collapsed with laughter. There he stood, completely naked except for one thing, a loud necktie!

"I felt silly taking *everything* off," he explained. His joke helped to overcome his shyness and the two of them had fantastically good sex that night.

HAPPY BIRTHDAY

Birthdays seem to be good times for couples to apply a little imagination to their sex lives. One wife sent the children away to her parents on her husband's birthday. When he came home from work, she greeted him at the door with a big smile, completely naked except for a big ribbon bow around her neck, holding a cupcake with one burning candle. "Happy birthday, honey," she said. "I'm your present." Years later he still said that was the best birthday present he ever got.

"You are on the air."

"Hello, Dr. Ruth."

"Yes."

"My name is Bud and I live in Manhattan. I am thirty-six years old and I suppose that I'm a bachelor. I have had relationships with many women. I can't even count them—a few hundred probably. And there is one thing—I have a problem. Everytime I have sex with a woman I can probably read the Gettysburg address as I am ejaculating. What would you feel would be the cause for something like that?"

"How long does it take to read the Gettysburg address?"

"I use that as an expression. What I am saying is that I'm fully aware of when I'm going to climax and I am not spaced out. When I was twenty-four years old, I was engaged, and at that particular point I was younger and I was a little bit more emotionally involved with this particular woman and I do remember specifically a few orgasms which were—when I was spaced out."

"Okay. Are you saying that you do not feel the kind of orgasm when you ejaculate, that you don't feel a tremendous release? Is that what you are saying? Or are you talking about how fast you ejaculate?"

"No, it's not how fast. I can hold off on ejaculating, that is why I suppose that women do appreciate me. I can go a half hour or forty minutes. I have no problem holding back."

"But when you do ejaculate, does it seep out instead of kind of coming out in spurts?"

"No, no. Sometimes it seeps out. Sometimes it comes out with a full thrust, but the whole idea is I am totally aware of when it is taking place. It is not like when I was twenty-four and I was spaced out. I am wondering if it is that I am not emotionally involved with a woman."

"I'll tell you something, Bud, that is difficult to answer over the air because there seems to be nothing wrong with the mechanism, in terms of arousal."

"No, I am physically healthy. I'm in good shape."

"It might be that you are so much aware with whom you are and that this is again a partner that you might not really be interested in, because if you tell me that it is a couple of hundred people, then maybe . . ."

"It has been quite a few. In other words, I might be taking up with the wrong women on a constant basis. Is that it?"

"Yes. What I think it might be is that you just get involved with the wrong women and you are so aware of that that you don't really kind of lose yourself in some kind of fantasy of good, good feeling. I would suggest that, maybe, hold off before you have the next sexual relationship. And try to find a woman that you really care for."

"You mean one that I really feel is my equal? Is that it?"

"Right. Absolutely. Try that. In the meantime, just masturbate and have some good fantasies, but try to really go out and find a woman that is more to your liking. Don't think way back to when you were twenty-four, because nobody can recreate the exact same feelings of an earlier age.''

''In other words, just don't settle—find someone I really find that I would love to be with.''

''Right. Don't settle.''

''Dr. Ruth, I want to thank you very much.''

''Thank you for calling.''

There is a case of what I mentioned earlier—a good strong sexual appetite. Yet he is bored. His erection is fine. His mechanism and physical performance bring no complaints. His boredom is from another source, and it looks as though a lasting relationship with a woman he respects, who interests him, may be the cure for it.

Stimulating and maintaining sexual appetite requires some work and some imagination. You cannot always wait for the right mood to hit you or for sexual inspiration to come down like manna from the heavens. But, with a little effort, two people can keep sexual appetite alive between them for all the years of their lives together.

10

SEX AND THE ELDERLY

Of all the people who have phoned in to my radio show to ask questions about their sexual activities, Martha is certainly one of my favorites. During the course of each sixty-minute program I announce several times that it is a program for mature listeners. Well, that certainly described Martha—she was a sprightly, intelligent, well-spoken woman of seventy-three. Here was the way the call went.

"You are on the air."

"Hello, Dr. Ruth. My name is Martha. I'm calling from New Jersey. I listen to your show every weekend. I think it's just marvelous. I think it's one of the best shows on radio."

"I like to hear that! You make my evening."

"Well, I have this problem, you see. I'm an elderly woman. I'm seventy-three years old and I have trouble finding men my own age who are as sexually active as I am. Sometimes I can find younger men, but I just don't relate to younger men as well as I do to men more my own age. But they're usually just not as sexually active as I am."

"I really am very, very pleased that you called, because one of my special interests is sexuality and the older adult."

"That's wonderful!"

"I just finished a chapter in a medical textbook, and if you do send me a letter, to the radio station, I'm going to send you—if you'll just remind me—I'm going to send you this chapter. Because this is specifically geared toward sexuality and the older person.''

"I'll do that.''

"Now, Martha, as you and I do know, we do have more older women than older men.''

"Yes, it certainly seems that way. I'm a widow myself.''

"Right. We have no solution for that. Actually what we could say in theory is it would be very nice if we lived in a society where one man could service more than one woman. But we don't live in a society like that. One thing that I would suggest is, number one, do not despair, and do continue to go out to clubs or wherever you do socialize.

"But let me give you an example of what I did with another older woman, a widow, who came to see me in my office, and who had the exact same problem that you are reporting. She used to go folk dancing with her husband. When her husband passed away, she was very sad, and after a proper time of mourning she came to see me—not for a sexual problem—she really came to see me because she had a problem with her daughter-in-law. And when we were talking about 'What are you doing Saturday night?' and so forth, she said that she didn't go back folk dancing. I did send her back folk dancing, saying by all means this is a kind of activity where you don't have to have one man to each woman. But she was very upset when she left after the dance when she went home, because she felt sexually very aroused. Because that was exactly the type of activity that she and her husband were engaged in, and then afterward they went home and had good sex. So I did tell her that she ought to masturbate. Now, she had never masturbated in her adult life. She doesn't remember if she did it as a youngster.''

"That's a good idea.''

"In her adult life she did not masturbate, and I really encouraged her. If I may make a suggestion, Martha, I would like to suggest, rather than to feel the sexual tension and to feel kind of unhappy, I would rather suggest that you do masturbate.''

"Oh, I see. I could try it.''

"Absolutely, and number one, Martha, do use a lubricant. Don't touch the clitoris directly. Go around the area of the clitoris.

Maybe put a finger, or even a cucumber, or a banana—it doesn't matter—in the vagina, and fill your head with good fantasies.''

"Oh, boy, I could try that."

"All the good-looking older men that you could think of—let them all take turns with you in your fantasies."

"It's an interesting idea. I'll have to try that."

"Please do let me know. And if you do send me a letter, I will send you those pages of the chapter that deals specifically with sexuality and the older adult. In the meantime, keep on going out and try to meet . . . There are plenty of older men out there.''

"It's not so much finding the older man, as I said. But they're usually . . .''

"Not sexually so active. Let me make one more suggestion. I'm so pleased you called. If you find a man whom you do like, and he does not seem to be as sexually active as you seem to be, do have an open talk with him, because sometimes men at that age are a little worried about their erections. They are worried if they will have an erection, and, if they have an erection, will they sustain an erection, will they be able to penetrate, and so forth. What I would like to suggest to you is that you have a talk with a man that you have a relationship with, and tell him that Dr. Westheimer and you discussed over the radio, right here on WYNY, that it's perfectly all right for him to masturbate you to orgasm, without him having to feel sexually aroused.''

"Yes, okay."

"Will you try that?"

"I certainly will. I want to thank you very much. I'm going to take all your suggestions.''

"And you will let me know."

"Yes. I will let you know, and I will write to you."

"Good luck to you, and thank you for calling. Bye-bye."

"Bye-bye."

After that came a commercial. When I came back on, I was still bubbling about Martha's call.

"I want to tell you that I really want to congratulate my producer, Susan, that she didn't miss that last call, because a caller like

Martha, this is really what this program is all about. That it's not only young people, that it's middle-aged people, that it's older people, it's disabled people, and that everybody has the right to pursue happiness in terms of sexual functioning.''

The week following that program brought a number of letters from older people, all obviously encouraged by Martha's call. That was what I had been hoping for since the program began—that some brave senior citizen would phone in to *Sexually Speaking* and mark the beginning of older listeners taking an active part in our Sunday evening discussions of sex. And two months after Martha's call, I got a letter from her saying she had met a new man, in his seventies, and they were hitting it off wonderfully!

> *Dear Dr. Ruth:*
> *I am troubled and disturbed. Please answer as soon as possible.*
> *After performing sexually for forty-seven years with my wife, I have been having trouble lately in keeping an erection. I am sixty-five years old in good physical health. I am a diabetic which has not been a problem to my health. Thank you.*
> *Stanley*

First, I have to congratulate Stanley on having reached his age without any troubling failure of his penis. It makes me happy just to think of it. I would wish that for every man.

Then, as to his very serious wish to go on being a good husband, having no intention to give up, bravo!

What can he do?

People think of foreplay as something for the woman. She has to be brought to readiness in a leisurely way. Talked to tenderly, petted, kissed, caressed, the way she likes to have it done. It is loving and considerate to do that so that she can have fun at the party, too.

The whole pace of life begins to change long before life is over, and that is true of sexual life as well. After a certain age, the majority of men need that kind of attention as much as women. The penis has to be fondled into an erection. It needs the touching and physical attention that the clitoris requires most of its life.

In old age a couple may have to pleasure each other more, take turns giving each other pleasure with manual or oral attentions to each other. It isn't necessary for both to have orgasms every time. And a penis will give good service long after it has stopped having psychogenic erections—if enough kind attention is given to it before attempting penetration.

> Dear Dr. Ruth:
> Would you be so kind to give me the name of the publisher of Dr. Zilbergeld's book.
> I am seventy-one years old. Tell me how to improve my life. I am in excellent health. But always willing to learn and improve. . . .
>
> Ralph

That's the spirit! That's what I like to hear! I sent him the name of the publisher and said I would be glad to tell him how to improve his life if he would write again and be a little more specific about any problem he might have!

I am delighted with these letters because they mean that more older people will come forward and take part in *Sexually Speaking*, bringing the fact of sexuality in aging human beings into wider acceptance.

Until recently the idea of elderly people having any kind of sex life was considered ridiculous and unseemly. After a certain age—teenagers still think it begins around thirty-five!—people were supposed to give up sex gracefully. The trouble with that is—and I at fifty-three am glad—the trouble with that is, the sex drive goes right on long after people begin drawing Social Security pensions.

I don't know offhand what the record age for having an erection or a female orgasm may be. I don't suppose it's in the *Guinness Book of World Records*. But if someone writes in and says it was at the age of one hundred ten, I won't be surprised, because medical science has set no top age limit for sexual activity. Or sexual problems, of course.

THE OLDER MALE: MAKING A COMEBACK

Not long ago a couple sought my advice as a sex therapist because their sex life had ended abruptly—and they both wanted it to continue. The interruption need never have happened, as it turned out. But it *had* happened—only because they were unaware of a change that occurs in men after a certain age.

Howard and Paula were in their late fifties and had enjoyed a vigorous sex life all the thirty-five years they had been together. But one night, even after kissing and hugging with Paula for a while, Howard was unable to get an erection. When Paula reached for Howard's penis, she was surprised to find that it was still limp. They decided that Howard was simply too tired, and so they went to sleep without any further sex play.

But when the same thing happened the next several times they tried to make love, they both began to worry. While Paula tortured herself with worries that she was no longer sexually appealing to her husband, or that he was having an affair with another woman, Howard worried that he had become too old to have sex anymore. When Paula told him of her suspicions, he swore that he was not seeing another woman and that he still found Paula very attractive. He couldn't understand what had gone wrong.

Paula and Howard didn't talk about the problem any further, but they began avoiding opportunities to have sex. If Howard started yawning and saying he was ready for bed, Paula suddenly discovered that she was terribly interested in the late-night movie on television. If she mentioned beddy-byes, he suddenly got involved in a story in the evening paper. They became very good at these bedtime evasions.

Soon they became convinced that Howard was too old, that their sex life was over. Howard's self-image took a dive. Paula began to feel guilty about still having a strong sexual appetite and to wonder if there were something wrong with her. She was also concerned about the years of sexual frustration that lay ahead of her. They were both miserable.

When they finally went to see a family counselor, they learned what was responsible for so much of their emotional pain and how to deal with it. This was the first time these kind and well-informed people ever heard of the psychogenic erection. When he was younger, Howard would often get an erection just by thinking about sex. Sometimes it had embarrassed him. Once, while he was riding home on a bus, he began thinking about Paula and had an erection that was so big and obvious through his pants that he was too embarrassed to stand up. He had to let the bus pass his stop while he thought about his income tax and mowing the lawn and anything else nonsexual that came to mind until it had finally gone down. By then he was four stops past his regular bus stop and he had a long walk home.

When he told Paula what had happened, she laughed. And they both became aroused. They went to bed immediately and made passionate love.

But, as men grow older, they lose the ability to have psychogenic erections. That is, erections stimulated solely by the mind. Erotic thoughts are no longer enough. They need physical stimulation of the penis. If Howard and Paula had been aware of this fact, she could have stroked and caressed his penis until he had an erection, and then they could have engaged in sex. But since neither knew about the passing of psychogenic erections, they both assumed that their sex life was over.

Once they had decided that sex was a thing of the past for them, their decision became a self-fulfilling prophecy and kicked off a vicious cycle. They stopped having sex because they believed Howard wasn't up to it anymore. The sad day had come long before they were ready for it.

It would have been nice if this couple could have drifted from one stage of their sex life into the next, if they had always had a more playful way of acting with each other in their most intimate moments. But a certain antigenital attitude, one that is very common even among sexually active people, worked against this. Even if they like sex a lot, many people think of the organs of procreation and pleasure as ugly, smelly, nasty, as the pudenda—the parts to be ashamed of.

The crotch and its parts are like the rest of the body. When they are stale and unwashed, they are stale and unwashed, and when they are fresh and clean, they are fresh and clean. Male semen—which is the only kind there is, of course—has a nice fresh smell unless you have persuaded yourself otherwise. Vaginal fluids smell good to many lovers. Why not? They are fresh excretions of the healthy body, harmless as tears and certainly not as sad!

Playful lovers like the private parts. Women who like men (and male lovers in particular) like to make friends and playthings of their lovers' parts. A lady said to me, "It's like that girl in *On a Clear Day You Can See Forever,* who talked to her plants. It grows if you talk or sing to it." Women like to fondle and watch the penis grow, if they are on good terms with it.

Now, if Paula had just gone on playing with her husband's penis—her old friend of years standing (and lying down and standing again)—the pair of them might have drifted lovingly from the era of psychogenic erections to the era of physically stimulated ones.

Or it would have helped if in all the talk they had heard, or if in any book or magazine they had read in their lives, they had come upon the information that with the passage of time the penis may get tired of all those messages from the brain and say, "Come on, stop all the talk and show me how you love me. Pat me, play with me."

Frequently the older penis is in a way more reliable. When the time of psychogenic erections is past, the penis may be able to stay hard much longer once it is erect. A friend told me this rhyme he heard from an old farmer in Vermont, about fifty years ago:

> A thought that's of comfort to ladies forlorn—
> The older the buck, the harder the horn.

That little rhyme is a piece of what we call positive thinking about sex.

Getting back to my clients Howard and Paula, after they learned that sexual activity *was* still possible, when they went to bed, Paula made it a practice to rub herself against Howard's penis and to take it in her hands and gently stroke it. At first they were both anxiously watching and waiting for "something to happen," and that anxiety prevented Howard from having an erection. Not only was he a spectator to his own erection, Paula was a spectator too, with both of them watching and wondering, *Will* Howard get an erection or will Howard *not* get an erection?

Finally one afternoon when they returned from a pleasant day together at the beach and were feeling in a particularly good mood, they decided to take a shower together. They took turns soaping each other and forgot to be anxious watchers and simply relaxed and enjoyed each other's bodies. Howard got an erection, and they were able to make love. And once they believed that their sex life was possible again, it *became* possible again.

SHE AIN'T WHAT SHE USED TO BE

That old song about the Old Gray Mare always had a "naughty" connotation. But an old mare who balks at being hitched to a heavy wagon can still kick up her heels. Not the way she used to, no.

While sexual appetites do continue past retirement age, sex at sixty is not the same as sex was at twenty. Some time after menopause the walls of a woman's vagina lose some of their elasticity and become thinner. She also tends to lubricate less and she may find that sexual intercourse, especially the kind of rough-and-tumble intercourse she may have been used to, is sometimes painful. Some women take this as a sign that the days of their sexual activity are over, and they begin to avoid having sex. But their sexual activity does not have to end. If she uses a vaginal lubricant such as K-Y Jelly, to make it easier for the penis to enter her vagina, a woman can usually enjoy sexual intercourse without pain.

The intensity of a woman's orgasm may be somewhat less after menopause than it was earlier. But even a less intense orgasm is still an orgasm, and it can still provide a great deal of pleasure and release. No damage can be done by having an orgasm. On the contrary, a great deal of physical and psychological good results, since the woman's image of herself as a healthy, sexual person can contribute a lot to her happiness and sense of vitality.

A woman may sometimes experience some pain when her uterus contracts during an orgasm. If she does, she should discuss it with her physician. But even that pain does not have to be taken as a signal from her body that she has to stop being sexually active.

HE AIN'T WHAT HE USED TO BE, EITHER

For men too, sex in later years is not what it was way back when. But it can still be very good. After a certain age, which varies from one man to another, men may no longer get a full erection. But they can have sexual intercourse even without a full erection. The penis can be inserted into the vagina when it is only partially erect. Very often, during the thrusting of intercourse, the penis does become fully erect.

"I've been making love with a limber member so long," one elderly fellow said, "I could row a boat with a rope."

A man's erections may not be as strong and his ejaculations may not be as powerful as they were when he was younger, but if a man and his partner are aware of the changes age brings, they can continue to enjoy sex long into the sunset years.

A particularly bitter joke tells of an elderly man who was walking down the street when he saw a little boy sitting on a stoop, crying.

"Why are you crying, little boy?" the man asked.

"I'm crying because I can't do what the big boys can do," replied the boy.

And so the man sat down on the stoop and began crying also, because he couldn't do what the big boys do either.

The tragedy is that many elderly people *believe* the myth that sex ends at a certain age.

Just as a person moves a little more slowly in the later years, so too the pace of a sex life alters with the years. But even though a man may not be able to run the four-minute mile, he can still walk quite well. And while he may not be the sexual athlete he once was, he can still enjoy quite an active sex life. And keeping this moderate flame alive brings much warmth into an elderly couple's relationship.

CHANGING EXPECTATIONS

Because the muscle tone of elderly people is not what it was when they were younger, they may have to adopt somewhat less rigorous and demanding positions for intercourse. Partners may find they enjoy sexual intercourse more when they lie facing each other side by side or while sitting together in a chair.

With the children grown up and out of the house, one couple finally had enough time and privacy to concentrate on each other and to have relaxed sex together.

They discovered they enjoyed having intercourse in a large

rocking chair, she sitting on his lap as they rocked back and forth. They were convinced that the effectiveness of the technique was responsible for the lasting popularity of the rocking chair in America. To keep off the chill when they made love, the wife did a little creative sewing on her flannel nightgown and designed a special movable flap at the back, so that when her husband unbuttoned the fly of his pajamas and she moved the flap aside, they could have intercourse comfortably as she sat on his lap on the rocking chair, still warmly dressed, sometimes while they watched their favorite television programs!

Think about that, Johnny Carson, during your monologue!

It is true that their bodies are not what they were when they were younger, but that doesn't mean elderly people have to give up sex. Sexual activity is not a matter of all or nothing. People can adapt their behavior to meet the changes nature brings.

Elderly people may find they have sex less often than they did when they were younger. But just because there is less of it, doesn't mean sex has to stop.

An active sex life may require some changes in routine, however. For example, it is not a good idea to have sex when you're tired or when you are feeling ill. Men and women may not be as agile as they once were, and neither partner should be disappointed if intercourse does not always include hours of vigorous thrusting and grinding.

No one remains nineteen forever. Both men and women put on extra pounds and wrinkles. Your hair loses some of its luster and your skin some moisture. It is foolish to spend time lamenting the loss of youth, to devote energy to recalling how handsome or beautiful you or your partner were twenty or thirty years ago. But while her days of wearing a bikini may be over, and you may not look as good as you once did in bathing trunks, you can go on having an active physical and sexual life.

BELIEVE IN IT OR LOSE IT

Elderly people who are in relatively good health are depriving themselves of a gift of nature if they fail to take advantage of their own sexuality. It is possible to continue an active sex life indefinitely. It is also possible to start up a sex life if some time has passed since

132

the last time—even years. You *can* teach an old person new tricks.

For older people sex is truly a matter of "use it or lose it." If older people believe they cannot be sexually active, they will be unable to *be* sexually active. The first task is to believe that one's sex life doesn't have to end.

The well-known worship of youth in American society suggests that if you are no longer young, you might as well lie down and die. This cult of youth is one of the more destructive attitudes faced by elderly people who may, tragically, subscribe to it themselves.

As long as they live people should believe that sex is better sometimes than others. The earth doesn't always have to move. Sex can be a quiet pleasure. As one sensible old man from West Virginia put it, "Even when it isn't perfect it's pretty good."

THOUGH THE TEMPO MAY BE SLOWER, THE MUSIC IS STILL SWEET

As people age most of their senses become less acute. They may have to give up many of their pleasures as a result, but sexual activity need not be one of them.

Your eyes and ears may not be as sharp as they once were, but you can still see and hear your partner. The sense of taste and smell may fade somewhat, but that doesn't have to affect the enjoyment of sexuality. The last of the five senses, the sense of touch, frequently assumes a greater importance with age. The sensation of hugging and being hugged by another person can provide a measure of joy and pleasure that is especially appreciated by the elderly.

GERIATRIC DATING ROOMS

People at geriatric facilities report that elderly couples often discreetly arrange to spend time together to have romantic liaisons. There is nothing wrong, and a great deal right, with elderly people being sexually active. Some more advanced geriatric facilities have even set up "dating rooms." And though some staff people and some of the inmates' relatives may complain that such arrangements are "improper," most of the elderly themselves welcome this recognition of their sexual needs.

Sometimes when a person moves from a solitary apartment to a home for the elderly, there is a change for the better. Loneliness isn't one's constant companion. There are people around to talk to. And being around one's own age group is like going back to college or to one's courting days.

A grandma may have played being grandma, living with her children and their children. But in a setting where most folks are her own age, she can become a "live one" again. It's a new lease on life, when it works out right.

A man whose mother was in a nursing home would visit her and take little walks with her around the building and the grounds. One day they passed two old ladies strolling together. The man's mother nudged him and whispered, "They're *libyans*." In an "old folks home" you soon learn that life goes on to the end.

"I GAVE IT UP A LONG TIME AGO"

Sam came to see me about a year after his wife had passed away. He had cared for her very tenderly during the last two years of her life. After a period of mourning, he began going out with an old family friend, a woman he and his wife had known for many years. They met for lunch and dinner several times, and a warm relationship developed between them. When Sam asked her to go to see a new play on opening night, they both sensed that the evening would mark the beginning of their sexual relationship, something they were both looking forward to.

Sam met Betty after work, took her to dinner, then to the theater and to several nightclubs afterward. By the time they returned to her place in the small hours of the morning, they felt very close and were both ready to have sex. But when they went to bed, Sam was unable to get an erection. Embarrassed and confused, the next day he went to see his doctor, who gave him a thorough physical examination and informed Sam there was nothing wrong with him.

Sam told him what had happened the night before, only to have the doctor laugh at him.

"What do you expect, Sam? You're sixty-three. I gave it up a long time ago."

Afraid that sex really was a thing of the past, Sam grew despondent and decided that he and Betty were finished before they had begun. When he came to talk to me, I tried to undo the damage the doctor's well-meaning but ill-informed advice had done.

I told Sam that while he might not always be able to work all day, stay out all night, and then have sex, the way he had when he was younger, his sex life did not by any means have to be over. Following my advice, Sam and Betty went away for a weekend together. They slept together the first night and hugged and kissed but didn't try to have sex. Then, after a good night's rest, and feeling very relaxed and comfortable together, they enjoyed a mutually satisfying sexual encounter.

Sam called me after the weekend and his voice was positively glowing. He said that he and Betty had spent a wonderful weekend together "behaving like a couple of kids." Some months later Sam and Betty were married, and while they never went into details about their sex life together, they both had a happy sparkle that spoke far more eloquently than words.

LONELINESS

It is a fact of nature that women tend to live longer than men. As a result, there are many more elderly women in the population than there are elderly men. Many of them face the prospect of loneliness in their later years.

The loss of a spouse is one of the great traumas people have to deal with in life. After a suitable period of mourning, however, it is important for the surviving partner to take steps to overcome loneliness.

There are plenty of books on the market with advice on how to get back into circulation; how to find new interests, new friends, and a new partner. It is a good idea for a person to become involved in a relationship with a new partner, but until that new partner is found, it is important to keep the sexual apparatus intact. Self-gratification is a good way for a man or a woman who is alone to keep sexual response mechanisms functioning.

Men are more apt to masturbate than women, and so for men, keeping everything in working order may be relatively easy. Many women, however, cry the first time they try to masturbate, because, as one woman put it, "I felt so damn alone!" But such reservations need to be overcome.

Even if a person has not masturbated before, it is possible to learn how. Books, such as this one, are available, or a person can see a qualified sex therapist. With some experimentation, people can teach themselves how to masturbate. Sexual gratification, even if it is self-gratification, makes for a happier old age.

Masturbation has long been regarded as shameful, even by sensible people who don't think it a sin or a crime or bad for the health. "It's no crime, it just isn't an accomplishment," one man said. He was wrong; it *is* an accomplishment and a great aid in much of sexual therapy.

Among the Arabs the term for it is *the secret*. I would like it to be an open secret. I don't want to see people doing it on park benches, but I often advise it—in private.

DANGER TO HEALTH AND DIGNITY

It goes without saying that at any age vigorous activity or excitement can be harmful at times, when one is ill. Heart patients especially have to be careful. But a great deal of needless forbidding of sex has been prescribed in the past. Now doctors order reasonable exercise as part of the treatment for heart patients. And, if asked, doctors may well say that moderate sexual activity is all right or even beneficial. The point is, the patient has the right to know.

As for dignity, older people should have all the control over their own privacy and their own actions as other reasonable people. The grandchildren don't have to "know" what Grandma and her nice man friend "do" when they are alone. Whether Grandma has a liaison with some gentleman or not, the grandchildren will respect her dignity pretty much according to how dignified she actually is.

Each generation has to accept the sexuality of the generation above it and below it. Mature people have a right to their own sex lives. If people are dignified, they will carry off their sex lives in a dignified way.

People in the prime of life will always worry about the safety of their children and their elders. The best advice to anyone seeking sexual encounters, at any age, is "Use your head before going to bed."

UNTIL FOREVER

It is important to realize that sexuality is a gift people are born with. But it is a gift that has to be cultivated, like a taste for good food or fine wine.

People need to think about their sexuality at any age. If you put some thought into your sex life in later years, it can make those years more pleasant for yourself and for your partner.

Sex can be very good, very late in life. It is foolish to deny yourself and your partner a basic human pleasure. To ignore sexual needs, or pretend that they don't exist, is to deprive yourself of a great gift, part of the wonder of being alive.

11

IN DEFENSE
OF THE
QUICKIE

"You are on the air."

"Hello, Dr. Ruth. I have been listening to your show constantly, and now for the first time I have a problem here. My name is Hy and I live in Queens. I am getting married in a few months."

"Congratulations!"

"Thank you very much. Now, I have a problem here. This past weekend my future wife was working, and I was over with my future mother-in-law, and what happened was, I had sex with her. Now, I don't know if that's going to constantly haunt me in the future, and if I can live with that situation."

"First of all, don't tell your future wife. Did you tell her already?"

"No, I didn't tell her."

"Do not tell her. If you want to keep this relationship with your future wife going, then make believe that this one episode—It was only one time?"

"Yeah, this was the first time."

"Okay. Make believe that this one episode never existed. All right?"

"What happens if it comes up again in the future?"

"Do not—absolutely do not have a sexual relationship with

your wife's mother. This sounds to me that, if you would have asked me before it happened, I would have told you: 'Run! Take your running shoes and run, but run very fast.' But it happened, it happened. The one important thing is to make it absolutely clear to that future mother-in-law of yours that whatever happened, happened, and not ever to repeat it. But I would not tell your future wife, unless you want to break up the forthcoming marriage. Do you want to get married?''

"Definitely. But the problem is, do you think this will ever come out, with that situation, of having that in the back of my mind?''

"No, I hope not. I hope you are going to consider it as something that happened and it's over with and it will never happen again. One thing that you might want to do is to tell your mother-in-law that you decided not to tell her daughter, but if that would ever happen again, that you would tell her daughter.''

"What would happen if she told her daughter?''

"I hope that she doesn't.''

"What happens if she does?''

"If she does, then you have a very serious problem. Because if she does that, there's something on her mind that she doesn't want her daughter to get married—that maybe she does want you for herself. I don't care about what she minds. I find it a real serious problem that it did happen, but if she does tell her . . . Did she say anything that she would tell her daughter?''

"No, but you never know. But she definitely wants me to marry her daughter. It's not that she would try to break up the situation.''

"But then what I would do is, I would make very clear to her in no uncertain terms, that you tell her: 'Cut it out, and don't you ever tell your daughter, and don't you ever make that situation available again.' And for you also to know that you just have to be careful. All right?''

"Right.''

"Good luck for your marriage.''

"Have a nice evening.''

"Thank you, you too. Bye-bye.''

*   *   *

In the disgraceful little episode Hy talked about, one finds one of the most stimulating elements in sexual experience—forbidden pleasure. Everyone knows this kind of thing is forbidden. That in itself adds zest to the deed. And danger—that is stimulating, too. And the folly—"What are we doing? We are mad!"

And spontaneity!

Not for a minute do I recommend this kind of thing. In a moment of silly gratification a man can wreck his hopes for a marriage that he wants very much. And the anxiety he may have for years that somehow his wife will find out will probably make him regret the action even if the worst never happens.

But so often things like this are the basis of harmless fantasies that even the most well-behaved partners may find delicious. Married people and partners in a responsible relationship enjoy having their "little secrets"—their moments of mutual naughtiness, of doing what the impulse tells them to do, thumbing their noses at propriety—all within the framework of a perfectly acceptable, sensible partnership.

And that is the special charm of the hurried, furtive, and reckless sexual encounter known as the quickie.

Okay, so I am turning around 180 degrees and saying the exact opposite of things I have said over and over before this. I go on and on about it during the radio show and I have said it in this book— don't rush, have a private time and place, take time for intimate talk and physical foreplay, lots of time. Learn to prolong your sexual encounters until both partners are gratified fully, then lots of afterplay. And when you read other writers on sex, you read much the same thing.

You're not catching the bus, we tell you, or running with a letter for the last mail pickup. Why this mad rush to get through this pleasure we think about so much of our lives and regard as life's great gift to us? Do the deed right. Soft lights, music, pleasant surroundings, a little wine. Make a leisurely art of it.

That's what I say, and I'll stand by it; all the same, there is something to be said for the occasional quickie! Despite all that has been said about the importance of two partners having full sexual encounters, there are times when a quickie is just the thing.

REMEMBER THE APRON?

Often a quick moment of passionate sex becomes a prelude to more leisurely sexual encounters.

Let me tell you about a couple and how they had a quickie they remembered happily all their lives. They had been married for only a few months when they woke up late for work one morning. While he took a fast shower she slipped on an apron and quickly cooked him up a couple of scrambled eggs. He wolfed down the eggs as he got dressed, kissed her good-bye, and was headed out the door when he turned to wave. The sight of his bride standing in the kitchen wearing nothing but the apron struck him as the best turn-on he had ever seen. So it would make him late to work! The hell with it! He closed the door again, ran back into the kitchen, swept her up in his arms, still wearing the apron, and carried her back to the bed, where he made passionate love to her. His excitement aroused her, and though she didn't have an orgasm, she was tremendously turned on. When he was finished, he kissed her and ran on out the door, and she luxuriated in bed, recalling the scene over and over in her mind as she masturbated herself to orgasm. Disgraceful! Both of them spent that day in a secret, rosy glow.

For years afterward this couple shared a special, intimate joke about that morning, which they kept alive between them as a memory of their early passion. None of their friends ever knew why every anniversary, in addition to a "real" gift, he also always bought her a fancy new apron.

One of the nice things about quickies is that they are so spontaneous, a way of stepping out of a couple's usual routine of sexual activity. It can be very nice to just suddenly sweep your partner off her feet—or to be swept off your feet by her—in a burst of lust.

Because a quickie is so erotic by nature, the memory of the experience can serve as a good base for fantasy during future lovemaking.

"CAN I WATCH WHILE YOU SHAVE?"

One morning while a certain young husband was shaving, his wife joined him in the bathroom to discuss getting the car fixed. He stood there naked, half his face lathered, as they debated the wisdom of replacing the shock absorbers. It was anything but a romantic moment, but she suddenly felt very aroused. She reached for his penis and started playing with it while they talked, and he found himself very pleasantly distracted. She laughed as she continued to toy with him until he finally dropped his razor in the sink, said "The hell with it," and they made love on the rug in the bathroom.

Their quickie of the morning was an unplanned and unexpected delight for both of them. All day she grinned to herself, feeling mischievously erotic and happy in the knowledge that she was a very sexy lady who could get her man aroused whenever she chose. He strutted around like a bantam rooster all day, grateful for his good fortune in marrying such a sex kitten.

This happy pair went on having sex at sudden, unexpected times, and they both felt that never knowing when they might give themselves a sudden present—shoving aside the humdrum world to indulge in this lively pleasure—did a lot to keep sex alive in their marriage. Good for them!

I have heard many women complain that their partners were only interested in satisfying their own needs, not caring about theirs. "All he ever wants," they say, "is a quickie." If quickies take the place of full sexual encounters, the result can be a lot of unhappiness for the partner who is left unsatisfied. That is what gave quickies a bad name in the first place!

Quickies should *not* take the place of full sexual encounters, complete with foreplay and afterplay, but they can be a welcome addition to a couple's sex life. If a full sexual encounter is like a twelve-course meal, a quickie can be like a delicious, unplanned midnight snack.

A quickie is not a good idea for a person's first sexual encounter. The first time someone engages in sexual intercourse the experience should be full of warmth and tenderness. A lot of time should go into foreplay and into holding each other close in leisurely, undisturbed afterplay.

But after the first time, when the circumstances are right, the erotic spontaneity of a quickie can be one of the delights of being part of a close and loving relationship.

12
BEYOND THE MISSIONARY POSITION

The way of having sex with the man on top and the woman underneath is called the missionary position, because the natives of the South Sea Islands, the Polynesians, called it that. When the missionaries arrived on the islands, they found happy half-naked people playing in the surf and sun, in the firelight and moonlight, with no shame about showing their skin—and not much about their lovemaking, which the missionaries found startling. The missionaries felt that the natives had too many ways of doing it. When they came under the missionaries' influence, the native women put on Mother Hubbards—long loose gowns covering them from neck to ankle. And they were told by their new teachers that there was only one godly way to copulate—woman underneath, man on top, in holy wedlock. So the natives called that the missionary position, and we call it that now.

Until just a short time ago, Americans generally regarded making love any other way wrong, nasty, and perverted. And they are still startled to dial WYNY and hear a conversation like this:

"You are on the air."

"Dr. Ruth. I am married for the second time, and my husband at present prefers oral sex, and I don't care for that type of sex."

"He prefers to give oral sex or to receive?"

143

"Receive. And I feel abnormal. I feel there is something wrong with me because I don't enjoy this."

"Do you love him?"

"I do."

"Okay. Let me say something. Not everybody has to be engaging in oral sex. So after having said that, if your husband likes it a lot and really craves for that, then one of the ways that you might try—I'm not sure if it works, but you can try—eat an ice-cream cone. Eat it very, very slowly, kind of licking around it, and then when you do perform oral sex, think of that ice-cream cone. Don't tell your husband. Just put an ice-cream cone in your head. . . . But let me ask you something important. Are you worried that he would ejaculate in your mouth?"

"No, no. It's just something I never grew up with."

"Right. But there is nothing abnormal about it."

"No, I guess not."

"I am not saying everybody is involved in oral sex, but if your husband likes that a lot, you maybe at least should try. The one thing that I can say with assurance to you is that there is nothing abnormal about it. Now, sometimes it's the technique that is needed, because some women are so worried about it because they feel that, you know, that he is so big in their mouth. And there is a technique. That is why I told you about an ice-cream cone, just licking around it and licking around the ridge of the penis. Hold the penis in your hands, in both hands, or in one hand, which is very pleasurable for the man, and it still doesn't mean that you have to take the entire penis in your mouth. Maybe what he also likes is you could hold with one hand, and touch the testicles a little bit. Just try that. If he craves it, then you might want to give yourself a push just to try it. But don't tell your husband that you are having ice cream in your head. All right?"

AN ERA OF TRANSITION

The fact is that people born after World War II have much more varied sexual repertoires than their parents, in the main, but they still have some likes and dislikes. So there are plenty of people to call me up and ask me is it all right, is it clean, healthy, normal, and have they got to do it if they don't want to.

So we are in a state of transition here about adopting ways of having sex that are in fact as old as the hills. In older countries a varied sex life is taken for granted.

The walls of the Sun Temple of Konarak in India, for generations a special treat for travelers who wouldn't see anything like it in downtown Wichita or even New York or London, are covered with large carvings of men and women having every conceivable kind of sex.

In Japan they have a nice custom. The bride and groom are given a lavishly illustrated book showing all the ways to do it. It is an honor to be the person who gives this book to the newlyweds. They place it under their pillow on the wedding night.

In most of the world variety has been traditionally considered the spice of everyone's sex life. When one partner says to the other, "You're a good lover," it means an imaginative and versatile one.

In the United States, until the Kinsey report in 1948 and then the work of Masters and Johnson in the 1960s, nothing but the missionary position was considered normal sex. Anything else was done by perverted foreigners.

The new generation has developed quite extensive sexual repertoires, which, as a sex therapist, I have to regard as a very healthy trend. A good repertoire makes for a long sex life and a happy one.

POSITIONS FOR ALL OCCASIONS

So, the missionary position is with the man on top, the woman underneath and on her back, and they are facing each other. It is a very popular position; if you think of a sexual repertoire as a kind of cuisine, this is the meat and potatoes of it. It has advantages. It allows the pubic bone to stimulate the area of the clitoris. It brings the two bodies together in a way people like—mouth to mouth, breast to breast, belly to belly, loins to loins. The hands are not as free to stroke and roam around as in other positions, but still it is a fine position. I am defending it because many people feel that it has become unfashionable and that they shouldn't admit to liking it.

A knowledgeable lady who liked good Scotch said, "The mish posish is the Scotch of positions. You keep coming back to it."

The man should rest his weight on his elbows unless he is a very light man! Simple variations on the missionary position are to

145

have the woman raise her legs up to the man's hips, or over his hips, or over his shoulders. Doing these things lets the man get his penis in deeper, which is pleasurable to men and women alike.

So it is a very good position but, like a diet of nothing but meat and potatoes, it can become routine and boring. It is a good thing to come back to, as the lady said, but people with a more varied repertoire last longer with fewer complaints of the sexual blahs.

For a vacation you can try lying side by side, facing each other. Or a position much favored in the movies, because you can see the woman in motion, the female superior position. That is with the woman on top, lying facedown on the man, or straddling him and sitting up.

Then there is dog fashion. The woman is on hands and knees, and the man enters her *vagina* from the rear. I am not talking about anal intercourse. Then there is doing it in a chair (the man getting a waffled bottom from the cane seat unless he protects himself!), with the woman sitting on the man's lap, straddling, facing him, or with her back to him.

The usefulness of these varies with each set of partners. Some positions let the man touch the woman's clitoris with his fingers while his penis is inside. Some make it easier for the man to rub this particular woman's clitoris with his penis while he moves his penis rhythmically or while she moves up and down on it.

Other positions are better for intercourse than the missionary one when the woman is pregnant. After all, you don't want Daddy's weight squashing Baby!

A great many big, tall men have a special liking for tiny women. They seem like little dolls or Lolitas and make the men feel even bigger and more masterful, some say. Now, the missionary position is not the best for the little lady in such a partnership, but in former times many small women had to tolerate it because it was the only one they believed to be ordained by God. Such women had dreams of being seven-foot Brünhildes and married to midgets.

"I hate it under there," one tiny matron said after years of marriage. "I can't breathe and I'm squashed to death, and it's so dark and sad and lonely." Ultimately, I'm glad to report, she trained her man to let her get on top. He did it first out of kindness and after a while he learned to like it better.

That female superior position is good when the woman is lively and randy and the man is tired. "You just lie on your back, Daddy Bear, and I'll do all the work; don't you move a muscle." Sometimes she can do this when she wants to do it one more time.

If you listen to me on Sunday nights, you have heard me talking to callers asking about oral or anal sex. Very often one partner wants this and the other doesn't. Obviously, the outcome is that one or the other gives in. I always hope that lovers find ways to accommodate each other. I try to explain that the one who wants it is not a monster of depravity with perverse tastes, because if you think about your mate that way, it doesn't help; it colors your attitude toward your loved one. Whether you do it or don't has to be your choice, though. Being pressured is in violation of your rights as a person and as a lover.

The point is that it is all right to explore the land of love with your partner, and you don't have to let the world know all your little secrets, either. Go into it all with the idea that you can try something once or twice and if it doesn't work for both of you, if it is unsatisfying, or uncomfortable, or you have to be an acrobat and you're not, don't do it anymore.

Don't turn something down flat just because it sounds silly, however. You are not doing this for an audience, like Fred Astaire. Your bedroom is not a place to stand on your dignity.

WHY MEDDLE WITH SUCCESS?

Very often when I suggest to a couple that they try some new positions, they look at me with astonishment and say they never thought of doing it that way. The problem here is that sex *does* need to be thought about, the partners have to put serious thought and effort into their sexual relationship if they want to avoid sexual boredom.

Often a couple gets used to having intercourse in only one position, and the woman trains herself to have orgasms in that position. When the couple then tries other positions, she may not experience orgasms at first and she may want to give up and go back to the usual position. But if a woman gives herself some more time to practice other positions, often she will discover that she can have orgasms using those, too.

One suggestion that is often helpful in trying out a new position is to use it during intercourse until the woman is ready to have an orgasm. Then she can shift into the more familiar position that is efficient for her. In this way she can explore new positions and still be sexually satisfied. In this way too the new position becomes both a part of foreplay and a part of sexual intercourse, as it should be. There is no firm line between foreplay and sexual intercourse; one should flow naturally into the other.

It is important to get away from the idea of sexual activity being "cost-effective," the idea that sexual activity is only worthwhile if it leads directly to orgasm or ejaculation. Sexual encounters should not be engaged in solely for the sexual "salary" of an orgasm or ejaculation. They should foster warmth and intimacy and a sense of caring about each other's happiness.

One couple I know went to an art supply store and bought two dolls, one male and one female, of the kind that artists use for practice in drawing the human figure. As part of foreplay, they took the two dolls to bed with them and used them to work out different positions for intercourse. They had so much fun with those dolls, they joked that it was like having four people in bed.

Sex doesn't have to be only a penis in a vagina. Anything that works and doesn't hurt is worth trying a few times. If you like a particular position and your partner doesn't, you can take turns using each other's favorite. It is all right occasionally to go along with your partner's preference, even if you do not care for it much yourself, and to ask your partner to go along with you, even if he or she is not particularly crazy about your preference—just as you take turns with food, one day going to a seafood restaurant because she likes flounder and another going to a steak place because he likes steak.

THE PLEASURE MUSCLE AND HOW TO USE IT
Women who are preparing for childbirth are often taught how to tighten and relax the pubococcygeus muscle in the vagina as an aid during labor. That muscle, which some people call "the pleasure muscle," has a tremendous number of nerve endings. Stimulation of the muscle can create intense sexual pleasure for a woman, and if she uses it correctly, for the man as well.

Over fifty years ago a noted urologist named Kegel invented an exercise for the pubococcygeus muscle to help women control the flow of their urine. A woman can easily locate that muscle by momentarily tightening it when she urinates to cut off the flow. She can tighten and relax the muscle at will. Once she has located it, she can later explore it with her finger to find which part of it is the most sensitive. The particular area of sensitivity varies from one woman to the next.

She can stimulate it herself by rubbing it as part of masturbation, and by teaching her partner to stimulate the sensitive part of the pubococcygeal muscle, she can add an additional pleasuring technique to their foreplay and lovemaking.

A woman can do exercises for the pubococcygeus muscle by repeatedly tightening and relaxing it. She can do the exercises several times a day, and she can do them anywhere—while she is sitting in the office, while she's watching television, while she's having lunch.

One young woman told me she did the exercises while driving to and from work each day. She found she had to limit herself after a while, however, because the pleasurable sensation was so intense, she was afraid she might have an accident. She decided to do the exercise only when she was stopped for a red light. And now, whenever she sees another woman driver stopped at a red light, wearing a look of intense concentration on her face, she smiles to herself and thinks, I know what *you're* doing.

She taught her husband to stimulate her ''pleasure muscle'' and also began using her tightening and relaxing exercises during intercourse.

If a woman tightens and relaxes the muscle when a man's penis is inside her vagina, she can give him an intensely pleasurable sensation. Though many men have never heard of the technique, most of those who have experienced it say it is pleasure such as men dream of but never expect to come true.

''The first time I did it,'' she told me with a laugh, ''his eyes went all glassy and he smiled a big, delighted smile. When I asked him if he liked it, he just nodded his head up and down and moaned, 'More! Please, more!' ''

ORAL SEX—FELLATIO

"You are on the air."

"Hi, Dr. Ruth. Happy Mother's Day!"

"Thank you, to you, too."

"My husband and I were introduced to you a couple of months ago, and we really do enjoy your program. We get a real kick out of it."

"Great!"

"I am twenty-seven. I have been married for two years. My husband and I have great sex with contraceptives."

"Good, good, good. I like to hear what you are saying! Ha ha! I am glad you got through."

"It is not really a problem—not a real problem but . . . I am pretty liberal-minded, and my husband and I, like I said before, we have good sex, but when it comes to oral sex . . . With me, I can go so far with my husband, having oral sex with him, but then I stop."

"You mean you can't have an orgasm?"

"No, I have an orgasm with him, but when I go down on my husband . . ."

"You don't want him to ejaculate in your mouth?"

"You got it! Now he has been very understanding, and he has shown me surveys from *Penthouse*. Can I mention that?"

"Of course."

"And material such as that about how women enjoy this and they really love it, and it's the best way to have sex and everything. I feel like I'm kind of strange. He hasn't really been putting any pressure on me, but from your vast audience I am wondering if I am the only weirdo."

"No, no. First of all, you sound like a terrific woman. Let me tell you that I'm getting many, many questions. For example, in the hundred letters a week that I get, I get this question over and over, and, you know, I don't mind when I get repeated questions, because this shows that there is a concern about that. Let me tell you something. Number one, what I like to hear is that your husband doesn't put pressure on you. That's great. Don't let anybody talk you into such nonsense as if this is the only way to have good sex."

"He is very, very understanding and really trying very hard.

He's been very sympathetic and understanding, but I know that at times he gets very frustrated."

"Let me tell you what you could do. Let's try if it would work with you. You don't mind to do oral sex, but you don't want him to ejaculate in your mouth?"

"I feel uncomfortable about that."

"And there is no need that you have to, but what you could do is the following. Do have oral sex, and then have a box of Kleenex right next to you. Do tell your husband that as soon as he feels that premonitory sensation, that is, that moment of inevitability, that moment when he is just about to come, and tell him that you want him to let you know when that moment is, and then just take the tissue and let him ejaculate into the tissue. That should be very enjoyable for him. Tell him—what I suggest is in his mind, in his fantasy—he can make believe as if he ejaculated into your mouth. Tell him to use his fantasy, since that's what fantasy is for—to make believe as if he does ejaculate into your mouth, but to actually ejaculate into a Kleenex. All right?"

"Dr. Ruth, is this really difficult for most women?"

"Yes. Some women do get used to it. For some women it is very difficult, and some women never get used to it and it's okay. Not everybody has to be involved in every aspect of sexuality or in every position. That your husband would like to have it, there is nothing wrong with that. You know what else you could tell him? Who knows what life brings. Maybe next year you suddenly will think that that's the greatest thing to do."

"He would love that."

"Tell him that, who knows? Tell him that maybe by reading books or things like that—maybe by next year you might change your mind. Nothing is all the time the same. . . . There is nothing dirty about the spermatozoa, you know that."

"Yes, I know."

"But it is not something that everybody has to be worried about. I have seen many women, also in my office, who say, 'I don't mind going down on him. I don't mind to pleasure him that way, but I don't want him to ejaculate!' And there are many men who agree with that and who accept it. But just leave the hope open of saying 'Who knows what happens next year.' Okay? Good luck.''

"Okay. Thank you so much."

"Thank you for calling and for listening."

Some women say they are not comfortable having an erect penis in the mouth because it makes them feel like they are going to gag. In this case a woman can take just the tip of a man's penis into her mouth and lick along the ridge near the tip, a sensation many men find very pleasurable.

It is relatively easy to learn how to perform fellatio by practicing on a banana or a lollipop or a Popsicle. Women who wonder if they are doing it "right" should ask their partner what feels good to him. As in everything else in sexual relations between two partners, it is always a good idea to overcome whatever shyness you feel and discuss with your partner how he or she likes to be pleasured.

Some women wonder whether swallowing a man's semen can make them pregnant! Since something you swallow goes to your stomach, not to your ovary, there is obviously no risk of pregnancy.

Some women swear that the vitamins in semen are good for the complexion. While it is doubtful that ingesting semen is beneficial in any way, it is definitely not harmful.

In addition to being a good variation in a sexual routine, oral intercourse is sometimes the ideal way for a woman to pleasure a man when she herself is not in the mood to have sex.

ORAL SEX—CUNNILINGUS

While many men enjoy having oral sex performed on them, many do not enjoy performing oral sex—cunnilingus—on a woman. Often they say they feel that a woman's vagina is unclean.

One possible solution to the problem is for a woman to take a shower or a bath immediately before going to bed. If she then encourages her partner to perform oral intercourse on her, and gives him a lot of positive feedback by letting him know how much she enjoys it, a man's reluctance can sometimes be overcome. There are sprays and flavored spermicide for men who like a woman to smell like a flower or taste like jam!

Lots of men find the genuine female odor stimulating. "If anything is truly sexy, that is it," one man told me.

Different women enjoy having the clitoris stimulated by a man's tongue and lips in different patterns, at different rates, and with different degrees of pressure. The only way her partner can know what she likes is if a woman lets him know. Many women also find it pleasurable for the man to insert one or two fingers into her vagina while stimulating her clitoris, others enjoy a dildo or a vibrator for this purpose. And some women like to have their anus stimulated or penetrated with a finger.

A dildo can be bought at a sex shop. Either the man or the woman can go to the shop, in case one of them is too shy.

The only way a woman can discover her sexual preference is to explore different styles with her partner and then let him know which she likes. As in everything else in a sexual relationship between two people, overcoming a shyness and reluctance to talk with your partner about what you like and what you don't like in your sexual encounters is the best way to expand and refine your sexual repertoire.

If, after trying it a few times, a man is still not comfortable performing cunnilingus on his partner, it may not be worth making an issue of it. There are plenty of other ways he can give her pleasure.

ORAL SEX—NEW ATTITUDES

Oral sex, both fellatio and cunnilingus, is generally much more practiced among younger people than by the rest of the population. This seems an encouraging sign of a willingness to explore and an openness about the body. While there is nothing good or bad about oral sex itself, there is something very good about people getting away from the idea that their bodies—especially the parts of their bodies that used to be referred to as "down there"—are nasty or dirty.

A natural, healthy attitude about the body and about sex is the necessary first step to good sexual functioning.

ANAL INTERCOURSE

Like oral intercourse, this was long considered unnatural in western countries, where Judeo-Christian morality prevailed. While being condemned in those countries, it was also widely practiced in those same countries! Both by men with men and by men with women.

Today the practice is considered by some simply as another sexual variation. With sufficient lubrication, there is pleasure in it for both partners, since there are nerve endings around the anus that can be pleasurably stimulated, and until quite recently I would tell people, "Do it, if both of you want to do it." Only I would warn that without lubrication, there could be soreness and damage, and that a penis should never go from the anus into the vagina without being washed first, because germs that flourish in the intestinal tract can cause very uncomfortable infections in the urinary tract of the woman. But lately urologists are cautioning people against it more strongly—not forbidding, but cautioning—because some very serious illnesses are apparently connected with the practice. Do read the chapter in this book about sexually transmitted diseases.

Men sometimes get to prefer this above all other sexual practices because the anus is so snug around the penis, and women have complained that they can't get their men to do anything else once they get used to anal intercourse. Between men and women it is best kept as a variation, not the only pleasure. Women too have become addicted to it—for one thing, there is no danger of pregnancy.

Caressing the area around the outside of the anus with a finger can be a stimulating part of foreplay. But don't put that finger inside the vagina. Not without washing it first.

The principle to follow in sex is to do anything pleasurable if there is no harm in it, and both partners accept it. But we live in a world of reality, and avoid activities plainly marked DANGER.

There is so much else to do, in the playful land beyond the missionary position, that we can forego one thing for the sake of health.

The dangers of sex must not become a fixation. After all, we face germs and the possibility of illness every day in the street, shaking hands, kissing, riding the bus. In return for all our pleasures in life, it isn't too much to behave sensibly.

13
CONTRACEPTION

"*Sexually Speaking;* you are on the air."

"Good evening, Dr. Ruth. My name is Yvonne. I am calling from Queens."

"Yes?"

"I have two questions. First of all, I want to tell you, because of you, I went to my gynecologist and got fitted with a diaphragm."

"Bravo! I love it. I also know where your accent is from!"

"Tell me—first of all, when I put the diaphragm inside, it is burning. I would like to know why."

"Okay. Please do give a call tomorrow morning (tomorrow is Monday morning), call the same gynecologist who gave you the diaphragm, because this might be a medical question and I cannot answer that."

"Only in the first few moments when I put it in it is burning. After that it is not burning."

"Let me ask you something. Do you put spermicidal cream around the edges of the diaphragm when you insert it?"

"This cream is the cream that comes with the diaphragm?"

"That's right. Then you should go back to the physician. Don't neglect it. Go back because maybe there's an infection. Maybe there is something, because there should be no burning even if it is only a few seconds. I would not neglect it. Okay?"

"The second question is also about the diaphragm. When I put the diaphragm inside, the gel tastes very bad, and my boyfriend says maybe I can get a different taste of diaphragm gel."

"Yes. One is a strawberry, the other one is a raspberry flavor. You just have to do a little bit of research to find out where it is available."

"In a pharmacy I can get it?"

"Yes, try that. If the pharmacy doesn't have it, call up one of those sex shops. You don't even have to go there, you can call up and ask where are those creams sold."

"He says it tastes *terrible*."

"Okay. Try the other creams. But I am so pleased that you are using a diaphragm because of this program."

"Because you scared me!"

"I am very, very pleased. Bravo to you! Stay in touch. Good luck to you. Bye-bye."

"Bye-bye."

I know it makes people laugh sometimes when I say it, but I am serious about it. *Use contraception.*

Maybe not for gay sex or oral intercourse! But be sure you don't make a baby by mistake—a baby you aren't ready for.

"My boyfriend and I are getting into whips and chains," a girl told me on the air. "With contraception?" I asked. That made my friends in the control room laugh. Well, it's a funny show sometimes, but I was serious.

You can start pretending with whips and chains and end up having a real baby or an abortion.

I have often said, on the air, in my private practice, and in my college classes, that if I can help prevent just one unwanted pregnancy by convincing someone to use contraception, then all the talking will have been worthwhile.

The first question I ask someone who tells me he is sexually active is, "Are you using a contraceptive?" To be sexually active *without* using contraception is one of the stupidest things anyone can do, especially since there are so many different methods of contraception readily available today.

Despite this fact, due to sexual ignorance and sexual illiteracy, the rate of unwanted pregnancies is at an all-time high. The high rate of unwanted pregnancy among teenagers—according to some estimate, the number is as high as one and a half million teenage girls each year—is particularly disturbing.

Part of the problem is that we are bombarded with sexual messages from the moment we wake up to the moment we go to sleep. If visitors from another planet were to come to Earth today and watch our television and see our movies and our magazines and our advertising, and listen to the popular songs on the radio, they would be convinced that we think of nothing else *but* sex all day long. But among many people, there is a tremendous amount of sexual ignorance.

WHEN A MIRACLE CAN BE A TRAGEDY

When teaching contraception in my college classes, I often begin by asking my students how many sperm cells it takes to make a woman pregnant. A few students invariably call out the correct answer: "One!" And I usually say, "Yes, one. One fast one."

The male ejaculate contains literally thousands of spermatozoa. Upon introduction into the vagina, these microscopic cells immediately begin moving up toward the ovaries, "swimming" by means of a kind of tail. When one spermatozoon reaches and penetrates a fertile egg, the egg seals itself off, preventing penetration by any other spermatozoa. The genes from the father in the spermatozoon combine with the genes of the mother in the egg and, when everything goes normally, approximately two hundred eighty days, or nine months, later a baby is born, bearing a composite of inherited traits from both parents.

It is all a wonderful miracle—when the baby is wanted. When a pregnancy is *not* wanted, that same miracle can result in terrible human tragedy.

"You are on the air."

"Good evening, Dr. Ruth."

"Good evening."

"This is Frankie. My question deals with contraception. I know it is one of your favorite topics."

"That's right. Yes?"

157

"Is there any particular time during the month where it is most important to use contraception? I know it is somewhere around the middle of the month. What are your feelings on that?"

"Right. First of all, I like when you call and talk about contraception. I am really very pleased about that. You know I am not a gynecologist, but my feeling is that a couple who are sexually active actually should protect themselves the *entire month*. You hear me clearly saying protect themselves, because what I like is when a young man like you calls and asks about contraception, because I get so many women constantly complaining that the man leaves the entire contraception responsibility to them. Here you have now proven to all of our listeners out there, thousands of them, that that's not so—that here is a young man who is concerned.

"I would use a contraception the entire month, and let me tell you one of the reasons. It's true that during the middle of the month you're in ovulation, and there is more likelihood. But many women don't know when they ovulate and sometimes they can ovulate more than once—if there is an emotional upset, for many, many reasons. So, I would say just to make it into a habit.

"Use contraception as part of foreplay. Remember, I say very often that to place it—let's suppose a couple uses a condom—to place the condom on the erect penis during foreplay ought to be very enjoyable. Or for the guy, especially a guy like you who is so responsible, to actually learn to put a diaphragm into the vagina as part of foreplay should really be fun. This way, if people can incorporate— I see the people in this studio, even the engineer is laughing! I think he hasn't heard that one yet— You know, this way you could incorporate the contraception as part of foreplay.

"Then, I want to say one more thing. Let's suppose she's not protected, there is nothing wrong with stimulating her to orgasm, or stimulating him to orgasm, but far away from the vagina. Because, as you know, those spermatozoa can travel very fast."

"Oh, yes—they can be speedy little rascals!"

"That's right. Thank you so much for calling."

"Thank you. Bye-bye."

THE NOT-SO-PERFECT PILL

At present, the safest and most effective contraceptive methods available are the condom and the diaphragm.

To many people the coming of the birth control pill in the 1960s meant that at last we had the ideal contraceptive. Easy and convenient, it was a means of preventing pregnancy that did not require any action on the part of either the man or the woman either before or following intercourse. But even in 1967, when I counseled people at a Planned Parenthood clinic in New York, I had reservations about the pill and was advising women to use a diaphragm instead. Perhaps it was my old-fashioned, European background, but I was not comfortable with the idea of women altering their hormonal balance and their body chemistry by using the pill. Since that time a number of side effects of birth control pills have come to light. Today it is said that women over thirty-five, women who smoke, and women with varicose veins should not take the pill.

My feeling now is that while in *some cases* the pill may be the best solution, used only after conferring with a gynecologist, the condom and the diaphragm are far safer and surer means of contraception.

RUSSIAN ROULETTE

Even some otherwise very intelligent people behave with remarkable stupidity when it comes to contraception. They approach the subject as though it were a game of Russian roulette that they somehow can't lose.

I got very angry not long ago at a woman who called me on my radio program and told me she'd had three abortions and didn't want to get pregnant again. But, she said, though she was very sexually active, she wasn't using any form of contraceptive. When I asked "Why not?" she answered, "Oh, I don't know. I just never think about it."

I was so overwhelmed by the woman's attitude that I simply told her, "Tomorrow morning, first thing, call Planned Parenthood and make an appointment for yourself." There was nothing more I could say to the woman until she realized that she *did* have to think about it.

That woman's attitude, which, unfortunately, is not uncommon, goes beyond ignorance. It is an attitude of indifference and callousness, and I find it absolutely infuriating.

Abortion is not a form of birth control.

THE DIAPHRAGM—DON'T LEAVE HOME WITHOUT IT

The diaphragm is one of the two best contraceptive methods available. A diaphragm can be used by most women, but it must be fitted by a gynecologist. When it is properly fitted, a diaphragm can be easily inserted and easily removed and should cause no discomfort during sexual intercourse or at any other time.

If it has been properly fitted by a physician, a diaphragm can be kept in for many hours. Since it rests on the cervix, a woman should not be able to feel it—if she does feel it, it isn't properly fitted. And the fit is important. You should not, as one pregnant woman sheepishly told me she had done, borrow your girl friend's diaphragm and expect it to work!

A woman can insert the diaphragm into her vagina in the morning, walk around with it inside her all day, and have intercourse that afternoon or evening. All she has to do is add contraceptive jelly or cream before the sexual encounter.

Too often I see pregnant women who tell me they always use a diaphragm. When I ask how they came to get pregnant, they respond with something like ''Oh, I always keep my diaphragm in my night table, but that day we were at his place, and I didn't think anything would happen. . . .'' or ''I left it at my boyfriend's house, and that night I was with another guy. . . .'' or ''I always carry it in my purse, but that night I changed purses. . . .''

As foolish as these stories sound, I hear excuses like these all the time.

Often I advise a woman to have two diaphragms, one to keep at home and one for her purse. One of my clients went one better and gave her second diaphragm to her fiancé for a birthday present.

"WHY DO I HAVE TO DO ALL THE WORK?"

I have no patience with women who complain that it is unfair that they have to take all the responsibility for contraception. ''Why doesn't *he* take some of the responsibility?'' they ask. Some women feel so strongly on this point that they send their husbands for vasectomies, a subject I will deal with later in this chapter.

In the case of one couple I saw, it took many sessions until the woman finally made an appointment with a gynecologist to get fitted for a diaphragm. Eventually she came to see that, whatever the merits of her argument, she was cutting off her nose to spite her face and being foolish to allow her attitude to prevent her from experiencing the pleasure of good sexual encounters.

THE CONDOM—LIKE WEARING A RAINCOAT IN THE SHOWER?

Like the diaphragm, the condom is a simple, reliable method of contraception. Because the thin membrane stretched over a penis lessens the sensations of intercourse slightly, some men complain that using a condom is like taking a shower with a raincoat on, or washing your feet with socks on. But the lessening of sensation is really very slight and, to illustrate the point, when teaching classes in human sexuality, I sometimes open a package of condoms and ask the students to put one on their finger and then touch that finger with their other hand. "Can you feel the contact well through the condom?" I ask. The answer is always yes. Then I ask, "Is the penis more sensitive than a finger?" Again, the reply is always yes. The sensation is there, and while not exactly what it is *without* the condom, it is certainly enough for sexual enjoyment.

In the past, some condoms were manufactured from cheap materials and without the receptacle tip that is common today. If a man did not leave a little space at the end when putting the condom on his penis, the force of his ejaculation was sometimes powerful enough to burst the condom. As a result, many women got pregnant even though the man had tried to take contraceptive precautions. Today, however, condoms manufactured by reputable companies are safer and much more effective.

One man told me that he began carrying a condom in his wallet when he was fourteen, a holdover from his boy scout training to "be prepared." He carried the same condom all through high school and still had it when he went off to college. It is a good idea for a man to carry a condom at all times in anticipation of the moment it will be needed, but a condom tucked away in a wallet, in the back pocket of his jeans, for three years, is not going to be a good condom. And will not do the job it is supposed to do.

A woman can also carry a condom as a contraceptive measure. She may run the risk of a man's assuming that if she carries a condom with her, it means she is ready to go to bed with every man she meets. But if a man does react that way, he probably doesn't know her very well, there is no mutual trust and understanding, and he probably isn't a good person for her to go to bed with anyway.

Some men, and women, say they don't like using a condom because the flow of their sexual encounter is interrupted while the man puts it on. There is a common fallacy that lovemaking has to follow a rigidly ordained sequence, like a military lockstep. This is not so. Rather than seeing putting on a condom as an *interruption* of a sexual encounter, it can be seen as *part* of it. The woman can place the condom on the man's erect penis—something many couples find very erotic.

In some instances, a condom is *not* a good contraceptive to use. For example, if a man has a problem with premature ejaculation, he may use a condom to lessen the sensation of intercourse so that he can hold back his ejaculation longer. But Dr. Helen Singer Kaplan has developed a method by which a man can overcome the problem of premature ejaculation relatively simply by learning to recognize the premonitory sensation that immediately precedes ejaculation and training himself to halt intercourse for a moment until that premonitory sensation fades. While learning this technique it is better not to wear a condom. Another type of contraceptive, such as a diaphragm, would be better.

A condom is also not recommended for a man who is experiencing erectile difficulties. The most common cause of erectile difficulties is a man's anxiety about how he will perform and especially about whether or not he will be able to obtain and then maintain an erection. If he begins to worry whether he will be able to maintain his erection while he puts on a condom, his anxiety may increase even more.

Condoms are now being manufactured in different colors and styles. While these variations may not have much actual physical benefit, the novelty can have a psychological effect and be a sexual stimulant that enhances the sexual encounter. Sex is more in the mind than it is between the legs. Anything that stimulates sexual appetite can be a welcome addition to a sexual encounter.

YOUR TURN TO CURTSY, MY TURN TO BOW

Whether or not a couple chooses to use a diaphragm or a condom during their sexual encounters is a matter of personal preference. The important thing is that they *do* use an effective method of contraception.

Some couples take turns, the woman using the diaphragm one week and the man using a condom the next. This system has the virtue of sharing the responsibility for contraception between the partners, an important point to some couples.

If they make it a practice for the man to insert the diaphragm in his partner's vagina and for her to place the condom on his erect penis, taking turns with contraception can also provide some extra variations in foreplay, a very necessary ingredient in maintaining sexual appetite between two partners in a relationship.

OTHER METHODS OF CONTRACEPTION

While I do recommend the diaphragm and the condom as the most effective methods of contraception, I will briefly mention some others in common use today.

Catholics are advised to use the rhythm method for contraception, and many couples, *who have been properly taught how to use it,* report that the rhythm method works. But you must learn how to use it.

The intrauterine device, or IUD, is a method some women find works for them. It is inserted surgically and removed only when the woman wants to conceive a child. But some women have experienced problems with infections related to the use of an IUD, and women who have not yet had babies may find that their bodies expel the device.

Several contraceptive methods make use of spermicides that neutralize the spermatozoa in the vagina. These include spermicidal suppositories inserted in the vagina that dissolve and coat the vaginal walls with a chemical agent that kills any spermatozoa that enter within the next several hours. This is similar to the active spermicide in the jelly or cream used with a diaphragm.

The same principle is at work in spermicidal foam, which a woman can spray into her vagina prior to intercourse. Some men find this foam distracting.

Another method of contraception, the Knaus system, which originated in Switzerland, involves a woman measuring her body temperature to determine when she is fertile and when she is not.

The natural method involves measuring the consistency of vaginal fluids and requires that a woman be consistent in her ovulation cycle and keep very precise records to determine her periods of fertility.

COITUS INTERRUPTUS—A NONMETHOD OF CONTRACEPTION

Very often I hear women say something like, "Dr. Westheimer, he told me that he had a lot of experience; he said I shouldn't worry, that he would pull out in time. And I swear to you he really *did* pull out. I could feel his semen on my thigh, so I *know* he pulled out. But I'm pregnant."

The drop of liquid that appears on the tip of a man's penis when he gets an erection contains many thousands of spermatozoa. The moment a man inserts his penis into a woman's vagina, he is also introducing spermatozoa into the vagina. And it only takes one spermatozoon to make a woman pregnant. Even if he *does* withdraw his penis before he ejaculates, there is a fair chance that the damage will have already been done.

Besides being ineffective as a contraceptive method, coitus interruptus (interrupted intercourse), or the "withdrawal method," is a very bad and destructive method of lovemaking. During intercourse both partners worry whether the man will withdraw in time and neither one can really yield completely to sexual abandon and fully enjoy the sexual encounter.

VASECTOMY—"THE CRUELEST CUT OF ALL"

Dear Dr. Ruth:

I was married to a woman of thirty-one ten years ago. We wanted children and the clock was running out for her to have them safely so we got to work and had four children in seven years. A year ago I was divorced. I have visiting rights to my children, of course. But now I have met another woman, and we want to get married. And she wants to have children. I have been to a doctor and he says to have a vasectomy reversed is almost impossible. You see, I had a vasectomy after my fourth child was born, as I did not realize that my marriage was not going to last. . . .

What could I tell him? I referred him to a certain clinic, but the fact is, the future is not bright for him as far as fathering any more children is concerned.

All of us have our own particular biases. Mine is against mutilation of the body.

In a vasectomy the small tube leading from a man's testicles to his penis is surgically severed, thereby preventing spermatozoa from reaching the man's penis. A relatively simple surgical procedure to perform, it is always difficult, often impossible, to undo.

Unless there is some compelling medical necessity for a vasectomy, as, for example, in the case of a couple who cannot use any contraceptive method and pregnancy or abortion would endanger the woman's health, I don't recommend vasectomies.

I have heard too many stories of tragic fires and car accidents leaving couples childless and desperately wanting and needing to rebuild their lives by starting a new family for me to be comfortable with the idea of vasectomies. When a man has a vasectomy, in effect he is saying, "I'll *never* want to have any more children."

Life is too uncertain for anyone ever to say never.

RECREATIONAL LOVEMAKING
I would like this country to put its resources toward finding a perfect contraceptive.

Research may develop it someday, but until it does, or until people are educated about the proper use of existing contraceptives, millions of people each year will experience the deeply personal trauma of an unwanted pregnancy.

Ideally it should be possible for consenting adults to engage in recreational lovemaking without having to worry about procreation.

Good contraception is important for the peace of mind people need in order to abandon themselves into the never-never land of sexual excitement and pleasure and ecstasy without having to worry that somebody may get pregnant. It is foolish to allow the danger of an unwanted pregnancy to enter into the lovemaking experience, or to ignore the matter and have to deal with options like raising an unwanted child, or giving a child up for adoption, or having an abortion.

ABORTION—DEALING WITH CONTRACEPTIVE FAILURE

Abortion is *not* a method of contraception. Abortion is a method of dealing with contraceptive failure.

I get incensed when I see ads in college newspapers that read ''Abortion only $125,'' followed by the words, in very small print, ''contraceptive advice available.''

Many abortion clinics do a big business, servicing the abortion needs of people too sexually ignorant, or too irresponsible, to use proper contraception. What ads for such clinics imply is that it is okay to play Russian roulette, it is okay not to worry about contraception, because even if you do get pregnant, it doesn't matter—having an abortion is no more serious than having a wart removed. This callous attitude is terribly destructive to the value people place on human life.

Abortion should be legal. Nothing is perfect, and some women are going to have contraceptive failures and need to have an abortion. We should never go back to the way things used to be in the past, when a woman who needed an abortion was forced to go to some back room and lie on a counter while an unqualified butcher ''operated'' with a coat hanger. But people must learn about their own bodies and become sexually literate enough to take the proper contraceptive measures.

A CASE OF OVER-CONTRACEPTION

Occasionally in matters of contraception there can be too much of a good thing.

Jean was a fashion designer in her early thirties who had the unique distinction among all her friends of being the only one never to have had an abortion. While this fact says a lot about the carelessness of her friends, it made Jean determined to be very cautious about contraception.

Whenever Jean began a relationship with a man, she began to worry about getting pregnant. This poisoned every relationship. Whenever she and her boyfriend made love, Jean inserted a diaphragm and also insisted that he wear a condom. Even with these precautions Jean worried so much about getting pregnant that she looked for ways to avoid sex. And every month, about a week before she was due to have her period, Jean began worrying that she would miss her period and was pregnant. Her anxiety was so great that it sometimes did cause her to be irregular, and then she would begin agonizing over having to have an abortion.

Jean's nervousness inhibited her sex life so much that every relationship would come to an unhappy end.

Despite my reservations about it, the pill is probably the best contraceptive method for a woman like Jean. With the pill she has had the security of knowing that she could not get pregnant, and that confidence has allowed her more relaxed sexual functioning.

CONTRACEPTION IN LATER YEARS
A woman can get pregnant from the time she begins to ovulate as an adolescent until she ceases to ovulate with the conclusion of menopause. When a woman is going through menopause, her periods can become so irregular that she may think she has finished and will stop taking contraceptive precautions, only to find that she is pregnant. If a woman thinks she has completed menopause and is no longer ovulating, she should check with her gynecologist to be sure. Only if she *is* sure can she stop being concerned with contraception.

A man, however, has to be concerned with contraception all his life. While conditions vary from one man to the next, many men remain fertile until they die. The mobility of the sperm may not be as great as it was in his earlier years, but if a man was fertile at thirty, chances are he will still be fertile, and able to father children, at the age of sixty, seventy, and as long as he can insert his penis into a vagina.

When it comes to reproduction, human beings are very efficient organisms. And because people can make babies so easily, it is important that they be aware of and use contraceptive methods when they do *not* want to make babies!

SEXUALLY TRANSMITTABLE DISEASES

"You are on the air."

"Hello, Dr. Ruth. I hope you can help me out. I don't see how you can. I listen to your show a lot, and when I should have been listening to it two weeks ago, instead I was out fooling around on my wife. To make a long story short, I was at my doctor's yesterday, and we confirmed that I have a communicable . . ."

"Sexually transmittable disease."

"Now, I've been flipping out, Doctor."

"Of course."

"I don't know how to tell my wife. She senses something. And she knows something's wrong. What can I say to her?"

"What does the doctor suggest?"

"He told me that the disease I have is of the herpes strain, or something to that effect."

"Which is very prevalent, in epidemic proportion now. What did he say that you could tell your wife?"

"He didn't really offer me any suggestions. He just said see if you could tell her that you got it at work, in a bathroom, or something to that effect. But I don't want to give it to her. I've been refraining from sex, and she senses it. I don't know what to do. I've been drinking. I've been smoking pot."

"Let me think for a moment with you. It's very difficult for me to give advice on that in general because I don't know you and I don't know your wife. Let me ask you this. Let's think about it together.''

''I've been married a year and a half.''

''What do you think will happen if you do tell her the truth? You see, very often, I tell people not to say anything, if it's not necessary, but here it seems to me that it's necessary.''

''Yeah. She's been bugging me. I can't even get dressed in front of her. I'm afraid she'll see something. It's been like hell these past few days. I'm ready to run away.''

''No, don't run away. Don't run away and don't start drinking. And don't start doing something foolish. From the way it sounds to me, I would suggest that maybe you could talk to her. Make it sound like it was something that just happened. It will never happen again, and tell her . . . because it doesn't sound to me that you can hide it.''

''Doctor, I could maybe do that. I have the disease—it was confirmed. I called the girl. I work with her. For a year and a half she's been trying to seduce me, and I finally succumbed, and I'll regret it for the rest of my life.''

''But wait. Let me tell you something. These things do happen. For you I think the most important thing right now is not to think about regretting for the rest of your life, and not to think what you ought to have done, because it happened. I think what you ought to do is take your wife out for dinner, or a ride, and then go home. Don't do it someplace outside, because if she does want to be angry, or cry, or whatever, she should have that freedom either in the car or at home. Do you have a car?''

''Yes, that is true. Yeah, in the car would be a good idea.''

''Not while driving. You know, go into someplace and park. All right?''

''Yes.''

''And do tell her, 'Look this woman has been after me.' Do tell her that you had a few drinks too many. That's what I would do. I would say, 'I had a few drinks too many,' even if it's not so. Okay?''

''You're saying I should just face up to the problem like a man. I did my thing and it was wrong, and I own up to it now?''

170

"Yes. Absolutely. I think that's what you should do. All right?"

"It's going to be tough, but I guess . . ."

"I think you have no other choice."

"I guess you're right."

"It's going to be tough. You take a deep breath. But don't be drunk when you talk to her."

"Not even one drink?"

"Not even one drink, because you have to be absolutely sober and to have all of your wits with you. You should really sit down, talk to her, tell her, 'Look, it happened. I had a few drinks too many. This woman in the office has been after me for a year and a half. It happened.' "

"Does it happen to a lot of people?"

"Yes, it does. To men and to women. And herpes right now is in epidemic proportion. And then what you would probably have to do is go and talk to a doctor exactly how to do it, so that you transmit it the least possible. But I think you have to talk to her. Will you let me know?"

"For sure."

"You promise? All right. I will think of you, all right?"

"I have a small question. What do I do about my family, as far as visiting them. Should I use different towels?"

"That you have to ask the physician, since I'm not a doctor."

"Doctor, I feel better."

"Okay. But do it soon. Okay? And without drinking. Thanks for calling."

Poor guy, he has a rough evening ahead when he tells his wife. In the last few years while the herpes epidemic has been growing, a lot of people, women as well as men, have had to tell their wives or their partners in serious relationships that they have had a fling with someone else and picked up herpes.

It would be easier nowadays to tell your spouses that you were unfaithful and have gonorrhea or syphilis, because people are more tolerant about infidelity now. Some regular partners even give permission to each other. And gonorrhea and syphilis can be cured if you catch them in time—penicillin and other "miracle drugs" have

171

taken the big terror out of these diseases. But herpes is something else. It won't kill you, it won't destroy your brain like the last stage of syphilis, but, unfortunately, there is at present no cure for it.

THE HERPES EPIDEMIC

Herpes is not a new disease. It has been around for centuries, since biblical times. But they only identified it as a virus in the 1940s, and it is only in the last twenty years that it has become a modern epidemic. It seems to have been epidemic in ancient Rome and in Paris in the 1700s, but they did not have it labeled as herpes.

In the August 1982 issue of *Time* magazine there was an article, "The New Scarlet Letter," about this incurable epidemic disease. Under the title on page 62 was the subhead "Herpes, an Incurable Virus, Threatens to Undo the Sexual Revolution."

Now I think that the change in sexual attitudes of the last twenty years is here to stay. Some people will get herpes, or learn about a friend getting it, and swear off sex entirely for a while. Or there will be people who will decide not to risk it anymore with people they just met in a bar or in the dark in a park. Or with known swingers, who risk the disease frequently.

A lot of people will decide that the thing to do is to go back to the old way of having one partner, someone they can be serious about, get along with in many ways besides sex, *and who doesn't have herpes!*

According to that article in *Time,* about twenty million Americans now have genital herpes, and another new half-million cases are expected in the coming year.

There are two known strains of herpes, called HSV-1, which causes sores on the mouth for the most part, and HSV-2, which causes sores on the genitals. Those mouth sores that people call cold sores are often caused by HSV-1.

You can't count on herpes to stay in the area of the body where it originates, however. A good many causes of HSV-1, mouth herpes, have been found on or in the genitals. One survey shows one third of women under twenty-four who are suffering from herpes on or in their genitals actually have HSV-1, the mouth herpes.

Now, you can get mouth herpes from kissing an infected person. (Will this cut down all that kissing we see on TV shows?) And you can get mouth herpes on the genitals by having someone do oral sex with you, go down on you, when that person has an open sore discharging the herpes virus.

Whether you are a man or a woman, you can usually tell when you have a case of herpes—at least, within from two to fifteen days. You may get a tingling sensation or itching, then blisters within days or a week or two, accompanied by high temperatures and headaches in many cases.

These big symptoms die down without medication, go away for weeks or months, then come back, on and off, for as long as you live. I do not want to be depressing, but I must bring this information forward in a book about good sex. Because good sex is certainly better without this disease.

If you catch herpes, you must tell people, even at the risk of ending the relationship. I'm not saying you should take an ad in the paper, but you do have to tell your wife or husband, your lover or lovers, anyone to whom you might transmit the disease. Unless you have no conscience at all, you must tell that person and anyone else you have sex with *before having sex*. A person who loves you may be willing to go on having sex, with precautions.

You have to go to a doctor who can give medications that relieve the symptoms, though he or she can't cure you of the virus that causes herpes. And a doctor will tell you how to keep from transmitting the disease to other people by sexual contact, using a common towel, and so on. You don't have to give up all sex forever, but only a physician, a medical doctor, can give reliable advice about that.

Herpes afflicts people of all kinds, but of the *reported* victims, according to *Time,* ninety-five percent are Caucasian, eighty percent are from twenty to thirty-nine years old, fifty-three percent had at least four years of college, and fifty-six percent earn twenty thousand dollars or more a year. Of course, these figures may mean that cases in the higher incomes, and among the more educated, are the cases that get reported by doctors.

The effects are not only physical. The psychological effects can be very bad. People who have herpes often feel dirty, ruined for life, unworthy, permanently frightened of sex. They might go into alcoholism or drug abuse. For these additional problems the herpes victim should go to a psychotherapist or seek help from a mental health clinic. You can live with herpes, and you owe it to yourself to get help. Many people cannot handle this problem by themselves.

A TALK WITH A UROLOGIST

Recently I was very glad to have on my radio show a physician who is a prominent urologist to talk about herpes and other diseases you can get by having sex, because to have a show like mine and never talk about this problem would be ridiculous and harmful.

I spent the whole hour talking to him about herpes, other sexually transmitted diseases, and certain ailments of the urinary and reproductive systems.

Dr. Jack Forest is a good friend of mine, a diplomate of the American Board of Urology and the director of urology at a hospital in Queens, New York City.

As the regular listeners to my radio show know by now, I do not try to move in on the urologist's field and tell people things that they should go to a urologist to hear. That would be bad popular educating—first, because I do not know that field the way a urologist does and would be telling people things that are wrong and harmful; and second, because a show like mine should tell people to go to a urologist for medical advice related to sex—to a urologist, or a gynecologist, or to a general practitioner, a family doctor, who will steer you to the right specialist.

This program with my friend Dr. Forest was a very good one, with information of great value, some of it correcting some wrong ideas that we have been living with until very recently.

I want to present what Dr. Forest had to say in his words because the information is vital and should be stated correctly and because we all should get used to listening to the right authorities for information on sexually transmitted diseases.

I will be quoting Dr. Forest and leaving out my own questions and observations because of course these programs do ramble in a nice, friendly way, but the essential information is what should be emphasized here.

"Sexually transmitted diseases," said Dr. Forest, "in some areas have reached epidemic proportions, and it's wrong not to deal with them, especially in these days when sex is more permissive. I remember when it was very difficult if someone had a sexually transmitted disease, such as gonorrhea, to explain to his wife that he'd been with another woman. Even if he weren't married he would find it difficult to explain to his girl friend. It is necessary not only to cure the disease in the person who has it but to track down the person he might have transmitted it to, or the one that he received it from, who in turn is transmitting it to other people if he or she is engaged in sexual activity. There is no way we can give anyone permission to keep this a secret. It must immediately be talked about, it must immediately be treated.

"With men, detection of gonorrhea is easier than with women. They have a painful discharge out of the urethra. The discharge is thick, it is obvious, you can almost make the diagnosis by looking at it. With women, unfortunately, it is not so easy. Women get the disease through intercourse, but the vagina is mostly insensitive. Women are often unaware of any discomfort. One must look carefully for discharge from the area of the urethra to get a culture in order to determine whether the woman has the disease, or, unfortunately, she will come to us when the disease has already traveled up the uterus into the Fallopian tubes."

"Then she has pain?" I asked.

"Then she has pelvic inflammatory disease. That can be a serious matter," Dr. Forest replied. "I would like to see women who are sexually active with multiple partners checked frequently, depending on the degree of frequency with sex. If she's very active, as often as once a month. If she's not very active, at least every three to six months."

A NEW KIND OF GONORRHEA

"I want to mention briefly another subject, a special kind of gonorrhea that has become very serious. With the use of penicillin as a miraculous drug in the treatment of gonorrhea through the years, the gonococcus, that is, the organism that produces gonorrhea, has become very intelligent and sophisticated and it has developed new strains that know how to deal with penicillin. They manufacture a substance that is able to destroy penicillin. A very clever little organism. . . . We now feel that as many as ten percent or perhaps more of new cases of gonorrhea are due to this PPNG type of organism, and the Department of Health is now advising that in every

175

case that has a discharge, the man or woman should have a culture taken. That way we can tell if it is a penicillin-resistant gonorrhea, in which case there are many other medications we can use. It is no longer adequate to take a bit of the pus and do a smear of it to look for gonorrhea; we must know what kind.

"Let me talk about herpes for just a moment. Herpes is a disease which has become more commonplace and which is also transmitted by sexual contact. We have not yet developed a cure for herpes. Unfortunately, when the herpes virus enters the body, it is able to remain in a dormant state virtually for life. It is reactivated at intervals and produces these terribly painful, unpleasant sores which can occur on the lips, on the genitals, or anally. We now have a new drug which hastens the recovery locally but does not cure the disease.

"You asked me about hepatitis. Hepatitis, too, can be transmitted in the sense that the virus is excreted in the semen and transmitted to a partner. So if you have hepatitis and you are going to have intercourse, use a condom to contain the Hepatitis B virus and prevent it from entering the vagina."

I asked if you know when you have hepatitis.

"In the later stages you can almost function normally. But at the beginning you know that you are ill. You begin to feel weak and soon you have jaundice and you begin to know that you're a sick person—nauseous, loss of appetite; it's a serious matter."

Of late we have had some very disquieting evidence about anal intercourse, enough to make us much more cautious in talking to people about this activity. I asked Dr. Forest to talk to the radio audience about that.

Dr. Forest said, "Yes, I think that it is an absolute must that one must not go from the anus into the vagina with the penis, the hand, a vibrator, or any object whatever. Let me tell you about a case I had. It was a young woman who would get episodes of very high fever, 104 and 105 degrees, really seriously ill with bloodstream infection due to a urinary tract infection. In tracking it down we found that she had a preference for rear entry—not anal sex but real rear entry, penis-to-vagina sex. However, the penis was sliding past her anus every time it entered the vagina. And every time they did this she would develop these serious infections until we determined that that was her problem.''

I asked him to give us his opinion on anal sex in terms of both heterosexual and homosexual activity.

''It is such a big subject that what I am going to say in a sense is almost contrary to what I have said in the past.''

ANAL SEX: A WARNING
What Dr. Forest said next was in fact a reversal of what many of us have been saying about anal intercourse, and I want to emphasize that Dr. Forest has always been ready to permit as wide a variety of activities as anyone in the field, and only limits patients when there is a serious medical objection to an activity.

''I want to say this not in a very strong way,'' he went on, ''but I want to call to people's attention that in this era of sexual liberation, when we are encouraging people to be experimental and to seek out every form of sexual pleasure, suddenly I'm about to say that I have some reservations about anal intercourse.

''And this brings up a host of new anal diseases that are sexually transmittable. Among them is Kaposi's sarcoma. For years it was known as an endemic disease in Africa, almost entirely limited to women. They would get big purple malignant spots on the legs and lower torso. Rarely did anybody die. Some people did die of it: It did get involved in the bloodstream, the liver, and it would kill them. But it was a minority of cases that were fatal. Suddenly now we have come across Kaposi's sarcoma in the last few years in almost epidemic proportions and almost entirely limited to gay men, and it is related statistically to the number of partners that they have and to the amount of anal intercourse.''

I put in ''So when a gay couple lives together for a couple of years they would be less likely to have that particular disease.''

''Particularly,'' said Dr. Forest, ''if their preference is not to be involved in anal intercourse, as many gay men are. I don't want to frighten the gay men into believing that everybody is going to develop Kaposi's sarcoma. They are only too much aware of Kaposi's sarcoma now; if anything I would like to make it less frightening. All we know at this time is that it is epidemic, limited to gay men, and related to the frequency of anal sex with different partners.''

So it would seem that people must be cautious about having casual anal sex, about being promiscuous with this form of sex, in order to avoid this type of sexually transmitted disease.

A final word. I am not going to join in with those people who say, ''Good! I'm glad these diseases have come as a scourge to punish all this permissive sex, this riot of immorality, this new Sodom and Gomorrah.'' Even though I do believe there is greater happiness in sustained relationships, in not trying to go on too long in life overemphasizing sex as just a physical pleasure, something to have with every stimulating person one meets, I do not feel glad that anyone suffers any of the misfortunes that can come to people through sex when it is not enjoyed cautiously, with common sense. Disease, like unwanted pregnancy, can come from sex. But disease is not a punishment for sin. What of all the other diseases that cause suffering or death, that have nothing to do with sex?

I think it is too bad that anybody suffers from enjoying sex, even if that person's way of having sex isn't mine, or the kind I believe is most rewarding. But the facts of life and health are not even concerned with our happiness—that happiness is a creation of the human mind. Disease strikes the good and the wicked alike. It is only foolish to risk sexually transmitted diseases recklessly.

You know what I think? I think they will find a cure for herpes some day. But only an idiot will risk catching herpes tonight on the chance that the new miracle drug will be in the drugstores next week. They have been looking for a cure for cancer for many, many years, and it may take that long to find one for herpes as well.

15
GAY SEX

I get phone calls and letters from many listeners asking about their problems as homosexuals.

"You are on the air."

"I am twenty-three presently. I have been sexually active since I was seventeen, and I am gay. I am fairly attractive, so I don't have a hard time finding partners. My problem is that it's gotten to a point in my sexual life that I've really lost interest in partners, that I can't seem to find one person that I really like. The longest I'm attracted to someone is, like, for the moment I'm with him or for one night, then after that I seem to lose interest in the person."

"Let me ask you something. Where do you mostly find your partners—in bathhouses?"

"Exactly."

"Okay. You are not the only guy that I have ever heard with that problem. Because very often when you meet people in the bathhouses, it's just for the sexual encounter and for the sexual release. Maybe one suggestion that I might have is to join one of the groups where homosexual men do congregate. Call the Institute for Human Identity and ask them where there are places you could go. A good thing is to find some hobby where you will meet other people. And if you can find an interest to share, that's the best way to find a relationship, because what you are really looking for is a lover, not just a one-night stand.''

"It is almost as if I can't stand sex itself—that sex has become an addiction.''

"Right. And what you really want is a rewarding relationship. So, what I would do is, try to find a hobby and try to find a place, or take some courses or something, but specifically a place where other homosexuals do congregate, so that you have the two things at the same time—an interest and the possibility of finding a lover.''

"What do I do at times when I really feel like I have to have sex?''

"Just continue. Continue what you are doing, but keep some energy and your time open for finding a relationship. Go actively looking for a relationship. Don't just sit home and expect a relationship to be brought to you on a silver platter. Okay?''

"Thank you very much.''

Many people, gay or straight, are sexually promiscuous. Especially when young. And during this phase they can get into a sex-for-sex-alone pattern that is hard to break. They find it hard to relate seriously to others as love partners.

Straight people have a great curiosity at one time or another about what gays "do.'' There is less of this curiosity now because so many books have been published about gay behavior, full of specific gay sex. And this way people have learned that gays do the same things straight sex partners do with the exception of putting a penis into a vagina.

Gays masturbate, they masturbate each other, they have oral sex, they rub against each other and have anal sex. They use dildos and vibrators and other substitutes for the erect penis.

They use fantasy and have a variety of relationships including long-term, short-term, one-night stands, quickies with total strangers (male gays more than lesbians). In these relationships they act like other sexually active people. Sometimes they are good to each other, sometimes not. They have tender feelings, romantic feelings, want security and reassurance, and sometimes they get bored and let a relationship go to pot. Like the rest of us, they do the right things and the wrong things.

WHAT DO THEY SEE IN EACH OTHER?

No one really knows why one person is sexually attracted to some particular kind of person. Some men find tall blond women irresistible; other men go for petite brunettes. For some women, muscular men with black curly hair may be terribly sexy, while other women are aroused by a man who seems little-boy shy or by the bearded professorial type. Everyone has seen a handsome man with a plain woman or a beautiful woman with a nondescript man and wondered, "What does he or she see in him or her?" The reasons for sexual attraction between particular men and women are a mystery and they will probably always remain a mystery. In the same way, no one is really sure why some people are sexually attracted to members of their *own* sex.

CHANGING IDEAS

The stereotype of a male homosexual that was once popular, as a weak, effeminate, "pretty" man, may still exist in some people's minds, but the reality is that gay men are as varied in personality and life-style as straight men. The myth that every homosexual man had an overpowering, domineering mother and a weak, submissive father has long since been debunked, partly by the recognition of the obvious fact that many homosexual men have brothers who grew up in the same home who are totally heterosexual.

Similarly the myth that all lesbians are man-haters who at the same time somehow wish they could *be* men has pretty much faded away as more and more gay women have "come out of the closet" and revealed themselves to be very feminine, well-adjusted women who interact quite well with both men and women.

Few people worry any longer that if a little boy spends a rainy afternoon helping his sister arrange the furniture in her dollhouse he will grow up to be gay, or that if a little girl pitches for the local softball team she is bound to grow up to be a lesbian.

With the new freedom in roles and role models, society has increasingly accepted the fact that men are not any less masculine if they cry at weddings and sad movies, and that women are no less feminine if they are capable of changing a light bulb or fixing a carburetor.

Homosexuality and heterosexuality are both aspects of human sexuality. Sexually speaking, in terms of sexual functioning and sexual relationships, there is surprisingly little difference between homosexuals and heterosexuals. In my work with the Institute for Human Identity I have counseled many homosexual couples and I deal with them in basically the same way that I deal with heterosexual couples. Often the problem and the solutions are similar and sometimes identical.

Perhaps the chief difference is that homosexuals frequently need support in getting their families to accept their life-style and their partners. Since life is more difficult for homosexuals and since many parents are disappointed when they realize that there are not going to be any grandchildren, this aspect of counseling is particularly important. But many heterosexuals also face problems with their parents accepting their partners or a lack of grandchildren, so even this aspect is not unique to homosexuals.

FIRST HOMOSEXUAL EXPERIENCE

Having a homosexual experience does not make a person a homosexual. Some people have homosexual encounters when they are young, and the experience does not have to prevent them from having heterosexual experiences later on.

I had a client I'll call Ella. Ella was convinced that after a homosexual experience with another woman, which was the first sexual encounter for her of any kind, it would be impossible for her ever to have a sexual relationship with a man. When Ella was seventeen she met a woman several years older than herself at a party and was soon totally infatuated. The woman swept Ella off her feet and took her to bed and Ella enjoyed the experience tremendously. Afterward she was afraid to go out with any of the many boys who asked her for a date, because she was sure that if a boy started to make love to her, he would somehow *know* that she had had a homosexual encounter. Though she was not sexually attracted to any other woman,

Ella was also afraid to socialize with her girl friends for fear that she might find herself sexually attracted to one of them.

After I assured Ella that there was no way anyone could tell she had had a sexual encounter with another woman and that the experience did not necessarily mean she was a homosexual, she was able to begin enjoying her social life again. I encouraged her to have a relationship with a man, to relax a little and to see what life would bring. Human sexuality is not something that is determined by one experience or one relationship. It is a composite of all that a person is and wants and loves. When she asked whether she should tell a man about her homosexual experience, I told her not to. People should not feel obligated to present a detailed sexual history of their lives to every new person they become involved with. It's a mistake to believe that it is somehow good to bare one's soul to relative strangers, to be totally frank and honest. That approach can be destructive. It is often best to hold some things back until there is a basis of mutual trust and understanding between two partners. In the case of a homosexual experience, it may be best not to mention it at all if there is a risk that your partner may throw it up to you during a quarrel, saying something like, "Anyway, you're a lesbian."

FANTASIES AND SURROGATES

Sometimes a man who has always been a homosexual decides he wants to become involved with women. Often he finds it difficult to make the adjustment. But it happens a good deal.

Ray was thirty-two and had been a homosexual since he first became sexually active. He had never had a sexual encounter with a woman. For a number of reasons he decided that he wanted to try being heterosexual, but he honestly had no idea how to go about it. When he learned he was going out of town for a week on a business trip, he decided it was a good opportunity to try out heterosexuality.

Ray worried that he would not find a woman sexually appealing and that he might not be able to obtain or maintain an erection with a woman. I suggested it might help him to fantasize that he was making love to a man. As Dr. Kaplan suggests, there is nothing wrong with using whatever fantasy comes to mind to stimulate sexual appetite.

On his first night in town Ray asked a woman out to dinner and when he took her home, she invited him in. They went to bed, and Ray did have difficulty obtaining an erection until he began to fantasize that he was really in bed with a man. He became sexually aroused and was able to have intercourse with the woman, but Ray ejaculated in only a few moments and had no idea at all how to bring her to orgasm. The woman suspected Ray of nothing more than being a clumsy lover, but Ray was disturbed. If he was going to do this thing, he was determined to do it right.

The next day he made discreet inquiries and obtained the phone number of a very high-priced, very accomplished call girl. When he saw her that night, he explained the situation and offered to pay her for a series of lessons on how to make love to a woman. Delighted with this new facet of her profession and with the high fee Ray offered for the lessons, she agreed to teach him how to be a heterosexual lover.

A surrogate can be very useful to a man in Ray's situation, or to any man who lacks either the knowledge or the confidence to function sexually with women. In Europe there was quite a tradition of experienced women teaching men the ropes. Some were courtesans—high-class prostitutes—some were older women looking for interesting sex, and some were simply kind-hearted women.

Ray was shy and awkward at first, but the woman was a very good teacher and she soon put him at ease. During Ray's week in the city she gave him a detailed course in how a woman functions sexually.

By the time Ray's business in the city was over, he had acquired the confidence to function sexually with women. He put his newly learned abilities to work and discovered that he very much enjoyed heterosexual sex.

Ray went on to establish a warm relationship with a woman whom he eventually married, and they had two children. Though he was very much in love with his wife, and was never unfaithful to her with another woman, he did occasionally have sexual encounters with other men. But Ray was happy being a family man, and his lapses from fidelity grew fewer and further between.

COUPLES

I have counseled many homosexual couples who have been together for ten years or more, and find that the problems they confront are generally the same problems confronted by any two partners in a sexual relationship. The same techniques of sex therapy often apply in dealing with their problems as well, including instructing the partner in means of sexual enrichment, such as new positions, new techniques, and the importance of varying the time and the setting for their sexual encounters to prevent boredom from setting in.

Midge and Kitty were both in their twenties and had been living together as a homosexual couple for three years. They had a good relationship and cared very deeply for each other. Midge had had heterosexual experiences, though Kitty had not, and both had had other homosexual experiences in the past. Their problem, which is familiar to many heterosexual couples, was that one of them, Kitty, was unable to have orgasms. I treated them as I would have treated a heterosexual couple, urging Midge to continue to be patient, and teaching Kitty how to pleasure herself and bring herself to orgasm through masturbation. Eventually Kitty was able to have orgasms, and her relationship with Midge was strengthened by their having dealt with the problem together, just as a heterosexual couple's relationship is reinforced by sharing the experience.

Gay or lesbian couples often face a problem familiar to many heterosexual couples—a difference in the level of their sexual appetites. Take Bella and Lynn. Bella wanted sex much less frequently than Lynn did, and I explained, as I explain to heterosexual couples, that sexual appetites do not always coincide. Just as they could accept that Lynn might be in the mood for a big steak while Bella only wanted an egg salad sandwich, they could similarly accept their differences in sexual appetites. If Bella was not in the mood for a long sexual encounter and Lynn *was* in the mood, Bella could just give Lynn an orgasm, pleasuring her in the same spirit that she might make Lynn a cup of hot cocoa even if Bella wasn't in the mood to have any herself.

They were as surprised by the suggestion as many heterosexual couples often are, and at first they worried that Bella would begin to feel that Lynn was using her. But, as I explained, that could be avoided if they had a frank and open discussion and honestly decided to recognize the difference in their levels of sexual desire and to deal with that difference in the most effective way. Sexual appetites do not always occur at the same time or with the same intensity. Recognizing the differences and resolving the varying needs of both partners in a relationship is always important.

I have also counseled many gay men who were involved in couple relationships and were experiencing sexual dysfunctions such as erectile difficulties and premature ejaculation. The treatments were essentially the same as those I have prescribed for heterosexual men with those same problems.

"You are on the air."

"I have a very serious problem. I have a boyfriend of almost two years now and I suspect he has a homosexuality problem. I came down the basement of his house one night and found him sitting there with his friends, and when the lights went on, he had such a nervous look on his face. Now, every time I want to make love to him, he gets turned off by the idea. This has only been happening within the last six months."

"How old are you?"

"I'm eighteen. I'll be nineteen."

"And how old is he?"

"He is seventeen."

"He had a look—but did he say anything?"

"He didn't know what to say. And this is really upsetting me, because I really love him."

"Of course. Did you ask him if he is attracted to men?"

"No. I'm afraid he would hit me. Should I confront him with this problem?"

"I would say, wait awhile. Wait awhile. See if it's only a passing episode, since, after all, you know him for quite a while and you really do love him. I would say, wait awhile. If afterwards you are going to ask him, you can also tell him that you are willing to go for some counseling with him, and if you do write to me, I'll give you a few referrals."

"Okay."

"Thank you for calling."

*   *   *

"You are on the air."

"Hello, Dr. Ruth. I am a Kinsey three, a bisexual. I really don't want to be. I've never had a relationship with girls, but I know I do like them and I prefer them to men, but it's just that the men are easier to come by."

"Okay. I understand that."

"I don't know what to do."

"There are some therapists, like at New York Hospital, in the Human Sexuality Clinic, like Dr. Helen Singer Kaplan. If you write to me, I will send you a couple of names of people who work specifically with people like you who would *like* to start a relationship with a woman but haven't had any opportunity, or didn't dare, and so forth. If you do write to Dr. Ruth Westheimer, WYNY-NBC, Thirty Rockefeller Plaza, New York, New York 10020, I will send you a list of people. All right?"

"Okay."

"Because I think that for you it's worthwhile to talk to somebody, since you do want to have a relationship with a woman. And there are Kinsey-three people who definitely can have a relationship with women, even if they have had only homosexual experiences up to now, or even if they're now attracted to men (or with women, to women), and still they can learn to have a relationship with the opposite sex. If that's what they would like. Okay?"

"Okay. Thank you."

"You are on the air."

"Hello, Dr. Ruth. This is Lou from Elmsford. I've got a problem. My friend Sean drinks a lot, and when he gets a little drunk, he wants to get me in bed."

"Okay. Two things. You are not interested in Sean?"

"No, I'm not."

"When he isn't drunk, does he also try to make a pass at you?"

"No, no, I don't want no part of that."

"I know that, but when he's not drunk, does he also try to make a pass at you?"

"He did once."

"Did you tell him absolutely no?"

"In no uncertain terms I did."

"Good. Before he gets drunk, when he is sober, I would tell him, 'Look, when you are drunk, this is what you are trying to do.' Tell Sean maybe you are doing it without really wanting to do it, but that you don't want any part of it, and do tell him that if he does try that again, then you can't be friends with him. You have to threaten him a little bit. All right?"

"All right. Thank you."

"Good luck to you."

"You are on the air."

"Hello, Dr. Ruth. I am twenty-five years old and I am gay. My roommate is my gay partner. About three months ago she started working at a new job, and she has been getting a ride back and forth from work with another employee who is a man, and they have gotten really close, and I am worried about our relationship."

"Of course. This is exactly the type of problem that *anybody* has—gay or not gay. The important thing here is, did you have a talk with her?"

"Not yet."

"Not yet. Well, you can't prevent her from liking somebody else—if it is a man or a woman. In this particular instance, it doesn't matter. What you are worried about is losing the relationship. The only thing you can do is have an open talk and maybe what you could do is . . . You do like her, in addition to having a sexual relationship?"

"Yes."

"The only thing I would suggest that you could do is to say to her, 'Look, if that's what is developing between that man and you, let's at least try to be friends.' Ask her about maybe not talking to the man about your relationship with her. If she really falls in love with him, then there's very little you can do except trying to keep a friendship. Do you understand?"

"Yes. So, therefore, I will know whether I should start looking again."

"Absolutely. If she really does develop a relationship, then you, after a certain period of time of being sad and mourning, and being upset about losing a lover, you are going to look around for a new lover."

"How long a period of time do I wait?"

"That's difficult to say. You know, I will tell you something. I have known some people who come to my office, very upset because they have lost a lover, and they are so sad and so upset, and we talk about it and I say, 'Give it a little bit of time, and just get over the loss of this relationship.' And sometimes, you know what happens, the next week they come in beaming for happiness because they just happened to have met the right partner and fallen in love again."

"You are on the air."

"Dr. Ruth, I'm Harry from New Rochelle and I have a serious problem. I've been living with this girl on and off for about the past two years. Three months ago she came home from work unexpectedly and found me in bed with someone else, and she refuses to have sex with me since then. Well, this someone else was a male."

"Okay. And she's still friends with you? She wants to be friends but not to have sex?"

"I think she's mad."

"Let me ask you this. Since that time do you feel sexually more aroused by men or by women?"

"Well, since she doesn't want to have sex, I have been having sex with this one man."

"With the same one that she found you with?"

"Right."

"Aha."

"We work together, so I see him all the time."

"I'll tell you something. It's really up to her. The one thing that I could suggest, since you have had a long-standing relationship, is that the two of you go and talk to a counselor, you and your girl friend. Because, look, you can't force her, and she certainly did not know that you have homosexual tendencies, or that you are what is called a Kinsey three."

"A what?"

"A bisexual, which means that you can have sex with both. Right?"

"I guess so."

"I would say there is an Institute for Human Identity in Manhattan. If I were you I would make an appointment with your girl friend, because otherwise you probably are going to lose her. And if you really care, you have to talk it out with somebody so that the two of you— Either she can forgive you and say that she wants to continue the relationship and she forgives you, or whatever conditions she's going to put. Otherwise, if you just let it ride, you might lose her. So, I would certainly see somebody. If you can't get an address, send me a letter, and I'll get you some addresses."

"Okay. Thank you very much, Dr. Ruth."

"Thank you very much for calling."

"You are on the air."

"Hi, my name is Gerry. I live in a town where everybody knows me, and I have a friend. I lived with her in New Mexico with two other people, and we came back for the summer—she was going to school out there. Now that I'm here everybody thinks that she is gay, and now they think that I am too because I spend a lot of time with her."

"I understand. Is she gay?"

"I don't know. I'm not sure."

"Okay. Do you have a boyfriend?"

"No, I don't. I see guys, though."

"That is the best thing to do. Ignore what people say and ignore what people think and just you go out and be good friends with her, and as long as you go out with guys, then they're going to stop thinking that. Okay? Thanks a lot for calling."

"Thank you very much."

A MATTER OF CHOICE

If two consenting adults decide to have a homosexual encounter or relationship, whatever feels good between them should be acceptable.

But it is important to realize that society does make life more difficult for a person who wants to function as a homosexual rather than as a heterosexual. It is much easier, for example, for homosexuals to find social and sexual contacts in large cities that have relatively liberal social attitudes than in small towns where homosexuals may be actively persecuted.

Even in large cities, however, it is not always a good idea to proclaim openly one's homosexuality. Old myths and old prejudices die hard, and though a person's sexual preferences should have nothing to do with the qualifications for a job, or the right to live in a certain neighborhood, or to do anything else, in real life people do make judgments based on such things.

It is hard to hide homosexuality entirely. Lately many gays have "come out of the closet," stopped maintaining the pretense of not being gay. But the pretense was often no more than a formality. Gays lived as though they had no sex life to advertise, but in most cases the people who knew them surmised that they were homosexual.

But not all homosexuals are ready to come out and be counted as soldiers in the gay movement. I don't advise people to declare that they are gay until they are absolutely certain, ready to make a mature choice. Especially not until they are sure what they want to be, gay, heterosexual, or bisexual. I am against pressure in sexual matters, and the pressure to be forced into a gay mold is as bad as any other.

Many people go through a homosexual phase and then into another sexual phase. A homosexual phase may be one of many in a person's life, like a promiscuous phase, an inactive phase, a living-together phase, or a settled married phase.

It also happens that people turn from straight to gay quite late in life.

I don't try to "straighten out" gay people who come to me for counseling. Many come with real problems but no desire to change from gay to straight at all. But sometimes the problem they bring to me is that they want to change. And sometimes they do change.

There are times when it is wrong to counsel a gay person to try to change, when every indication is that such a change could never really take place and would only cause needless suffering.

My last words on this subject: By no means do I want to leave the impression that as a sex therapist I am lying in wait, hoping for gay men and lesbians to wander into my office, always with the feeling in my heart that it would be better if they could be straight! I only think that people who are confused will be happier if they can be helped to find an identity that will make them happy, or happier than living under pressure to be what they feel they cannot be.

16
SEX
AND THE
DISABLED

"And no sex," the doctor told the man recovering from a massive heart attack.

The man was known for his very active sex life, but at this point he was mainly thinking about staying alive. He didn't really want any sex at the moment. But he knew he would when he got a little better.

"No women," the patient said.

"No partying," the doctor said. "I mean it."

"How about masturbating?" the patient asked.

"The heart doesn't know the difference," the doctor said.

Do what the doctor says. But do ask the doctor what about sex after something like a heart attack. You have a right to know, and he may suggest some quiet form of sex in your present condition, or he may say that later on you can go back to sex. He may give you something to look forward to while you are being a good patient.

Human beings have the right to pursue sexual happiness in sickness as well as in health.

As a sex therapist and sex educator, I try to help people who are disabled—and the health care professionals who work with them—to understand the importance of accepting human sexuality as part of being human. Unfortunately, society consistently discourages disabled people from thinking about themselves as sexual beings.

Patients who have damaging illnesses or who undergo surgery should be advised about their ability to function sexually after recovery. In the case of a recovering cardiac patient, for example, a physician will often carefully outline a long list of special procedures to be followed but will fail to mention anything at all about sex. Since many patients are embarrassed to ask direct questions about their sexual functioning, they often return home confused about their ability to engage in sex and are afraid of resuming sexual activity. The patient's spouse is often even more afraid of initiating sexual activity and worries about bringing on another heart attack.

Many people who could continue to have sex after their recovery, if they are properly counseled as to methods and limitations, simply give up sexual activity altogether out of fear and ignorance. If a physician does not offer the information, patients should ask about their ability to function sexually during and after their recovery. Much unhappiness could be avoided by such sex counseling.

AWKWARD MOMENTS

Ileostomy, colostomy, and ileal conduit patients face the delicate task of telling their potential sex partners that they wear a waste bag. A similar awkwardness is faced by a person with a prosthetic leg or a woman with a prosthetic breast. It is best to discuss the matter with a potential sexual partner before the sexual encounter begins, rather than waiting until the encounter is in progress. People may need some time to accept the fact of an infirmity, even if it does not inhibit sexual functioning.

Individual or group discussions with other people who have recovered from similar operations, or who have learned to cope with similar infirmities, are an excellent aid to recovery. Such sessions should include frank discussions of the effects of the operation or infirmity on sexual functioning. Persons learning to deal with their own difficulties need help and support from others who have experienced the same or similar situations themselves.

IN THE HOSPITAL

Sexual prudery among health care professionals can be bad medicine for the patient. Doctors, nurses, and other hospital staff frequently react badly to any expression of sexual desire by a patient. Many nurses get flustered when they come upon a man with an erection while they are changing his sheets. Instead of just covering him up and going away quietly, they may scold and embarrass him. Hospital personnel are often not trained to meet such very natural situations and perceive sex as an unwelcome visitor in the hospital. Training to recognize and deal with the natural sexuality of patients should be a basic part of the education of all health care professionals.

"Dating rooms" have been set aside in some hospitals. I wish they were in all hospitals. These dating rooms should be comfortable private rooms that patients can reserve for time together and for sexual encounters with their partners.

WITH A LITTLE HELP

When patients' disabilities preclude that they can be independent, the two handicapped lovers should be moved into the best position for exploring each other's bodies and then left alone. Many handicapped patients could derive great benefit from a sexual counselor who would aid in the sexual act itself.

For male paraplegics, for example, sexual intercourse is physically impossible. But they can be taught to stimulate their female partners by other means, such as by using their hands, or mouths, or toes, or a towel, and to gain as much pleasure as possible from being touched themselves. Even if they cannot have an erection, they may find anal stimulation pleasurable.

In some instances, semen is expelled back into the bladder during orgasm instead of ejaculated outside the penis, but the sexual release can still be very gratifying.

Despite difficulties in functioning, disabled people do have inalienable sexual rights. It is a great injustice to withhold sexual counseling and opportunities for them to satisfy their erotic needs.

There is information about this subject of sex for disabled people that should be available to them, from the doctors or nurses (but many of these people are untrained in sex counseling and therapy or are unwilling to take part in it), or in support group sessions for the disabled, or in those booklets that people get to take home with them. For instance, arthritic patients find many physical activities painful. Not in the genitalia but in the joints that are moved during sexual activity. But we know that arthritis sufferers have an easier time of it right after a bath. Bath time can be changed to just before bedtime. Or the time for sex can be in the daytime. There is no rule that sex has to be at night, with the stars and moon. One can create a romantic atmosphere during the day.

DISABLED SINGLES
Perhaps the greatest problem faced by the single person who is disabled is loneliness. Disabled people are often overprotected by well-meaning family members who want to shield them from being hurt.

It is important for disabled singles and their families—as for all chronically ill or disabled people and their families—to participate in support and discussion groups. In such groups sex should be a major topic for discussion. Ignoring human sexuality is never a solution to any problem.

SOME PHYSICAL PROBLEMS WITH SEX
Sex therapists tell clients to go to medical doctors for physical malfunctions and illnesses of the sexual apparatus. Physicians often refer patients to sex therapists for ''that sort of thing''—meaning help with lovemaking and related aspects of sexual behavior.

Everyone who has a sex life should have at least an idea where to go when things don't work sexually. It probably should be the family doctor first, and the family doctor can recommend a specialist if such is needed, if the proverbial friend has V.D. or a pain down there or some loss of sexual ability, or the happy or unhappy thought that a pregnancy has started. If you want to be sexually well informed, you should have the phone numbers of Planned Parenthood, a sex clinic, a gynecologist, a urologist, a general practitioner, and be prepared to seek their services rather than letting things slide.

In my mail and on the air, as my regular listeners know, I get many inquiries about physical problems.

Dear Dr. Ruth:
When I was born, only one testicle dropped down into my scrotum. The other one was surgically removed when I was

six. *Needless to say, now that I'm twenty-two, it can be sexually embarrassing at times. Is there a safe surgical procedure that is available to have a placebo placed in my scrotum? Please answer in a plain envelope.*

Joe

Dear Joe:
I am sorry that I am not able to answer your question since I am not a medical doctor. You must seek the opinion of the appropriate physician.

I would like to make one comment. If you are able to function normally, and your question involves a concern for the appearance of the scrotum, you may want to consider turning your special appearance into an advantage. You can tell your new partner that your special situation makes a very special lover! This may relieve any anxiety you or your lover feels.

Good luck!

Dr. Ruth

Dear Dr. Ruth:
Me and my boyfriend attempted to have sex but in the process he was unable to enter me. Please tell me what I should do. Should I buy a certain kind of cream, or would I need surgery?

All your answers would be appreciated. Thank you.

Deedee

Dear Deedee:
I understand from your letter that the reason your boyfriend was unable to enter you was due to a tightness in your vagina.

If this is so, I suggest several things. Firstly, it could be you were not sexually stimulated enough. Try having a very long foreplay session and make sure your vagina is very, very wet before trying to have intercourse. If that does not work, you can buy K-Y Jelly in any pharmacy. This will help lubricate your vagina.

You did not mention what type of contraceptive you are using. If you are not using one, call a Planned Parenthood clinic

197

for advice. The cream or jelly from the diaphragm, or a lubricated condom, might help as well.

If the problem continues, you should see a gynecologist to make sure nothing else is wrong.

Good luck!

Dr. Ruth

Dear Dr. Westheimer:

I have been engaging in sexual activities for seven years now, and feel that my vagina has become stretched out (which I understand is normal). I was wondering if you could recommend any positions for intercourse which would help the vagina grip the penis better? At times I can barely feel the penis inside me, and cannot feel when my boyfriend is ejaculating. . . .

Polly

Dear Polly:

I suggest you try a "doggie" position where the man enters you from behind and variations of that. It might be a good idea for you to buy The Joy of Sex. *It will give you other ideas as well. You may also want to try to strengthen your vaginal muscles by doing Dr. Kegel's exercises. As you are urinating, stop and start several times. After a while you'll recognize those muscles and you can exercise them several times a day even when you are not urinating.*

Dr. Ruth

Dear Dr. Ruth:

I am a girl twenty-one years old. I have been going with this man for about two years. My boyfriend has never had an erection. It's hard for him to talk about it with me, but he tries. I love him very much and he loves me and wants to marry me soon. I don't know if I can live the rest of my life without intercourse. Can you help us, please?

Beryl

Dear Beryl:

Your boyfriend has a very serious problem and he must see a sex therapist for it. I suggest you ask him to call the Human Sexuality Clinic at New York Hospital in Manhattan to make an appointment to see a counselor.

Dr. Ruth

Dear Dr. Ruth:

I'm nineteen years of age. I was raped at the age of eleven by my friend's father, who was in his mid-forties. I went to the doctor my mother works for, but she never told me the results.

I didn't start my menstrual cycle till I was about fifteen going on sixteen. Ever since then I've had bleeding problems. Example: it's either too heavy, too light and lasts longer, or it will go heavy for about three days, which is normal, then it will stop and go for about three more days. And every time my mom takes me to the doctor I never hear the results, and I'm too scared to ask her anything. But the question is, two years ago I made love to a lot of guys—no condom—and now I've been going out with this one guy for over a year. We have plans to get married in about four years. When I started going out, well about five months after we'd been going together, he told me that I can't get pregnant. We've been making love forty times (no condom). And I can't or haven't gotten pregnant. I would like to know if this is a mental or physical problem.

Claudette

Dear Claudette:

You have written to me with a kind of complex problem, that I cannot fully answer in a letter.

You had a terrible thing happen to you when you were eleven. You said your mother took you to the doctor but you didn't say if you ever discussed what happened with her. It does sound to me though that you should ask your mother what the doctor said each time. You may also want to make an appointment with your doctor just to talk about your past visits (without your mother) and to talk about your fear that you cannot get pregnant because of your slightly *irregular menstrual flow. At the same time, if I were you, I would ask the doctor to fit you for a diaphragm. You may think you cannot get pregnant but you should take every precaution anyway.*

I also recommend that you visit a human sexuality clinic in your area. There are many connected to various hospitals or call Planned Parenthood for a referral in your area.

Dr. Ruth

Dear Dr. Ruth:

I have a serious problem. I have good sex with contraception. I have a new boyfriend, Joe. We've tried to have sex but his penis just won't fit no matter what position we use. This problem has only come up with me about three other times.

Lana

Dear Lana:

I am very glad to hear that you use contraception.

If your boyfriend's penis will not fit in your vagina, try the female superior position (you on top) again but this time have your boyfriend be absolutely still with only you moving. Go slowly with you controlling the motion and relax. This might help.

Sometimes it happens with very large men and very small women that the penis cannot fit its full length into the vagina. This, however, is usually still quite pleasurable for the man.

It might also be wise to be checked by a gynecologist.

Dr. Ruth

17
RELATIONSHIPS

Human sexuality is best held within the protection of a relationship, nurtured there, keeping the relationship warm—like the fire that people used to keep alive on the hearth long ago, before there were matches. That's a nice way to think of it, because it has to be cared for and kept alive, and then it will keep the people who care for it warm.

I give a great deal of advice as a therapist and as a radio educator to people who ask only about the physical, what you might call the technical, aspects of sex. (Sex is never *purely* physical with human beings—it is always in the mind as well as in the genitals.) Sex, considered as something apart from relationships, apart from the rest of human life, is still a very interesting subject, and I am always glad to answer these questions that are purely sexual. How to learn to have an orgasm, how to learn to keep an erection, what position would be best to use when people have certain difficulties during copulation, etc.

And people love to hear these questions asked and answered on the radio, especially in the beginning, when they first listen. Because it is still startling to hear about things like adult masturbation on the radio! But when they tune in again and again (listeners have told me this) it is to hear "the stories." The wonderful stories of relationships that people phone in about, each story so human and yet not just like any other story.

Sometimes listeners or students will want me to generalize. "How should people approach a relationship?" I am very cautious about answering a general question like that. The reason is that I might say "Always have ground rules," or something like that. That will not work for everybody. Somebody might go around trying to set up ground rules and scaring people off. It might be that this person doesn't have a good way of expressing things, he or she sounds too much like a lawyer talking, and the other person says "Hah!" and goes away! So this person might do better to wait awhile and let the feeling with the other person grow before talking about rules.

I try to listen and get a picture of the people involved in the question, the mood of that relationship right now, and give some appropriate suggestions. And people should be like that in their own lives, dealing with their own sex and their own relationships. Keep in mind your own special character, your own wonderful human uniqueness and the uniqueness of your partner, and the uniqueness of the relationship that the two of you have together.

All humanity is alike in certain basic ways. Everybody eats, sleeps, goes to the bathroom. I like the way somebody put it, and I would give credit to the person who said this, but it doesn't seem to be in any book of quotations. This person said, "Everybody is the same as everybody else, but no two individuals are exactly alike."

Don't look for your sex life to match up with some model that you got from somewhere, that stuck in your mind and seems very hard to shake loose. It is *your* sex life, and it is your sex life as lived with this other person. So whatever is different about it is all right, and the differences make it your very own thing that only the two of you share.

Another thing about relationships—they all present difficulties. All right, someone will write a letter and say, "Not *our* relationship, Dr. Ruth, ours is perfect." Fine, I am overjoyed for the person who says that! But I am talking about all the *other* relationships in the world. They all have difficulties, and they have to be thought about and solved. Whether to speak up about something or keep quiet and see what life brings, for instance. Sometimes one seems to be the thing to do, sometimes the other. At one time silence is golden, at another you have to speak up or things will go from bad to worse.

So when a person calls me up at WYNY I do not have an answer on the shelf, to give without considering many different things I hear in the questions that are not really put into words. I try to make each answer suitable to the special problem that is put before me.

This chapter is devoted to phone calls and letters about relationships. I think you'll find them very interesting. I certainly did! And you may store up something that you can use someday, to help yourself in some situation, or to help you in giving advice to a friend.

"You are on the air."

"Hello, Dr. Ruth. I'm nineteen and I've been going out with a boy who's twenty-one, for about two and a half years now."

"How long?"

"Two and a half years. We just got an apartment together. We signed a fifteen-month lease for a two-bedroom apartment. I insisted on having two bedrooms because I definitely feel it's necessary, from having known him for so long, that we need our own space— you know, when you want to be away, and there's no place to be."

"Of course."

"So we got a two-bedroom apartment, and I wanted your opinion on something. We made certain ground rules. We love each other very deeply and we're basically very true to each other, at least in the heart. There have been times when I found out that he's had a casual fling with someone and I have too. This doesn't happen often. We made ground rules. For one, neither one of us is ever going to spend the whole night out—no matter what the circumstances— because that'll hurt, wondering where the other one is."

"Right."

"And the other rule is that we would never—if we were going to have some casual sexual relationship—bring anyone to the apartment in case the other one came home. My question is, do you think it's normal when you're this young, when you have a meaningless sexual experience—maybe it helps to build security in yourself, like help build your ego, or it makes you feel stronger in your relationship with the one person. Is it okay to not let the other one know about it? Because I've tried full honesty and I've always been crushed very badly, and I've gotten violent, and it doesn't get me anywhere. So then we decided not to tell each other about it at all. We figured what you don't know doesn't hurt you. Do you think this is abnormal, considering our age, or do you think that's a good arrangement?''

"Look, first of all, you told me you are nineteen?''

"Right.''

"You sound very mature. If those are the ground rules in the relationship that you have, if this is your contract, then I don't see anything wrong with it. It seems to me maybe, I'm not sure, but maybe what you really would like is a commitment.''

"That's right. That's very astute.''

"Aha. Then I would say that maybe the time has come for being a little bit honest about that. Even honest with yourself, because if that's really what you would like, then be a little bit careful of what you are doing with yourself, in terms of maybe using the flirtatiousness and the other sexual relationships just to get this fellow to make a commitment.''

"Using it vengefully, you mean.''

"Exactly. Exactly. So maybe you do have to have a talk and see where it leads you. Okay?''

"Okay. Thank you.''

"Thank you so much for calling. Let me know.''

"Okay. Bye-bye.''

"You are on the air.''

"Hi, Dr. Ruth. I have a small problem. I went out with this guy for a really long time and we broke up—not anything serious—but right now he has a new girl friend, and I sort of want to get back with him. We went out when we were younger, and now there's more of a chance for a relationship. I don't want to hurt her feelings because she's really nice. What should I do?''

"Well, you have to take a risk. You have to take the risk of letting him know that you are interested in him. And you have to say to yourself, 'Of course, if she also loves him she's going to be a little bit sad,' but that risk you have to take by being very open—not with her, because that's really not her decision—by being very open with him and saying, 'Look, I really care for you. I really like you a lot. I do know you have another girl friend.' And just be very open and say, 'Is there a chance for the two of us to get back together?' Because if you don't let him know, how will he know that you are even still interested? Do you understand? Don't discuss it with the other girl, because that doesn't seem to me productive. Because if the other girl is very interested in him also, all she's going to tell you is keep your fingers off. You know, 'Keep your hands off him—he's mine!' But I would let him know. Now, is there a way of letting him know?''

"We go to the same college.''

"All right. Have a cup of coffee somewhere and have a talk with him. And do say, 'Look, there are two possibilities. I am very interested. I would like to be with you.' But leave the door open by also saying, 'If that's not possible, let's be friends.' All right? So that you don't close the door.''

"Thank you very much.''

"Bye-bye.''

Here is a letter I read over the air:

"Dear Dr. Westheimer: My husband and I have been married three years; six months ago we had a baby girl. We love her very much. The only thing is that before I found out I was pregnant we had a great sex life. While I was pregnant the thought of sex turned my stomach. If we made love three times it was a lot. After the baby was born, we have sex maybe once a week. I'm always willing and able but my husband isn't. One time I caught him masturbating, which hurt me so deeply, and he said he'd been doing it for a few months. I could see him doing it if I rejected him, but I don't. For him to be masturbating, I feel as though I have failed him somehow. I haven't ever masturbated, but I would figure someone to do it because they don't have enough sex. I just don't understand. I hope you can help me. Thank you.''

And she signs her name.

"Let me tell you, Karen, this is a question that I'm being asked very often about sex life being different after a baby has been born.

What I would suggest is that maybe the two of you do see a counselor, because maybe there is something, since you are willing to have sex and since your husband obviously is turned on, because by masturbating—and there's nothing wrong with masturbating—by masturbating there is no question that he is sexually aroused. There must be something that maybe he also doesn't really know about, that is bothering the two of you, and I would say that the two of you should go and see somebody before it becomes a real serious problem. Sometimes what you also could do is just have a talk with him, saying, 'Look, is there something that I could do differently in order for the two of us to have good sex? Because'—tell him—'I don't masturbate.' And don't make a big to-do over him masturbating, but do tell him that you would like to see somebody instead of just starting to have problems like that. Maybe he is worried that your vagina, that it hurts you after the baby. That happens. Maybe he has the feeling that you are too tired. That happens. Maybe he thinks that you may be, despite the contraception . . . maybe he has some kind of a worry about you becoming pregnant again. It might be that by talking with an experienced counselor for a session or two, the two of you can really talk very openly and put it on the table. And don't let it slide.''

"You are on the air."

"Hello, Dr. Ruth. I've been seeing my boyfriend for two years. I do care for him very much. I always express myself to him, 'I love you,' I buy him gifts. He buys me gifts, too—expensive things—and takes me places, but I've never heard these words—'I love you.' I do want to hear these words from him. He never says 'I love you.' ''

"Mmm. There are some men who don't express their feelings—who don't say 'I love you'—who don't really *know* how to express their feelings, partly because we have never trained boys and men to be able to express, you know, to say these things or to deal with emotional implications and emotional aspects. But there are also some men who hold back and don't want to say 'I love you,' because they have a feeling if they say that, that would mean that they have to make a commitment, that that would mean that they have to get married. So, I really think that after two years, you should sit down with him and have a talk, either to discuss what is your future going to be or to say to him, 'How come you never tell me I love you? How come you never express that you really like me very much?' "

"The thing is that he does show me that he cares for me, but I never just heard it. That's what really hurts."

"I'm going to tell you something else. Sometimes knowing that he really loves you really takes the place of words. So it's difficult to know where that in-between is. You know what you could do? Does he speak any other languages? Does he speak French?"

"Yeah."

"You know what you could do? You could teach him how to say 'I love you' in French and then maybe in another language— maybe in Spanish. Because, you know why? Maybe in another language, it'll be easier for him to say 'I love you,' rather than to say it in English. Try that."

"Okay. God bless you."

"Bye-bye."

"You are on the air."

"Hello, Dr. Ruth. My boyfriend and I have been going together now for two years. We love each other very, very much and we live together. Our sex life is fairly good except for one problem. Every time we have sex, my boyfriend is very passive in the area of sexual foreplay. In other words, I always have to make the first move."

"Did you ever ask him why he wants you to initiate?"

"Well, sometimes he'll tell me it's because I'm always the one that does it. He never gets the chance to. But several times I've waited for him to make the first move and it hasn't worked."

"It hasn't worked. I'll tell you what I would do if I were you. Let's try the following, okay? Not for the rest of your life, but only for right now, try to make it a little bit regimented. Which means, tell him, that for this coming week, you are not going to initiate. Tell him that Dr. Westheimer says you're not going to die if you don't have sex for one week."

"Right."

"But tell him for this week—for this entire week—he is the

207

one who has to make the first move. And then tell him next week, it'll be your week. Do that. Try that. If you do that a couple of weeks in a row, maybe after six or seven weeks he will get into the kind of routine where he will initiate, and then you will initiate, and then he will initiate.''

"That's a really good idea. Thank you very much, Dr. Ruth.''
"Bye-bye.''

"You are on the air.''
"Hello, Dr. Ruth. My wife and I have been married for four years and we've had a great sex life with contraception. Now we've decided that we want to have a child and we've taken away the contraception, and ever since then I haven't been able to enjoy sex at all. It's just like a turn-off.''
"Let me ask you a question. Only your wife wants the child?''
"No, we both want it.''
"You both want it. Then there must be something . . . What was the contraceptive you used before?''
"The condom.''
"The condom. Do you miss the idea of putting the condom on when your penis is erect?''
"I don't think so.''
"You don't think so. Is the feeling inside the vagina different?''
"I don't know. It's just when the idea of sex comes up, I get really nervous, and it starts to shrink and I get very scared.''
"You get scared and your penis shrinks, and you don't have an erection?''
"No.''
"I'll tell you what I would do. There must be some other reason, which of course I can't help you with over the air, because there must be some reason . . . Even maybe just going for a consultation to a therapist.''
"I don't want to go to a therapist.''
"You don't want to go to a therapist. Well, how will you be able to find out? What does your wife think is the problem?''
"She doesn't know. She told me to call you.''
"Why wouldn't you want to go to a therapist?''

"I don't know. My friend went because he had problems, and he said it didn't help."

"You know, sometimes you have to shop around a little bit for a good therapist, because this sounds to me like something too deep for me to just give some advice or education over the air. Do you understand? That is something that might have to do with your entire life-style. Maybe there is some reason that you are worried about a child."

"No, I'm really not, because to tell you the truth I'm at a point where I feel it's ruining me."

"You'll have to see a therapist. Go to a mental health center or write me a letter, and I'll suggest some people, or some clinics. But you have to go and see somebody. There's no sense and no reason for the two of you to suffer. Okay?"

"All right. Thank you."

"You are on the air."

"Hello, Dr. Ruth."

"How are you?"

"I'm fine. Listen, you once helped me with a problem and it's no longer a problem. I have something else now I'd like to discuss with you. I'm living with my fiancé and his brother. He happens to be a Peeping Tom."

"Who? The fiancé or the brother?"

"His brother."

"Yes."

"And it never really got out of hand before, in fact, he had stopped, and then he started doing it again. Then one night I went into the kitchen. A telescope was there. I know it's funny—I used to laugh about it. It's just that we have to think about our reputation."

"Of course, you really have to be concerned about your reputation. You're quite right. Does the brother know that you know?"

"Well, we're living together. In fact, I'm getting married in three weeks."

"And he's going to stay living there?"

"Yes. He'll live there, and then we're going to get our own apartment."

"Fine. I would pull him aside—without your future husband

knowing. I would tell your future brother-in-law, 'Look, I understand what you are doing. I know you're doing it, but you have to cut it out!' "

"I've tried this and it really hasn't helped. But you know, the funny thing about it is that he is going for help. But I don't think the help he's going for is really helping him. In fact, my boyfriend, my fiancé, was seeing that therapist too, and he felt that he is not as caring as one should be. I think he's more out for the money."

"Okay. Let me tell you something. I can't talk about any therapist. I hope that my colleagues . . . that nobody is out after the money, but I would like to tell you something. I do believe that we have to advocate for people to shop around, and maybe this particular therapist, for whatever reason, is not the right therapist for this particular young man. There is nothing wrong with you saying this to the young man. 'Look, why don't you try and talk to somebody else?' Okay?"

"I understand. Thank you."

"You are on the air."

"Hello, Dr. Ruth. I'm nineteen years old. My fiancé and I have been together for a whole year. I've been living with him for seven months. He's terribly jealous, and I'm not living with him right now."

"He's terribly jealous because you looked at other guys?"

"I can't even look nowhere and he's jealous. I just get up to go to the bathroom and he's up to see where I'm going."

"Oh, my God."

"Really!"

"I think you have to find out . . . Do you have a specific question for me?"

"Well, I ran away. I'm with my father now, and my fiancé is putting pressure on me to decide if I'm coming back or not."

"How would you like to go back to somebody who doesn't leave you any freedom?"

"I have no freedom. He doesn't have faith. He's not sure of himself."

"Well, that doesn't sound to me a good relationship—somebody who is not sure of himself. This doesn't seem to me to be the right relationship. Maybe you have to stay living with your father for a while and see what develops.''

"Well, I'm having a baby.''

"You're having a baby by this man?''

"That's what makes it a tough decision.''

"Look, the best thing for you to do is to call a social work agency, and do discuss it with somebody. Don't just go back. Do discuss it with a therapist or with a mental health worker. Where do you live?''

"I live in Queens.''

"There is a good mental health center.''

"I'm not the one who needs it.''

"I understand that. But you have to go and talk to somebody. Then they might call him in. But you go as soon as possible and talk things over.''

"I have another question. He's telling me that the baby cannot be raised without a father. So I have to make a decision for me and the baby.''

"I understand that. But what you have to do, first of all, is to go and talk to some people. Okay? Go tomorrow to a mental health center in Queens. What religion are you?''

"Catholic.''

"Catholic Charities has a counseling center. Or any hospital has a mental health center. And you go and talk to somebody. Is somebody giving you prenatal care?''

"Yes.''

"Is there a social worker there, or is it a private doctor?''

"I think there's a social worker there. I called her once because I was leaving and I had nowhere to go.''

"Okay. Discuss it with her. Okay?''

"Thank you for your help.''

"Good night. Bye-bye.''

"You are on the air.''

"Hello, Dr. Ruth. I'm having an affair with my sister-in-law. I'm twenty-one, and she's forty.''

"And she's the wife of your brother?''

"Yes. We went to bed once, and everything was all right, but she doesn't want to continue it because she really loves my brother. I don't know what to do about it because I really like her.''

"Well, I tell you, you know what the answer's going to be. What's my answer going to be?''

"I don't know.''

"Absolutely stop it! You had an episode. You had an experience. You can continue liking her, but certainly not in a sexual, physical way. She's the wife of your brother. All right?''

"Okay. Thank you.''

"Thanks so much for calling.''

"I really like your show. Have a good week!''

"Thank you, and find yourself a girl friend! And then use contraception. All right?''

That was short and sweet! Imagine—he didn't know what I would say about that!

"You are on the air.''

"Hello, Dr. Ruth. I'm twenty-two years old, and about a year ago I met a guy at work (he's thirty-seven) and I've been seeing him.''

"You are twenty-two?''

"Yes.''

"I've been seeing him for the past year, and we've had a really good relationship.''

"Is he married?''

"Yeah. That's what it is. I just found out this weekend that he is.''

"The whole year he didn't tell you?''

"No.''

"What did he tell you?''

"I didn't find out from him. I found out from another person at work.''

"Hmmm. And the whole year he made believe as if he's not married?''

"Right. And we had a really . . . what I thought was a good relationship, and a good sexual relationship. I really don't know what to do about it.''

"You know what you should do?"

"What?"

"You should drop him, but fast! If you had a relationship with a man, and he would tell you he's unhappily married, or he is separated, or he is going to leave—or whatever—I would say, let's see if you could work it out. A man who for an entire year goes with you, has sex with you, and doesn't tell you that he's married! Thirty-seven years old, and deceived you for an entire year! You drop him right now. Don't even have coffee with him. Okay?"

"Okay—and thank you."

"You are on the air."

"Hi, Dr. Westheimer. I'm twenty-five years old, my boyfriend is twenty-eight. We've been living together for the last year and a half. About four weeks ago I found out that he had been having an affair with somebody he works with. I was angry. I was hurt. I expressed every emotion that I had. It got to a point where I felt we were communicating better than I felt we ever had before. We went on vacation for a week. We saw a friend of his, who happens to be a counselor, and we did discuss it with him briefly."

"Good."

"And we felt we were on the right track or getting back to it. For the past few days though, I've found that, well, the old actions-speak-louder-than-words syndrome. He says he loves me, that everything is fine, that he's not interested in her anymore. But it seems like he's coming home later from work. He went out today, and I seriously doubt that he's where he says he's going to be. I made a phone call to try to reach him, and he wasn't there. I find, though, that I don't know whether to trust him, my feelings, or myself. I'm very ambiguous about that."

"Do you love him?"

"Yes, I do."

"I'll tell you something. If you have these doubts, I would take them seriously. I would not just ignore them. But I also wouldn't spoil my life by being all obsessed by it. What I would do is, I would keep my two eyes and my two ears very open, and if you have any indication that there's another woman, I would certainly pack up and leave, or tell him to get out—whatever is more feasible.

I would keep eyes and ears open but not to the point where you become obsessed that every time he just—''

"That's what I want to avoid.''

"Exactly. I think what I would do is, I would maybe once tell him, 'Look, I really do care for you a lot, and we have been together for this period of time, and I really got over that one infidelity.' But I would say to him, 'Look, if you have any desire of going with somebody else, please be so kind and advise me so that we can end it.' That's what I would say. Not say 'I don't trust you' and 'Where were you today?'—that's a little bit useless. But what I would definitely do, is say to him, and in a very serious way, 'Please advise me if you have any intentions like that, because then I want out of this relationship.' Will you try that?''

"Yes, I will.''

"You are on the air.''

"Hello, Dr. Ruth. I've been seeing this guy for about a year or so. I care for him very much. Several times I've caught him in bed with other ladies. And this is an on-and-off relationship. I know he cares for me. You know how I know?''

"How do you know?''

"Because one day I spent the night with him. This was on April ninth, and a few days later I came over and his diary was open to April ninth, and I saw that he put down that he really loves me. I think that it is a kind of sickness. I mean, everybody he sees—he wants every lady.''

"I think what you will have to tell him is, first of all, don't tell him ever that you looked in his diary. Don't you tell him ever! Because that diary is something private, and it's not written for other people, even if he left it open. All right?''

"Right.''

"I would have a very serious talk with him.''

"You see, the thing is, one time I caught him in bed—he did this recently—and we had a very big dispute. It was terrible. He cursed me and he told me all these disgusting words. I just couldn't stand it and I burst out crying. Now he found out that I care for him, and now he thinks I'm at his mercy.''

"No, no, no, no. I understand, but just because you care for him doesn't give him any right to think that you are just available whenever he wants you, and in the meantime he can go with everybody else. I think you have to make it loud and clear to him. Stand up and say loud and clear, say, 'Look, either you are going to be my boyfriend and then you're going to be mine and mine alone, or, if that's not the case, I really do not want to be involved with you.' Because you're going to get hurt. Also, if he does it in such a way that you actually, like you say, can catch him, I really have some very serious questions about the gentleman. There is something that he is doing to provoke you, and I would watch out for that, because something doesn't seem right to me. What I would do is tell him, 'Hey, honey, it's either me or the others.' Okay?''

"Okay. Thanks very much."

"Thank you so much for calling."

"You are on the air."

"Hello, Dr. Ruth. I'd like to start a relationship with a divorced man that I know from work, but he is not responding at all. We've worked together and we're pretty good friends. What I'd really like to know is how long it's going to take this man to get over his ex-wife before he can begin having sex in another relationship."

"Does he tell you that he likes you a lot?"

"As a friend. He likes hanging out with me, and going out to dinner."

"You know what? If he likes to go out for dinner with you, and if he likes you as a friend, and doesn't make any movement to having a sexual relationship—after all, he's free, he's not married—then maybe you have to do some very serious thinking. Maybe he's not attracted to you, is one possibility. You know, sexually attracted. And then, what I would do is tell him to go on his way. You know that sometimes I suggest for people to learn by heart 'Wash That Man Right Outa My Hair.' "

"Oh, yeah, yeah."

"Go and get that song tomorrow morning and put it on your record player, because if he doesn't make any advances and he knows that you are willing to have a sexual relationship with him, and he is not tied to another woman, send him on his way."

"Okay."

"And you find yourself a man who is sexually attracted to you and to whom you are sexually attracted and who can give you exactly the type of relationship you want and you deserve. Why should you go out for dinner and spend your emotions and your time with somebody that doesn't make you happy because you want something else from him."

"Okay."

"Don't think of it the way you asked me the question 'How long will it take?' It might be never. You know what could be. He is just using you because he doesn't have anybody else right now, and he might be just using you for companionship, and the moment he finds that other woman that he does feel sexually attracted to, he's going to tell you, 'Honey, good-bye, nice meeting you.' "

"Okay."

"Do you need that?"

"No, not at all."

"So what I would do is you have to take a risk. You have to take a talk with him, by saying, look, it's very well that I'm sexually attracted to you, that I would like a relationship . . ."

"I should tell him this, right?"

"Oh, yes. Absolutely. And to say to him, 'I am sexually attracted to you. I want a relationship that is more than just going out for dinner. I want the kind of full relationship that I know I can have and that I deserve.' Okay?"

"Okay—and thank you very much."

"You are on the air."

"Hello, Dr. Ruth. My girl friend recently said during an argument that she had sex with my closest friend. Do you think I should confront him about it, and risk losing a good friendship if it isn't true?"

"Well, what do you think? Do you think it's true?"

"I'm not sure. But it makes me wonder, why did she choose that particular friend . . . because she was angry, that's true."

"Yes, but that sounds to me a very bad revenge. You know, it's one thing to be revengeful, but it's another thing to be so revengeful as to really have sex with your best friend. Let me tell you what I'm thinking. I don't think you should confront him. Because if it is true, that she did have sex, if he says to you, yes, you are losing a very good friend. I would rather question a little bit the relationship between your girl friend and you because, even if it was true . . . Let's suppose that it was true. Why would she want to tell you? Does she want to break the friendship between you and him?''

"I'm not sure. I think it just came out in anger.''

"In anger. Do you think it only happened once?''

"Yes, she told me about one time when she had the opportunity because I was away.''

"All right. I would not confront your friend. I would make believe as if you don't know. Because what can he tell you? All he can tell you is that he's very sorry. And then what? Then you're going to have a very strained friendship. What I would do if I were you, is I would just ignore it, and not pay any attention, because I can't see the productive argument that would result by you confronting him.''

"I was thinking the same thing, but I feel I would always wonder if it's true.''

"Do you love your girl friend?''

"Yes.''

"If you love her, maybe what you ought to do is forgive her, and put it behind you. Because if it's true, or not true, if you confront him and it's not true, then he is going to be terribly upset about your not having confidence in him, that he wouldn't have sex with your girl friend. And if it is yes, true, it's also going to strain the relationship. I think that if you love her, and if you ever talk to her, and if she does . . . Did she promise you that she would never do it again?''

"Yeah.''

"Yes? Then why don't you let it go and see how life treats the two of you, and just take it from there. Yes?''

"Okay. Thank you.''

"Good luck to you! And thanks a lot for calling.''

Lonely hearts and broken hearts are with us in this post–sexual revolution age. Nothing about an age of sexual liberation cures the pain of being a loser when the love cards are dealt out. There are still those on the outside and finding no one, and those with their hearts held out to their chosen ones who pass by vaguely with a "Haven't-I-seen-you-somewhere?" expression.

Dear Dr. Ruth:

My name is Olga and I am seventeen years old. I'm also bisexual but I really prefer women to men. The trouble is I can't find any women like me. Most of the women I try to get involved with don't think the way I do. I'm really hard up. I want to love someone, but I can't find anyone to love. I've been looking but I haven't seen or come close to finding the women of my dreams. But it seems virtually impossible. Should I give up? Should I forget about my dreams? Help me please before I lose confidence in myself. I'm not ugly. I attract men with no problem. It's the women I want. I'll be waiting for your response in the mail. I need you and your help! So write soon.

Love,
Olga

Dear Olga:

I can't give you specific advice about finding a woman lover since that always is a very individual situation. What I can do however is recommend that you seek out other women who think the way you do. You may want to contact the Women's Conference Identity House, 544 Sixth Avenue, New York City 10011. They run workshops for lesbian and bisexual women, and may be able to help. Good luck!

"You are on the air."

"Hello, Dr. Ruth. I have a problem. I've been going out with my boyfriend, Pat, for a year and a half, and he pressured me to go to bed with him. I didn't know what to do and I went to bed with him, and we broke up last week, and that's all I think about—that night. I still like him a lot, but I know we could never get together."

"Let me ask you something. First of all, did you use contraception?"

"Yes."

"Good. Why did you break up?"

"He broke up with me for his reasons."

"Do you know the reasons?"

"Well, he likes someone else."

"How long did you go out with him?"

"A year and a half."

"And how long did you have sexual intercourse?"

"One time."

"Just one time. And right after that one time he found somebody else. That's really very sad. You know what? If I were you, I would be glad to get rid of a guy like that. Absolutely. Any guy who goes with you for a year and a half and then has intercourse with you—and lucky that the two of you did use contraception—and then right away after that finds somebody else to like, I have certain questions about that guy. I think that you are very lucky, and get rid of him and find yourself a good friend. Now, don't tell that friend immediately that you have had sexual intercourse. Okay. It's nobody's business. It happened. It happened one time. Don't make a big issue out of it. All right? And if that fellow left you after one time having a sexual episode with you, he really doesn't deserve you. All right?"

"Yes."

"Will you let me know when you find a new boyfriend?"

"Oh, yes, and thank you."

"You are very welcome. Bye-bye."

"You are on the air."

"Hello, Dr. Ruth. I met a young man last week at a wedding. He's a distant relative of mine through marriage, not blood. We got along very well, we talked a little. I liked him very much and I think he liked me, but I was somewhat aloof, and he therefore didn't ask me for my number, or pursue anything. I can get his number and I am very interested in him. I just wanted to know, do you think it would be foolish of me to call him?"

"No, I think that if you are willing to take the risk that he's going to say 'I am not interested,' then I think it is perfectly all right to call him. But you know what, find an excuse to call. Either say that you happen to have two tickets for— What does he like, a ball game?"

"I really don't know. I didn't get that close to him. I didn't find out."

"You could ask him if he would like to go to a movie with you. Nothing wrong with that. But you have to be *very* clear that if he says, 'No, thank you so much,' that you can't be upset. That you have to say to yourself, 'Okay. I tried.' I'll tell you another idea. Is there anybody who knows him from that wedding party?"

"Oh, yes."

"Could you pick out some person that you trust and tell that person to let him know that you are interested? That might be even a better idea."

"That *is* a better idea."

"And just call that person and say, 'You know, I might have been a little bit uneasy'—don't call it aloof—'but I'm really interested in that guy.' And tell that person to make a phone call, and to tell him that you are interested. All right?"

"Okay. I'll do that."

"Good luck to you. Bye-bye."

"Thank you."

They used to say "faint heart never won fair lady." That was something you could say to a fellow to encourage him to risk looking foolish and to get him to take the first step. In fact, many a fair lady found a shy fellow utterly charming and went after him. Many a man found himself at the altar because a fair lady decided to take *him* in hand.

Still, people who are stymied, getting nowhere with the opposite sex, or with their chosen sex, are in danger of getting stuck that way. Without being overaggressive or obnoxious, you can get out of that predicament by deciding that you will take the risk of being turned down. What will that do to you, make you feel a little foolish or hurt for a while? At least you can say to yourself, "Well, damn it, at least I tried!"

I often hear people say that they would like to start a relationship with someone but are afraid to take the first step, afraid they will be rejected.

Taking risks does involve taking the chance of being rejected. If you never pick up the phone to ask someone out, you may remain safe from rejection but you will also remain safe from acceptance. Maybe the other person will say no, and if they do, you have to be prepared to go on with your life and not be devastated. If they say yes, you may have begun a whole new relationship. But you'll never know if you refuse to take the chance. If you do get rejected, you can't just give up altogether and become a hermit. If things don't work out with one person, put it out of your mind and go on to find someone else. That's Dr. Ruth Westheimer's advice to you.

18
PARENTS AND TEENAGERS

I got an amusing call one night from a father who was a little bit concerned about something that his son was terribly interested in. I liked the father's pleasant and sensible attitude.

"You are on the air."

"Hello, Dr. Ruth. I have a fourteen-year-old son, and we live on the twenty-ninth floor of an apartment building in Manhattan, and we have neighbors, a young married couple, who don't always pull down their blinds. He spends . . . ."

"A great deal of time?"

"He's *watching*. I realize it's an invasion of their privacy. My own feeling is, I don't really see too much wrong with it from his standpoint, except I did want to talk to him about it, and I wanted to get your opinion."

"I'll tell you what I would do. It is very possible that this young couple gets pleasure out of being exhibitionists."

"I don't think that's the case. I think they're just unaware of it."

"It is possible that a fourteen-year-old who watches—there is no way of telling him don't watch, if there is an opportunity like that—that he actually does get sexually aroused and masturbates. But on the other hand, in the society that we live in, if that were my son, I think I would make sure I know who that couple is and very politely, without a big to-do, but very nicely, I would say, 'I would like to ask you to close the shades.' I don't think that there's anything wrong with that.''

"Why do you think there's something wrong with him doing it? Would it harm him in any way?''

"No. I do think you should give him the opportunity to explore sexual activity in a few years with a girl that he loves, without being constantly tempted to watch now. Because I can absolutely visualize that once it happens down there in that apartment, it is very difficult not to watch. Where does he do his homework? Right at that window?''

"Yeah. He could probably do his homework near the window where he could watch.''

"If I were you, I would have a talk. Did he tell you?''

"Yes, he told me. We have a very open relationship.''

"That's good. You know what else you could do? It might be that after a while he might get tired of it.''

"That's what I thought, so I felt I shouldn't make a big deal about it and tell him he shouldn't do it.''

"To tell him he shouldn't do it, I would not do. Because that's very unrealistic. If something like this presents itself, and here's a free show—he really is getting a free show without having to pay for it. But my inclination is to let the couple know. I'll tell you something else. If your son is watching it, then probably the whole front of that house—I can just visualize that—the whole front of that house is probably standing there . . .''

"Taking tapes, or something.''

"Exactly. They're all getting a free show. You sound like such a great, concerned father. Don't tell your son not to watch, because that's unrealistic. And don't stand there and watch it with him. That's not the best thing to do. If you watch, watch from a different window. All right? And that's okay. Have fun! But I would tell that couple that probably they're providing a free show, and if they're really unaware of it, they might be very grateful to you.''

"I appreciate it. I think that's a good idea.''

"Thank you so much for calling.''

"Thank you.''

*   *   *

I think that boy has a very nice father, and I would guess that if any parent and son have a good chance of keeping communications open during the years ahead, it is these two. Though concerned—he wonders if this nightly free show can harm the boy in any way—he backs off about jumping on the boy, respecting his feelings, his privacy, as he reacts to this unexpected treat. The boy isn't really a Peeping Tom, is he?

Suddenly a parent is confronted with something that tells him or her that a baby, a child, is going into adolescence. Is in it already! How did this happen? It's like Tevye and Yenta in *Fiddler on the Roof,* wondering where their little girl has gone, how she has become this young woman who wants to marry. The wife has been working hard all day in the house, the father has been out selling milk from his cart, trying to keep his family fed. . . .

The most confident parent has a right to feel the heart sink a little at the prospect. What will guard this child during the next few years, so much celebrated as The Terrible Teens?

I have a strong belief in ideals. This is the formative period when the mind can take fire from any number of sources, and a strong idealism, moral goals—religious, political, humane—will supply the youngster with something very valuable: his own personal reason for behaving well, following desirable leads, conforming to good standards of behavior. To get the youngster at this age into a church or synagogue youth group, some kind of volunteer work, a summer camp affiliated with some sturdy belief, is most valuable. It is mind-forming, and it is outside the home, so it is both protective and adventurous.

The kind of group has to be the parents' choice, and it will, of course, reflect their outlook, and some will say that to do this is brainwashing an innocent child, forcing him into your religious, philosophical mold. It is—but someone else will influence your youngster if you don't. You cannot leave his mind a moral blank until he emerges from youth into adulthood, so that he may then opt for being something or other. By that time something will have taken the boy or girl over. Or worse, nothing will have done so, and you will have donated to the world another moral nonentity. Now, this is a basic idea of mine, and I have expressed it, and we can go on.

Suddenly it happens to nearly everyone, with the best intentions, we find we are suddenly supposed to be in charge of a teenager, an adolescent, half-child, half-adult. Sometimes impressing us with great maturity, sometimes relapsing into infantile behavior. We are not, frankly, ready to handle this.

This is the almost inevitable result of deciding, a few short years ago, to have a baby. Or of finding you are going to have one, without having really decided to do that!

"What do we do now?" a friend asked me recently. "What should we stock up on? Give us a list of books to leave around, words of wisdom, strategies, methods of coercion, condoms, tampons . . ."

Before cluttering the house with all that equipment, let me suggest more basic things that you really can use. Good sense—the best you can summon up—a sense of humor, patience, tolerance, and respect.

You have suddenly realized that this is a half-adult you must deal with, and those are all good things to use in dealing with grown people, or partially grown people.

Try to make it easy for yourself. Not that you can be lazy or neglectful, not that you can get away without being alert and ready to act in your youngster's interest, but you will function better if you face the immediate future in a mood of relaxed confidence. If you can't quite do that, fake it. It will help you and the youngster if you show a good presence.

And for goodness' sake, don't expect that the worst has got to happen! Having an adolescent son or daughter, or more than one, can definitely be pleasant and even a joy a good deal of the time. Take my word, I have done it myself. Avoid self-fulfilling prophecies about how bad it all is bound to be.

I hope that by the time you realize that your child is on the verge of adolescence, you have supplied some very important information. Before certain startling (if they are unexpected) events take place in your youngster's life, he or she should be prepared.

The age for this education is not precisely to be set, but because of what happened to one young person I met in my private practice, I suggest that age nine is not too early. I say this because at this age the girl had her first menstruation away at summer camp, and she was quite unprepared.

It is not unusual for this to happen earlier than you think it should, especially nowadays. All the vitamins, all the healthy exercise, something different in the physical makeup of today's children, makes this happen quite often. Breasts bud and fill out, and voices get deeper, earlier, and they become "women" and "men" at an earlier age.

This young lady noticed a spot of blood on her panties and panicked. She didn't know what was happening and she was ashamed to ask. So she hid the panties under her mattress. Later she hid another pair, and another. This cache was found fairly soon because a tentmate began to say, "Something *smells* in here." Very fortunately, the counselor who found the hidden clothes was a sensible young woman who quieted the tent down firmly and had a comforting talk with the child and got the pants laundered without fuss. But the child's anxiety was unnecessary; she could have been warned. Or, rather, prepared.

How to give this information comfortingly? I have thought it would be nice if little girls could expect a party when this event takes place, a little family celebration, with a cake!

There are many horror tales about first menstruations. One girl, back in Victorian days, was alone in her home when she had her first period. Her mother was away on a trip, and she thought that for some reason she was bleeding to death. She had heard of stopping blood with cold water, so she got into a hip bath with ice from the icehouse in it. *She* was sixteen at the time. Her mother had meant to be around when this happened.

Girls should be told about bodily changes they can expect, and boys should be informed about random erections, involuntary ejaculations, and wet dreams. There are good books on these subjects, and at least one should be in the house where there is a child so the information can be given in a nonalarming, reassuring way.

In homes all over the world parents now are undertaking to tell children "the facts of life" with varying success, still with a good deal of embarrassment on the parents' part, but they are plunging in and doing their duty, which is an improvement. It isn't a painful task in every society, however. Recently I read how a mother in an Egyptian peasant village tells her daughter everything about sex, over a long period of time, every conceivable detail in cozy, gossipy little sessions in their primitive hut. When the girl marries she is a virgin, as is expected, but she knows everything about sex to help her into her married sex life.

Western parents who have the best intentions of doing something warm and wise with their jeans-clad children usually settle for a few pained or strained talks. And when they try to reopen the subject, they often find that the youngster simply won't talk to them about this beyond a stony-faced "Yeah," and then a "Gotta be going." Maybe not that much. The moment has fled for this talk.

If this happens in your family, leave the teenager alone. Don't try to force this conversation. Keep books and articles in the house where anyone can see them, and let the subject come up if it does. Otherwise let the teenager discover the reading matter on his or her own. The material will be read.

During this period it happens in some families that fun is made of the young teenager—a terrible thing! Teasing is out of place, and the family jokers are to be suppressed, because some teasing is very, very bad for the youngster. The girl's new breasts are a very sensitive matter. She may not know how to appear unselfconsciously before others with these worrying advertisements of the changes taking place. She would rather be a child with no breasts or a grown lady with accepted breasts, but this stage is not what she wants. She worries that they may never become the right size or shape, like the ones in the movies or the bra ads; or she is mortified that they are so huge on her young, rather shapeless body. Nothing could be crueler than to draw attention to them with klutzy jokes.

The boy should not be teased about why he is in the bathroom so long. No jokes about how he must think he's a big shot, because he shoots all over his bedsheet.

I don't want to give the idea that no mistakes can be made or the youngster will turn into a neurotic, or that life during this time has to be a ballet of good behavior—never an angry argument, never a door slammed—but let the outbursts be genuine, the mistakes real mistakes. Don't invent tortures for your burgeoning young folk.

Youngsters this age are themselves not always tactful. They

may suddenly ask why Dad doesn't get rid of that disgusting pot belly, or betray the idea they have that Mother's sex life is dead and gone, things like that. This is a good time to show how nicely a well-behaved grown-up can deal with thoughtlessness and rudeness. Take criticism from your teenager calmly, as if meant for your good. That's how you'd like them to take criticism, isn't it? You don't have to accept very bad behavior abjectly, but once in a while at least show that a suggestion for one's own good can be taken as well as given!

Respect the teenager's privacy. Establish it in the family mind as a thing to respect. Knock on doors, especially bedroom doors. It isn't just to let them masturbate serenely, as it should be done, but for all the reasons a person earnestly trying new things needs privacy: reading that book you have left around and he doesn't want to seem interested in; trying out a stern expression in his mirror; pinning up her hair in elaborate ways she isn't ready to display; studying her upper body profile.

This is the privacy, you realize, that you would give any grown person staying in your home. You grant it now to the teenager in many ways. Don't check homework—let the teachers worry about that. Only, be there if a question comes up about homework or anything else. If you don't know the answers always, you show how one reaches for the dictionary or the encyclopedia, or plans to go to the library, or calls up the grown friend who knows about this subject. Then when other questions of a more personal nature come up, the youngster may think of coming to you instead of worrying in silence.

When a youngster is impressed with the way you tackle things like that, your stock goes up. You may be honored to find out that you are the one your child will come to first if he or she gets into one of those teenage difficulties, instead of going to a stranger, or instead of worrying you to death by running away out of desperation. Never open a diary. If a parent ever snoops in a diary, it always falls open to something the parent shouldn't see. And I think it is very good for teenagers to record their thoughts and feelings and personal events in a diary, knowing that no one would ever invade this privacy. The young diary keeper constructs a personal set of remembered emotions, of personal fantasies, to use in life instead of mass-produced ones from TV or movies or magazines. This sense of one's own identity, one's personal feelings and gratifications, is very good for a later emotionally steady life. It helps the person to feel the right to be the way he or she is—not bulldozed by the media or peer pressure. And when that diary is twenty, thirty, forty years old, what a glimpse it will give the author into a personal past!

And here's another important rule: Do not read letters not addressed to you.

With all this perfect behavior on your part, be tolerant of minor infractions by the teenager. Tolerance of shoes left in the middle of the room will make life easier for everyone. They don't have to stay there forever, but don't let anger over things like that get to be a pattern—your patience will be a better thing in the house than military neatness.

Let them take care of their own rooms. It is time for them to have this responsibility. I don't mean to be after them all the time about it—just let them deal with that room, with living in it and keeping things so they know where they are. I know a woman who did this with the most gratifying results—her children became models of neatness and order, and she herself was never very tidy! But beyond any question of producing efficiency in that youngster out of need for it, having total charge of that room builds his or her sense of being in control of his or her affairs, of being grown up. Both you and your youngster must get used to that new maturity, for the good of both of you.

Fostering independence has its poignant moments; you will feel sad and left behind. But it has its good side. A friend of mine took her children on skiing vacations, and stood endless hours on the beginners' slope, watching them, freezing her toes off and wishing she were skiing with her friends. All this loving encouragement ended with their saying to her one day, "You're too slow, Mom," and leaving her behind. Ingratitude! Silly tears formed in her eyes.

But presently she realized that now she was free to ski with her friends, with the nice feeling that she had helped them to gain their proficiency and to go off on their own.

*   *   *

Going off on their own is what you help them toward all the time you are bringing them up, of course. In the early stages of their finding a life outside the home you can't help some fears. You don't want them being with companions who will lead them to harm, so you try to get them into outside groups that are reliable, that will give them the experience of being on their own while reassuring you. This means attendance at church or temple and some committee work; envelope-stuffing, napkin-folding, and the like. What has all this to do with sex? Why is it in a guide to good sex? Here is where your teenager will make contacts with the opposite sex, at dances, and at group activities and excursions. Your youngster may fight being corraled into such a suitable social life. But it's worth the try, and with enough hearty encouragement and pushing from you, it may catch on.

Who has time for all this? No one, of course—but you ought to do it anyway. Don't try to raise your teenager alone, without all the aids that this society provides. The same society that offers so many threats to your youngster's well-being also has these protections and encouragements to go in a safe direction—and of much more interest to your teenager than what you can possibly supply on your own. Church, synagogue, community center, whatever you can find to give the teenager a social life, a chance to begin mixing with the opposite sex in a reasonably protected environment, make use of it. Don't tell me you're not a joiner! For your own good and the good of your teenager, pay your dues and take advantage of the stability-giving institutions in your neighborhood.

Now, if you think this is all too goody-goody, conventional, and bourgeois, I can't deny liking the protective aspects of this kind of community life. But I have my sex therapist's eyes open, too! This is a great way for boys and girls to meet and get used to approaching each other. You don't want your child too shy to speak to someone, to ask someone to the prom or to go for a walk. Mixing in these group activities is the civilized way to encourage courtship—in a safe environment, a *reasonably* safe environment. The kind of organization I am thinking of does not crush high spirits or prevent smiles, hand-holdings, or understandings.

I am not for young teenagers going in for sexual experimentation. For those strong sex urges you find in people at age thirteen, fourteen, and fifteen, I frankly recommend privacy with their fantasies, preferably fantasies formed by knowing real-life girls or boys, though the fantasy built on some screen star is all but inevitable and does no real harm, just creates some image-building that gets in the way of real-life relationships. At this early age, who is ready for the responsibilities of a sexual relationship? Fantasy and masturbation are the safe releases, and they should be the teenager's private affair, like the diary, the letters, the perhaps unkempt bedroom.

But sooner or later your teenager is going to—or at any rate is very *likely* to—begin one of those young relationships that you cannot chaperon completely. At what age should you permit it? I don't think you can prevent it, or should try. What you should do is influence your child to behave sensibly, responsibly, and hope for the best as your teenager moves from the early teens into the late teens. And, providing the best advice you can, and that includes how and where to obtain contraceptives, you should keep your nose out of the teenager's sex life and thank the teenagers to do the same for you.

I know that there are religious groups, ethnic groups, geographical locations, where a much more restrictive life for young adults is possible and very deeply wanted by their elders. Among my clients and my radio callers are many young people who know they are expected to go as virgins to their marriage beds. This is not a fairy tale to them; it is the way they are expected to live. Now, obviously, if I have some of these people as clients, then they are in need of a sex therapist—but I do not think they need one any more than people brought up less restrictively. They have many of the same problems as looser people, some of their own, but I do not want anyone to think I am dictating a "liberated" or "permissive" young sex life. In many ways the children of sexually repressive parents are fortunate, because they know where they stand with their parents, with their society, with their religion. They don't have the terrible burden of deciding how to behave sexually on their own, making up their own rules, or trying to find out what the rules are with no help from anyone.

Inside the permissive parent is also a person tortured with doubt about the way he lets his child go through sexual development without greater protection from the dangers of freedom. The modern parent is theoretically for liberated sexual attitudes, and privately anguished over his or her own offspring. I say this is typical—not universal. There are parents who give their experimenting teenagers support, contraceptives, and a safe privacy in which to conduct their lovemaking. But the parent tormented by indecision and worry while the youngster is feeling his or her uncertain way, plagued with fears and often going into sex unwillingly, out of a mistaken conformity, is the parent I encounter much more often.

I do not say, send out your children to have sex on their own, that is the way to sexual health and happiness. I infinitely prefer the parent who has strong guidelines to offer. But if you only think vaguely that you favor sexual permissiveness, yet dread granting it to your teenager, and rather than giving permission only maintain a worried silence, you are not doing as well as someone who has a clear purpose in mind and lets the teenager know what it is.

If you don't expressly tell the young person very definitely that you are against premarital sex, or sex under eighteen, or twenty-one, you should realize that you are tacitly giving permission, in this age, for premarital sex. If you do that, if you let your youngster go out and experiment with sex partners of his or her generation, you are still free to require the teenager to behave sensibly and in a way to protect himself or herself and to relieve you of the more dreadful anxieties. Being a seventeen-year-old lover does not mean having the right to wreck a school career or keep Mom and Dad awake nights worrying.

At what age do you tacitly give permission?

One mother was actually asked by her daughter, "How would you feel if I had sex with Ted?" The mother said she would have doubts, worry about the pros and cons, and accommodate herself to it uncomfortably. "But what did she mean?" asked the mother later. "The next week, or the week before?"

What you have to do is influence your youngster the best you can to behave as you want him or her to behave, and then hope that your influence will have some effect. Many teenagers, late teenagers, are reluctant to take on a relationship that means ultimate responsibility to them, ultimate commitment. But once permitted to date, to have attachments in some degree sexual, you should not pry.

I know a mother who used to lie in her son's bed so that he had to waken her when he came home after a date. Then she would interrogate him closely about where he had been, with whom, and ask if he had kissed her, touched her breast, touched her genitals, and so on. This is outrageous, and it darkens the young person's entire notion of sex as well as humiliating him deeply.

You can insist on a curfew, for safety, rest, and peace of mind. But if you grant the right to go out at night, no such questioning about these very personal matters should follow.

In some families the teenage lover has the privilege, either given in words or by never raising any objection, of having sexual encounters in the house, usually in the teenager's bedroom. This calls for pretending you think they are really listening to records in there, going out for a while, or some such evasion. But while this goes on behind that closed door, try not to build up anger that you take out on the young lover the next day for some unrelated thing—for those shoes in the middle of the room, for instance. Fair's fair—you have granted permission, don't go back on it sneakily, without admitting your mistake in doing so.

I am a great one for suggesting that people make up lists. If you have a teenage lover in the family, you might make a list of just what you want and what you don't want. You don't want neglected schoolwork, drinking, drug using, having sex without contraceptives, staying out after curfew without a phone call, etc. You do want a reasonably polite and responsible member of the family, a happy youngster, and a courteous boyfriend or girl friend when you chance to meet him or her. And so on. Even if you never show this list to the teenager, it will clarify for you what you want, and make it easier to insist on it.

"I accept his right to have a love life, but I can't stand the girl." That is a common feeling, often based on apparent reason. They don't always go out with just the kind of lover you would prefer. Class, ethnic, and religious differences, or just differences in attitude, are often quoted. But you can't control a liberated modern child that way. Your youngster is not required to fulfill your dreams. He or she must have the right to choose and to live his or her own life.

A terrible price to pay for bearing down on a youngster about a strong attachment that you disapprove of is for the youngster to run away. You have to respect the emotion of love, even if, in your judgment, it is merely infatuation.

"You are on the air."

"Hello, Dr. Ruth. I have this problem. It's not really my problem, but my sister's. My sister's nineteen years old. She's going out with a guy, twenty-seven."

"He's twenty-seven?"

"Yeah. Well, the problem is, all my sister's life my father's been treating her like she's twelve years old and everything. She's nineteen years old, and when she goes on dates, he expects her to be home at twelve o'clock. Yesterday, she didn't, and he was really mad about it and everything. What do you think she should do?"

"Okay. First of all, you are a nice brother for asking for your sister. I really like that. If she lives at home, there's just no choice. She will have to abide by those rules. Even though she's an adult. She lives at home, so there's no sense in making life more difficult, but one thing I would like to say is, she could once sit down . . . Is there a mother at home also?"

"Yes, she's home."

"What I think you might want to do—you, as the brother—to sit down with your mother and your father, and say, look, sister is now nineteen, she's not a little girl. Hopefully, she has taken the messages the parents have given her, in terms of how to behave, and maybe what they could realize is that on Saturday nights, when she doesn't have to get up the next day on Sunday, to make the curfew a little later. That is what I would do, if I were you."

"Well, that's what everybody's been trying to tell them. I just don't tell my father—I'm just a kid, he's not going to listen to me."

"No, not you. But your mother should talk. You should talk to your mother, and your mother should talk to the father and say, look, instead of making people unhappy right now, why don't we try and tell her that she can stay out longer but that she has to call us so we know that she's safe. You know, there's something about living in a big city, and I talk now like a mother. You know, I have raised two children. Sometimes parents are really sitting home rather nervously when the kids are out. That's not bad intentions. That's not wanting to control. There's a little bit of reality in that, because we live in a big city. So, what she should do is tell your sister that she can stay out longer but that around twelve she should call, and should say what time she's going to come home. Then the parents can go to bed and don't have to worry. Okay?''

"All right. Thank you very much.''

"Thanks a lot for calling for your sister. That's really great! Bye-bye.''

"Thanks.''

Now, there is a case of a family trying to control someone who is simply too old for that kind of treatment. It is an example of how not to deal with a teenager who is only technically a teenager. Nineteen, every sensible person knows, is really twenty or twenty-one at the least, very likely more like twenty-five. I really liked that boy for calling up for his sister like that! Furthermore, I felt that he might very well be trying to set a precedent that might be of benefit to himself. More freedom for Sis might mean that he could strike for more freedom for himself.

There are definitely situations you cannot handle by yourself. No matter how you want to handle family problems in the family, some things will be beyond you. Drug abuse and alcoholism cannot be handled by Mom or Dad. You may try, but in the end the youngster will need outside help. Get it sooner rather than later.

And situations within the family that are harmful to the youngsters call for outside aid.

"You are on the air.''

"Hello, Dr. Ruth. My name is Audrey. I have three teenage daughters—that's a problem to begin with. The real problem though is my oldest daughter. She became pregnant when she was sixteen. She had a miscarriage. She's eighteen now. Ever since then she had a fascination. . . . She wants to have a baby. She's not married. She broke up with a boy—he went into the Army—he left her. I'm going out with someone, I'm divorced, and she's seeing this boy who works with the guy that I'm seeing.''

"The boy works with your boyfriend?''

"Yes. She has this fascination for him, and that's all that's on her mind. . . . She just started going out with him, and all she talks about is having a baby. I don't know what to say to her.''

"Of course. I'll tell you something. What I hear in that is more serious than what I could deal with over the phone, or over the radio. What I would suggest to you is that you talk to her and tell her that you really are very concerned—that you love her a lot, that what already happened to her is past, but that you feel that she ought to see a therapist. Is she at a college? Is she enrolled someplace?''

"No, she's not in college. She was going to high school, then she was going to business school, then she dropped out of business school. She's not interested in working and she's also very lazy.''

"Is she working?''

"She's not working. She stays around the house and does nothing. She just thinks about this boy all the time. She thinks about marriage and babies. She doesn't want to work.''

"Who supports her? You?''

"I'm supporting her.''

"Well, that's another reason. I would say that you absolutely should get in touch with a family service agency, either of your religion or . . . You said you live in Brooklyn?''

"Yes, I do.''

"Absolutely do get in touch with some kind of health agency. What you could do is tomorrow call up the . . . What religion are you?''

"I'm Jewish.''

"Call up the Jewish Family Service and say that you have an urgent problem, that it does concern your daughter, and that you would like the name of a social worker or a therapist in Brooklyn as part of the Jewish Family Service. Don't let that slide.''

"Okay. Also, one more thing. I have a fourteen- and a sixteen-year-old daughter, and I'm afraid that my older daughter could be a bad influence, because all they talk about is sex all the time.''

"Of course. And especially in your particular case, where she does know that you do have a man friend, which is marvelous for you. This is a serious concern. I would definitely insist that she see somebody. You can insist, especially since she's not working. I would talk to the younger ones, the fourteen- and the sixteen-year-old.''

''That's what I'm worried about mainly, because they hear talk from her and they see she's promiscuous.''

''I would definitely talk with them. I would tell them that 'Look, whatever your sister is doing, I'm trying to help her.' Tell them that you're trying to get her into some counseling situation, but do tell them that you don't think that sex talk alone is enough to be an interesting person.

''How are the younger ones in school? Are they all right?''

''They're fine, though they think more about sex than they think about their schoolwork. It's rubbing off on them. They have me worried.''

''Of course. I think you definitely should get in touch with the Jewish Family Service. All right?''

''Thank you very much.''

''You're very welcome. Good luck to you.''

''Thank you.''

A situation like that is beyond anything that the mother can do to make it better, and the sooner she gets outside help the better.

I do not want to end on a dark picture of life with teenagers, especially when there are teenagers who bring home nice boyfriends or girl friends. Youth, let us remember, is supposed to be a pretty time, but it is never a pretty time if you scowl at it or fix it with a perpetually suspicious stare!

I don't mean that you should foolishly give in and learn to love the dangers our society presents to the teenager. But the experience of these maturing years is natural, unavoidable, and a better experience all around if you can approach it with a good spirit.

I know two women who are friends in the suburbs across the George Washington Bridge in New Jersey. ''Just wait,'' said the slightly older of the two friends. ''Just wait until that darling daughter of yours starts going with boys.''

"What's wrong with boys?" asked the younger one. "I like boys."

"You just *wait*," said the experienced one, the voice of doom. "You'll come to regard boys as bad news—destroyers, impregnators, and carriers of disease."

"Oh, come, now," said the lady who liked boys.

When her daughter became a teenager, she watched her go out with a series of boys. She liked them all. They were cheerful, manly young fellows who would do little repairs around the house or on appliances. For nothing. Well, not for *nothing*—they would raid her refrigerator pretty regularly. But she didn't mind that.

Maybe the younger woman was just lucky. Between her good attitude and the pleasant, unthreatening character of the boys her daughter went out with, she may have drawn good cards. But I feel sure that her attitude improved her luck.

Nothing bad happened to the daughters of either of these ladies. Both girls are grown up and they are joys to their mothers. But the older lady still thinks of the teen years as a terrible ordeal, and the younger one thinks they are a lovely time with the house full of nice boys.

Neither mother is sure how much sexual contact there was between the two girls and their boyfriends. That was a long time ago, and since everything has turned out so nicely, it seems silly to worry about it now, doesn't it? Whose business is it, anyway?

Certainly, with the proper attitude, The Terrible, Troubling Teens may, quite surprisingly, be neither.

19
TEENAGE CONCERNS

Dear Dr. Ruth:

I am seventeen years old and have been seeing a young man, who is now nineteen, for a little over a year.

We have a fabulous relationship in which we enjoy and respect one another and honestly I could not think of seeing anyone else right now.

We engage in foreplay; however, we have never had sex. Both of us are virgins.

We constantly discuss sex, but we really are not sure whether we are ready to take this step. However, if we were to, birth control would be the number one priority on our list.

My question for you is, how will we know when "the time is right"? Passion is one thing, but getting carried away isn't necessarily being sexually mature and ready.

Do you have any remarks, ideas, or suggestions concerning maturity, sexuality, or even birth control? It would be greatly appreciated because right now both of us are quite confused.

Thank you very much!

Missy

Dear Missy:

I love hearing from people like you! Your letter was just wonderful—thoughtful, intelligent, and caring! And you ask a very important question. How does one know when it is the right time to start having sex?

I wish there was an easy answer to that question, but there isn't. You and your boyfriend have taken all the right steps— you talk openly, you love each other, and you can distinguish between passion and love. All I can advise is that if you are asking yourselves these questions about sex, it might be wise to wait a little longer. Keep having foreplay and love each other as much as you can that way; you'll be getting to know your own bodies as well as each other's.

Maybe you should give yourselves some time to think about it individually—in other words—put off making a decision. Enjoy each other without worrying about a decision and then see how you feel. Giving yourselves a rest from the decision might help clarify your feelings and relieve you from any pressure you may feel.

I recommend a book for you to read called Our Bodies, Ourselves. *I think you'll find it quite useful.*

Good luck!

                                                        Dr. Ruth

KNOWING THE RIGHT TIME

When is the right time to start having sex, to have it for the first time? I am asked that question again and again, mostly by girls but not always. I must admit I think of it as a girl's question, probably because it sounds almost exactly the same when girls ask it.

This question is rooted in reality. It isn't a silly question. It means that a lot of heartfelt wishes for the first time have not been met. In her heart, though she wouldn't care to admit it, the girl would like to be married, although that would be a terribly definite commitment. She would like some reassurance that if the contraceptive didn't work, this fellow could be counted on to regard it as his problem, as well as hers, and see her through the birth or the abortion. She would like it if her boyfriend were older and had some real money of his own, in case he had to be responsible for her. She would like to look at him and feel that he would stand up better in comparison to any of a dozen movie actors, as far as looks and style and self-confidence go. But most of all she would like to be sure, very, very sure, that she knows what real love feels like so she could know if she is in love with this guy.

I always tell them, "Don't do it until you are sure you want to do it." That always seems to be just what they want to hear.

It's a concern of teenage girls that they feel they *ought* to start having sex any minute now but don't want to for an indefinite period, although they are "pretty old"—anywhere from sixteen to twenty, usually.

I am pleased that girls would like to be in love before they yield their virginity, because I sympathize with the feeling.

I just want any girl who feels that way to know that she is not a freak. Lots of other girls feel the same way!

Other teenage concerns, and I want every teenager to note these because one of yours may appear here, and that ought to make you feel proud:

"Am I normal?"

"Will I be a big mass-media-type lover?"

"How can I stop ejaculating while dancing with a girl or petting?"

"Where can I find a safe, private place to be with her?"

"Gosh, wouldn't it be heaven to be alone in a private place with him?"

"Is this really my body? Don't I get one like the movie and TV people's bodies?"

"Is this being in love, or what?"

"Am I really a stud or am I daydreaming?"

"Will anybody get the idea I'm really a stud?"

"If I let him, to show him I love him, will he tell everybody in school?"

"Will she let me, just a little, so I can tell everybody in school?"

"Are my feelings normal?"

"How come I get a hard-on during a *math quiz,* and the teacher is a *guy*? Am I *queer*?"

241

"How come I sit around daydreaming in class and really get wet down there?"

"Will I find that movie star I have in mind?"

"Am I too tall?"

And, of course, "Is my penis big enough?"

The question "Am I too tall?" is a girl's question that they ask themselves in the ninth grade, when they tend to be too tall for the ninth-grade boys. Also a question of some girls who are five-ten or six feet, really very tall. Because boys and men aren't supposed to feel confident with tall women.

I would like to make it a teenage right to learn the truth about all these questions. That's part of the purpose of my radio show, to give the truth and to give reassurance to young people, who listen to the show in great numbers. There should be a teenager's Bill of Rights giving them the right to readily accessible information and free discussion of all these questions about sex and sexuality, adequacy and normality. There is very little reference material. Just trying to find out if one's penis is an acceptable size is nearly impossible. That ought to be an easy thing to find out.

TEENAGE RIGHTS

What rights does a teenager actually have?

I don't mean rights defined by law, like the right to drive a car, vote, drink in a bar, do with his or her body what he or she wants, to be protected against physical abuse or sexual abuse by his or her elders. These are clearly defined, at least, though unfortunately the laws against abuse seem to be hard to enforce. But a teenager can find out what the law is and at least be sure what the legal rights are. If a teenager is deprived of rights guaranteed by law, he or she can go to a police station or a legal aid society or a social service agency and get assistance.

The rights affecting most teenagers most are those granted by his family. He or she is dependent on the family, living in his or her parents' home and negotiating for rights one by one. What rights can he or she reasonably ask for, feel justified in negotiating for with the grown-ups, who can withhold money, privileges, and approval?

Except for some very venturesome teenagers, most of them

want to be sure of support together with parental kindness and approval. Even if they behave very defiantly, seem to hate their parents, and sometimes go so far as to run away, they would prefer a protective home life with ways of gaining approval and at the same time having a chance to explore the world of their own age group, in which they would like to have warmth, affection, approval, and some degree of sexual gratification from people their own age.

I think the following are rights a teenager can reasonably negotiate for, supposing that they are not granted automatically by his or her parents. There is general agreement in our society about these rights and they seem fair to me.

The right to have a degree of privacy and respect in the home.

The right to have a life of one's own outside the home, to develop the ability to be a person in the world where the teenager will be on his or her own very soon.

The right to have friends of one's own choosing, with only reasonable control of this choice by the parents. For instance, the parents retain the right to keep the teenager from associating with criminals or with others who may exploit or get him or her to harm him- or herself.

The right to have clear guidelines about what he or she can do. The right to use these for his or her own protection, by pleading that the folks will scream and go wild if the curfew isn't kept, if the homework isn't done to the teacher's satisfaction, if school grades fall below a decent level.

The right to have relationships with the opposite sex of his or her age. This right is adjustable, according to the beliefs of the parents, who are supposed to be protecting the teenager and acting in his or her best interests, but the teenager has the right to ask the parents to be clear and consistent.

The right to negotiate for greater personal freedom, such as going farther from home, staying out later, using the car, having more allowance or the right to earn money for the teenager's own social life. For instance, if given the right to stay out later, the teenager can offer to stay within certain limits of behavior or lose the privilege. If given the right to go away for extended periods, the teenager can offer to phone home and say where he or she is and what the plans are.

The right to get privileges back through good behavior if the privileges have been taken away.

The point of all this is that while the teenager is home, he or she should consider the peace of mind of the parents who support him or her, and who are responsible for him or her to society.

The teenager has a right to good treatment from his or her parents according to the norms of the community the family lives in.

The teenager has a right to be allowed to conform to the ways of his or her peer group, at least as far as these are not harmful. To ask a young person to dress or behave in a way that will make him or her look weird, or to refuse harmless privileges that most young people in that community are granted, puts the young person at an unfair disadvantage.

The teenager has the right to expect increasing personal privacy and freedom as he or she grows older. This means that he or she is to be allowed to make moral decisions for him- or herself after a certain age, being more responsible for these actions to society than to the parents, without being questioned as to how he or she has used this privacy or freedom.

With regard to sexual behavior, this means that the teenager has, at, say, the age of seventeen, the right to have or not have sex, using personal judgment. This right is granted out of sheer common sense. That is, if denied, most people that old will seize this right for themselves—which doesn't mean that seventeen-year-olds will *all* have sex, whether given this privacy and freedom or not, but that the decision either way will be personal rather than in obedience to the parents.

Undue abuse of this particular freedom isn't necessarily to be tolerated by the parents, but it is no longer a question of authority. If an older teenager behaves flagrantly rather than discreetly, gets into ridiculous trouble through sex—involved in a pregnancy, or several pregnancies, or in police trouble, or the like—the parents can call it quits and let this aging teenager make his or her own way in the world.

Every teenager knows his or her own family and how likely it is that they will accede to this set of principles. In actual fact, many families will accede to them in practice while rejecting them in principle, and many will give in on some and not on others. But these rights give you a fair idea of the customs of the present time, and an idea of how you can negotiate.

I would not think of just leaving those rights standing there without pointing out that your family, teenager, with all its drawbacks, is probably not a foreign power to be dealt with out of policy alone. They are human until proven otherwise, probably love you, and can use any love or understanding you have for them!

Be prepared to forgive some injustices, teenager, and accept your parents' love, however strangely it comes out of them, in place of perfect fairness!

And keep this in mind—almost any way you have of hurting your parents will be more harmful to you. That is common sense.

I have here a collection of letters written to me by teenage listeners, all about teenage concerns, which I think you will find very touching and interesting.

Dear Dr. Ruth:

I am 17 years old and I am in love with one of my teachers. He is 29. We have been seeing each other for the past two years and there are a few problems. He is married, has children, and the kids in school suspect something because we have been caught making out in school. We don't use contraception because he can't function with it, but right now it is all right because I have never had a period yet. He says he is getting a divorce but he has been saying that for a year and now I don't know if I should believe him anymore. He's always saying he loves me and I am definitely in love with him but I don't know what to do. It hurts so bad always hiding and lying. I don't want to break it up but I feel like I'm being used.

Joy

Dear Joy:

First you should know that you can get pregnant before you ever have a period. Because you can be fertile before that. That is a medical fact. You are risking pregnancy every time you have sex without contraception. You should phone Planned Parenthood in New York City and make an appointment and you should do it today.

245

What I am going to tell you now will hurt but it is the only thing to do. You must tell this man you can't see him anymore, that you want to go out with boys your age and stop lying to your parents. After you stop seeing him it will hurt and you will cry but it will not be for long. You will become interested in boys and this will be behind you.

I don't know you or your lover, but I do know that married men who cheat on their wives with younger women almost never divorce. And when they do they don't marry the one they cheated with.

You are being used. Don't put up with it.

Dr. Ruth

Dear Doctor:

Hi! How are you? Hope you're fine.

I'm a girl of fifteen years. I have a problem. When I was younger, about seven or eight years old, I had sex with other girls. I'm on a guilt trip. I want to know if it was wrong. I don't think I'm gay. I love boys. It's just my past popping in from time to time. Please reply.

Lisa

Dear Lisa:

What you did when you were seven or eight years old you should not feel guilty about. You did nothing wrong. Many people have experiences like that when they are young and they grow up to be normal, happy adults. So, just say to yourself that you were young and it's in the past.

Look toward the future!

Good luck!

Dr. Ruth

Dear Dr. Ruth:

I am eighteen and still a virgin. I do not have a boyfriend. I have never been in a situation that me or a boy wanted to have sex. My question is that in September I am going away to college and I do know that most eighteen- to twenty-two-year-old men have had sex, and I am scared that I won't know how. I am also scared that the first time it is going to hurt, and also I heard that the woman usually bleeds. I am afraid of sleeping with anybody because of it. I have had boyfriends but if I do not love him I won't sleep with him. I won't sleep with just anyone.

I have one more question, and please do not laugh. What is an orgasm? *Are you laughing?*

Elyse

Dear Elyse:

Thank you for listening to Sexually Speaking. *I am glad to have the opportunity to answer your letter.*

You have expressed fears that are quite understandable and normal concerning a first sexual experience. I do have a few suggestions for you. First, you should never do something you have strong feelings about not doing. It is wonderful that you feel you need to be in love with someone before you have sex with him.

You say you are scared that sexual intercourse might hurt the first time and you might bleed. For some women this is true, but for others, it's a very wonderful experience. You should make sure you are lubricated enough and he enters you slowly.

You also asked about orgasms. For this question, I recommend you go out today and buy the book For Yourself *by Lonnie Barbach. This is a great book for women who have never had an orgasm and it is a good preparation for women who have never had sexual relations.*

Good luck at college. I'm sure you'll do well.

Sincerely,
Dr. Ruth

Dear Dr. Ruth:

I am a fourteen year old. I belong to a youth group where there is a girl the same age, and I would like to ask her out but I don't know how to do so. I've never seen her before. But some of my friends that I know from school hang around with her. I think she likes me, but I would like to know how to go about meeting her.

Sincerely yours,
Sean

Dear Sean:

Thank you very much for listening to Sexually Speaking.

You might ask one of your friends who knows her for her phone number. If that's not good, while at the club you might walk up to her and introduce yourself. After all, that's one thing youth clubs are for—meeting people! Good luck!

Dr. Ruth

Dear Dr. Ruth:

I come from a strong upbringing where sex before marriage is out of the question. My boyfriend, who is my first, is sixteen and so am I. I see my boyfriend about once every two weeks for one year now and each time we see each other the same thing happens. We kiss and I rub him to orgasm. When he is satisfied, it's all over with, no talk about it. That is the extent of our sex life. (Usually this happens in a park, because there is no other place to go. It is nighttime also.)

I have many problems. First, I don't get anything out of it. I don't like the way he kisses, and I get sick and tired of the same routine. But on the other hand I don't want him to rub me to orgasm because I think I don't want him to touch me down there, but I don't mind him fondling my breasts. It is unpleasant for me to rub him and I just want it to be over as soon as possible.

When I'm alone I can reach orgasm by masturbating, and I have many fantasies about him. I wish I could relax when I'm with him because I'm very stiff. I know he would never pressure me into anything, but I always worry about going too far. I never talked to him about this. I know we would feel very awkward if we did. Before each time I see him I say to myself that I'm going to be very relaxed and enjoy it, but it never works. I just get tense. Otherwise, our relationship is good, but it might be better if I didn't have these problems. Also, I dream about giving him the best kiss in the world, but when the time comes I just leave my mouth opened and let him do it all. Please, Dr. Ruth, help me! I don't know how to help myself.

Sincerely,
Kathy

Dear Kathy:
Thank you for listening to Sexually Speaking.

You seem to be very hesitant about sexual activity and about going too far. It's good that your boyfriend would never pressure you because you don't seem to want to have sex yet. This is good and normal—it's always better to wait until you are ready.

It is also important that you do not pressure yourself, too. If you do not feel comfortable about rubbing your boyfriend to orgasm each time you see him, don't do it. Tell him gently that you care for him and look forward to a good sex life in the future, but for now you cannot continue doing as you have been doing! He may have to do what you do—go home, fantasize, and masturbate to orgasm.

Maybe when this is settled, you will be able to relax and enjoy kissing him. Tell him gently, as if it were a game—how you would like him to kiss you. He, like you, has a lot of time to learn. And kissing is an art all by itself!

Thanks again and good luck!

Sincerely,
Dr. Ruth

Dear Dr. Ruth:
How are you? I'm pretty confused. I've got a problem and I'll try to explain it to you. I am absolutely crazy about this guy, Terry. Oh, by the way, I'm sixteen and I am a virgin. Anyway, I was at my friend's party about three weeks ago and she had about forty people there. Terry was there and I was really excited because I really liked him! I don't know who told him, but somebody did tell him I liked him. As the party thinned out Terry and I kind of slipped away to the bedroom. I really

249

thought that he liked me because he was hanging all over me during the party. I figured since he knew I liked him, then he would like me. I figured wrong! When we were in the bedroom, he asked me to give him oral sex. I totally refused because I've never done it before and if I can help it I never will. He acted kind of cold towards me the rest of the time we were in the bedroom, and he really made me feel like a piece of trash, like I was used. When we came out of the bedroom he stayed for five minutes, then went home. He left on good terms but the next day he acted like he didn't know me. That made me feel very bad and I was extremely hurt by him. My problem is: How do I get him to like me?

The thing is though that all my friends think I'm crazy because it got out that Terry and I went "all the way," but we didn't. When people saw us come out of the bedroom together they must of gotten the wrong impression. The other thing is Terry doesn't say "no, we didn't do it." He just says "let your imagination think for itself," which bugs the hell out of me. I still like him very much but he treats me like shit, and I still like him, no matter what! Is that love? Help please!

Maggie

P.S. I love your show and I know you love to hear that!

Dear Maggie:

I have just one thing to say concerning what you should do about Terry. You must forget about him. You sound like an intelligent and sweet girl and there is no reason why anyone should treat you the way he treats you.

You must say to yourself that you deserve to be loved by someone who is considerate, kind, and someone who cares about your feelings. Terry, obviously, only cares about spreading rumors. It may hurt for a while to forget him, but afterward you will be ready to be with someone who deserves to go out with you.

As far as these rumors are concerned, the only thing you can do is ignore them, and ignore Terry also. If you do, people will stop asking about it and things will return to normal. Just re-member, you did nothing to be ashamed of!

Good luck!

Dr. Ruth

Dear Dr. Westheimer:

I'm sixteen and so is my boyfriend, and we've been going out for almost six months. We love each other very much and he would like to have sex (no pressure on me) and I would too, but I've been brought up in a home where the idea "no pre-marital sex" has been pounded into my head, and so far I haven't had any sex. I am ready, and feel that it would be the right thing to do, but somehow I know I would feel guilty, not to myself but to my family. I don't want that to hold me back. Also even though we would use contraceptives *I would be so worried about getting pregnant. I do want to have sex because I love my boyfriend very much but how do I get rid of these obsessions I have?*

One more question: Do guys have control over their ejacu-lating?

Tanya

Dear Tanya:

Thank you for listening to Sexually Speaking.

Even though you say you are ready to have sex (responsibly, with contraceptives), and even though I believe sex is a beauti-ful and natural part of life, you might be wise to wait awhile. You need more time to sort out your feelings about sex from the values taught by your parents. Being sixteen, and probably still living at home with your parents, that is difficult to do. Your guilt feelings, worries about becoming pregnant—your obsessions—will probably diminish as you grow older and es-tablish your independence.

The answer to your other question is that men can control or delay their ejaculation up to a point, but this ability is limited. Certainly, this cannot be relied upon as a contraceptive.

Sincerely,

Dr. Ruth

Dear Dr. Ruth:

I am sixteen and I've been seeing a nineteen-year-old guy, Joe, who I love (so I believe). Unfortunately, my parents found out that he parties occasionally. He also hangs around with two to three guys, one of who my parents think is constantly drunk, though he may not be. They are all in college and I am a junior in high school. If my parents find out that I'm going out with them, they always say, "You have to be in by eleven," or "I don't like you going out with them." We don't always have to drink to have fun, and all of us realize when we've had enough. We even make sure one person stays sober to drive! My parents have never done anything about what I do and are always asking if I've been smoking. I don't smoke but some of my friends do. I don't know how to convince my parents that Joe is not as bad as they think.

Another problem is that Joe is very shy and "slow." Is there anything I can do to make him less shy and take a lead in sex without him feeling less masculine? We've never gotten past a series of romantic kisses but we are very close friends (lovers?) and get along well. I'm afraid that if I start leading, he may feel as if I am too anxious or trying to rush him. Is there anything you can recommend?

Jean

Dear Jean:

Convincing your parents that Joe is not as bad as they think may not be easy. First you must ask yourself if your parents might not have a good point, can your being with Joe hurt you? If not, stick with him and maybe bring him home so that your parents can see some of the qualities in him you admire. If that fails, let your parents know, gently but firmly, that your friends are yours to choose and that they cannot control your social life now anymore than they will when you become an adult.

About Joe's slowness: Sometimes caution is a good sign in men. He obviously is not seeing you to use you for sex, he likes you as a person. He also himself may not be ready for sex with you; be careful not to push him because he may need more time to feel closer to and comfortable with you. You might sug-

*gest to him sometime that you do want to make love, and see
how he reacts. Sometimes talking about it breaks the ice. A
good follow-up might be to visit Planned Parenthood together
so that the two of you can investigate contraceptives and start
your sexual lives together responsibly and on the right foot!*
   Good luck!

Dr. Ruth

And here's a phone call to finish up with:

"You are on the air."

"Hello, Dr. Westheimer. I'll get to the question and make it
very brief. I'm nineteen years old. My name is Judy. What I'd like
to point out is that this is not a sexual question. I've lived with my
mother for the nineteen years of my life. She always treats me like
. . . She puts a gate around me all the time. She's very protective
and demands all sorts of things. If someone has to go to the store,
she'll send my brother, or if I want to go shopping, she'll say, 'You
can't go alone!' I love my mother. I don't want to say anything to
her."

"Is your mother from the old country? Is your mother European?"

"Yes. My mother is Rumanian. She is very old-fashioned, because her mother was like that with her, too."

"All right."

"I have turned out to be a respectable girl and everything, but
it's just terrible. Everything she wants me to do, I do it for her, but I
don't want to say nothing. So what should I do? I can't afford to
move out now."

"Are you going to school right now?"

"Yes, I am."

"Are you going to college—a college away from home?"

"No, in New York."

"In New York. I would tell you. Is there anybody in your family who could have a talk with her, because it would be a pity to
make the relationship strained. Is there any aunt? Is there anybody?
Does your mother have a best friend?"

"Yes, she does."

"Could you have a talk, but in a nice way . . . First try to have a talk with your mother."

"Okay. I also have a second question. It'll be brief also. It's just that secretly I have loved somebody for a year and we don't get along—we don't talk or anything—the most 'hello,' or 'good-bye'—that's as far as our conversation goes. He's very shy. He's younger than me. I don't seem to mind—age doesn't matter. I love him for a long time and I just can't get myself out of this. What's the best thing for me to do?"

"Is he interested in you at all?"

"I really don't think so."

"If he's not interested in you at all, then I do have a little remedy that you could try. If he is not interested in you at all—if you know that—go and get yourself a record, from *South Pacific*. There is a song in there that is called 'I'm Gonna Wash That Man Right Outa My Hair.' And I'm telling you, Judy, it works. It really does work. Because, if you know that he's not interested—you sound like such a terrific, serious young woman—it's a pity to just be unhappy about somebody that you feel is not interested in you.

"With your mother, sit down and have a little talk. But do tell her that you do understand that this is the way that she grew up— with a chaperon, you know, not ever going out alone—but it is a different world right now, that she has to trust you, that she has to know that you are responsible, and that you know what you are going to do and what you are not going to do, and that it kind of bothers you that every time there is somebody going with you. The other thing I would do, if I were you . . . Do you belong to any church group, or synagogue?"

"No, I don't really. I just attend church on Sundays at the most."

"You know what I would do, if I were you? I would start to find a church group that has young people that go out on outings without chaperons. You know, these young people go out with a priest or somebody but not with parents, so that your mother gets the idea that it's okay for you to be out, and still to be somewhat protected. You see, being a mother myself, and having a daughter who is twenty-five, when she was nineteen—I do understand your mother a little bit, because we live in a crazy city. So, it's not out of bad intentions that she's so overprotective. On the other hand, you have to make a little bit of a stand by saying, 'Mother, I am very responsible.' Can you tell it to her in Rumanian?''

"Yes, I can.''

"That's what I would do. I would tell it in her language, and would say that I'm nineteen now and that I have to go out, and tell her where you are going. Also, when you are going to be late from an outing, make sure that you call her. And this way you're going to train her that you call her and tell her 'Mother, I'm going to be late,' and that she will slowly get the idea that you are nineteen and have to stand on your own. Okay?''

"Okay. God bless you.''

"Thanks so much for calling.''

20
THINK BEFORE GOING TO BED

Thinking before having sex is not just saying no, putting the brakes on. Not at all. There are those people who honestly believe that the brain, where erotic thoughts arise to make the genitals engorge and lubricate, is really a depressing organ and the enemy of lust, passion, and pleasure. The fact is that sex as we human beings experience it is impossible without the brain. And thinking before having sex does not always lead to no sex. Here's a good example of constructive thinking making the sex better!

A man going home at night thinks of having sex, and he thinks that's the best idea he has had all day! Every night he passes The Pleasant Hour, a tavern. That is to say, some nights he passes it and some nights he stops in to have a drink. But this night he *thinks* he won't go into the tavern. He *thinks* it will be better if he goes on to the liquor store and buys a nice bottle of wine instead. If he goes into the tavern, he may start talking to somebody, and one drink will lead to another and the ''pleasant hour'' will turn into the ninety minutes, and he will be a little late home, and the chops will be overdone and his wife will be cool. Whereas if he comes in right on time with the wine, she may decide that he is really a nice man after all, and the wine may put her in even better humor. It isn't that he has to get her cockeyed to have sex with her, but a little wine taken together will make them feel very nice together. This, his thinking tells him, may well be what will happen.

That is thinking before having sex, about three or four hours before, and it is good thinking and may indeed lead to very good sex!

Along about eleven he may be having wonderful sex with his lady instead of being turned down and having, in addition to being turned down, a little hangover.

I wanted to start this chapter with a positive idea of thinking before sex.

Thinking before going to bed includes lots of things like being sure to have contraception and knowing the lady well enough, so you're almost sure she doesn't have herpes—you knew Dr. Ruth would mention the contraception, and I wouldn't disappoint you. And it does mean that sometimes, having thought, you will decide to pass up the sex because *on this occasion* it isn't a good idea.

BAD SEX DRIVES OUT GOOD

My whole supposition is that you who are reading this book seriously mean to have sex sometime, and pretty often if you have your way about it. But a good guide to good sex must have in it some calm, friendly talk about avoiding bad sex. People who know a lot about money have a saying that bad money drives out good money. I believe this, although I don't know much about money. It sounds good. And I do know a lot about sex, and I do know that bad sex drives out good sex. The wise sexpot goes for quality in sex. I didn't say "quality, not quantity." Quality *and* quantity. I don't believe there is much once-a-year or once-a-month sex that is really very good!

But I run into lots of people who are having a lot of sex that is not good—having it more and enjoying it less.

A typical case: the man who was married a dozen years or more, and then he thinks he'll make up for lost time and get in on the singles' bar scene. Sure enough, it's really there, and now, even with the money he sends his ex-wife, he can spend more on pursuing strange women than he could the last time he was single. And anyway, these ladies have their own money and don't care. And he's saying "Your place or mine" every night about the same time he used to be saying "Well, I guess I'll turn in," out in New Jersey.

He used to think that if he had a lot of time on his own he'd do something like learn to play chess well or read all of Harold Robbins's books, but, in fact, he is either out in a bar or in his bed or hers almost every night.

A wonderful life! A fantasy come true! So, why is he in the sex therapist's office? Because he needs help in keeping up the pace?

No, he's bored. He can't relate to these women. He's turned into a sex machine, feeling as much interest in all this sex as a machine.

I tell him to take it easy, and not feel that every time a woman is willing that he must have sex with her just because she's there, like Mount Everest. Slow down, I tell him. Not get to be a hermit, but just wait awhile until he meets a woman who seems to mean something to him. And then think before he goes to bed with her, let the thing between them grow. Because there is no point in rushing into more dull sex, is there?

There was a great deal of doing it more, enjoying it less, since the sexual revolution that started in the sixties, and now there are many swingers, male and female, who have decided to think before going to bed. Because a life of unlimited sexual opportunities with strangers was turning into the sexual blahs.

I don't take great credit for this idea of thinking before going to bed, because it isn't a new idea from me; any good sex therapist, not to mention a good many other sensible people, has had it. But it's news to some people. The man in my office who is worried, not because he can't have or hold an erection but because supposedly good sex with all the trimmings and mutual orgasms has become boring. The idea that if something is boring, *then you don't have to do it*—he's never thought of that.

Armed with this thought, he can now ask himself, Do I want to do this? It's what they call a breakthrough for him.

SAYING NO TO YOUR BEST GIRL FRIEND

Many a guy has dreamed of a girl friend who wants it all the time. Perhaps he has prayed for it. You must be careful what you pray for—you may get it.

"You are on the air."

"Hi, Dr. Ruth. I have a very unique problem. Approximately five months ago I met this lovely girl, and almost immediately we hit it off very, very well. Our sexual activity is to the point where we make love three or four times a day, and this has been going on, and I no longer can keep up with it."

"But, wait a moment. Let me ask you a question. Don't the two of you either have to go to school or earn a living?"

"Yes, we both work, and we see each other from about six o'clock."

"I see. What I would do is just make sure that you find some other activity, with friends around, so that the pressure is not on you for continuous sexual relationship. But let's suppose that your girl friend loves you a lot, and let's suppose that she is sexually very aroused, you can give her an orgasm without your having to have an erection. That doesn't make you any less of a man. People's appetites are different. People don't have a sexual appetite, everybody the exact same way. So, what you could very well do, and you can discuss this with her—you can tell her that I told you so. You can actually bring her to orgasm and hug and kiss her, and you don't have to have an erection."

"When we do that, it just seems like she wants more and more and more."

"Maybe then there is a problem."

"And I'm tired. And now she's accusing me of seeing somebody else, and I've no time to see anybody else."

"How come she doesn't trust you?"

"I guess she does. We talked about it a little bit. My job is on the road sometimes during the day, and it's very difficult for me to find time to even eat lunch, let alone look at anybody."

"You know what. I think the two of you have to do a little bit more of talking, because you really can't walk around and have your job on the road and constantly worrying that she's going to think that you are constantly making love."

"The problem is that I've been getting really tired because I'm on the road all the time."

"Yeah. So you have to tell her, you have to tell her very openly. You have to tell her, 'Next time we're going to make love is

going to be Friday night, and Saturday night, and Sunday night.'
And in between if she does get sexually aroused, give her an or-
gasm. If that doesn't work, then there might be some other things
going on between the two of you that have nothing to do with sex.
You know, it may be the relationship needs some talking out.
Okay?''

"Thank you very much."

"Thank you for calling. Bye-bye."

The sexual appetites of partners do not always coincide. There
are times when one partner is in the mood for sex while the other
one is not. It is not a good idea to enter into sex feeling, To keep her
happy I better make a big production out of it this time even though
I'm really not in the mood. It is much better to talk to your partner
and to say something like, ''This is one of those times that you're
going to get pleasured. This time you can just lie back, let me do the
work, and enjoy.''

There is nothing wrong with giving your partner an orgasm,
even if you yourself are not in the mood. But it *is* important for the
two partners to talk about it together. One partner can say to the
other, ''I'm not interested just now—but I'll pleasure you.'' The
consideration and concern for the other's needs can establish a
strong bond between two people.

Consideration is much better than resentment at being used, or
feeling like a sex object, which is the common reaction of the partner with the smaller sexual appetite.

This kind of thinking before going to bed can save a lot of wear
and tear on the tired or preoccupied partner and on the whole relationship.

TURNING DOWN A CHANCE TO BE MISERABLE

Sometimes you meet somebody you really go for, and this person is
interested in sex with you but doesn't seem to understand how you
feel. This attractive and willing person isn't thinking the way you
do.

"You are on the air."

"Hello, Dr. Ruth. . . . I met a nice girl about two months ago, and we have seen each other for quite a few times—maybe ten or fifteen times. And it looks like she's sexually interested in me, but I haven't touched her yet. And I know she's seeing somebody else.''

"Oh, dear! She's seeing somebody else? Is she in love with somebody else?''

"No. Well, she was in love with a guy. They went out for a long while, and about five months ago she broke up with him. And she met this guy. And a month after that she met me.''

"But why is she still going out with the other one?''

"I'm not sure. I don't know. I asked her, 'Is this guy really important in your life?' This way I would know where I am standing and I would not get emotional and use my feelings as much.''

"Exactly. What does she say?''

"She said when she broke up with her old boyfriend, who she went out with for a long while, she was kind of depressed and this guy helped her come out of that depression.''

"So out of gratitude she has to be with him? You don't have sex with her, you know why? You will get hurt. You will get hurt. Do not have sex. Because you are going to give your whole soul and body, and you are going to be in love, and you are going to be *very* unhappy if she still goes and sees the other guy.''

"I'm not sure if she's having sex with him.''

"It doesn't matter. As long as she doesn't decide . . . You sound like you are really such a sincere fellow.''

"I am. That's one of my problems.''

"As long as she doesn't decide that it's *you* who ought to be the man in her life, just by her being sexually interested in you. . . .''

"I'm sure about that.''

"Yes, but even so. Even the sheer fact that she wants to have sex with you, and there's nothing wrong with that, especially not if you use contraception, right? But what would be wrong is if she is really not sure that you are the one, and if you then, because you are so sensitive, fall in love with her, and, if you are then not the only one. You do not want to share her, right?''

"Right, that's true.''

"And just because the other fellow has helped her to overcome some difficult times in her life, which is very nice and I appreciate that, and I understand that she appreciates it, that should not make you do something until you are sure that you are *it*. Do you understand what I mean?''

''Yes.''

''Once you are sure that you are the man in her life now, *then* she can become *the* woman in your life. Do you understand?''

''Yes, I understand. I want to add something. I saw a picture of this guy she met one month before me in her wallet and it kind of upset me. I tried not to show it, but she noticed, and I think I gave her the impression that I'm a little pushy.''

''Look, pushy or not pushy, there is nothing wrong with your saying, 'Hey, you, I like you, I want to have a relationship with you, but if I want to have a relationship with you, it has to be me alone.' Does she carry you in her wallet, too?''

''Pardon me?''

''Does she have a picture of you in her wallet, too?''

''I didn't offer it, and she didn't ask.''

''Aha! Then I would say, sit still for a while. Do go out with her, and do show her that you are interested. But do not engage in sexual activity. It would be too bad if you were just used. Do you understand? If you were just used for sex, because you really seem very, very attracted to her and very much in love. Then just enjoy the feeling of being in love, but don't do anything. Sit still. All right?''

''Okay. I have another question.''

''Go ahead.''

''One of my basic problems is I'm a very sexual person, and at the same time a very emotional person.''

''Why is that a problem? That's fantastic!''

''I don't think there is anything wrong with it, but sometimes I have a hard time dealing with this problem with different people.''

''I understand that, but I'll tell you something. The one girl who's going to be yours is going to be very lucky, because she will have the two attributes in one person—she will have the guy who is sexy, and sexually very tuned-in and attractive, and she also will have a very sensitive person. So don't you worry about that. All right?''

WHEN YOU WANT TO SAY "NO"

The pressure to be sexually active is very strong in our society, and that pressure is felt not only by young people but by all single men and women, whatever their age. Many women feel that everyone is casually having sex with everyone else and that if they *don't* have sex with a man they go out with, he won't call them again. The pressure to have sex has become so commonplace that many women say they go to bed with men they don't particularly care for and may not even know very well. And many a man feels that if he doesn't make an attempt to have sex with a woman, even if he is not in the mood, the woman may think there is something wrong with him— he is "undersexed," timid, unmanly, perhaps homosexual.

Using your head before going to bed means not having sex when you don't really want to. And when you *do* have sex, knowing that it is really what you want to do at that particular time.

WHEN YOU NEVER SAY "NO"—BUT YOU WONDER

"You are on the air."

"Hi, Dr. Ruth. I'm seventeen years old. I've been dating a guy for almost a year. We have sex a lot—like every time we're together. He tells me he loves me. Whenever I see him we always wind up in bed. Then, all of a sudden, he doesn't want to be with me or he doesn't want to have nothing to do with me. I feel like I'm not satisfying him."

"Ummm. Look. I'll tell you something. If all he wants from you is sex, and if every single time you see each other all he wants is to go to bed, I would question a little bit if that's the guy that you want to be friends with. You mean to say he doesn't discuss the weather with you, or politics, or literature, or school? All he wants is sex?"

"No, we talk. I mean, it just doesn't happen right away."

"Does he take you out to the movies?"

"No."

"No?"

"No, he sees his friends at night."

"I *really* have a serious question there. You mean he doesn't take you out and he doesn't take you for dinner?"

"He's not working."

263

"He's not working, so he doesn't have any money?"

"Right."

"And all he does with you is only having sex?"

"Right."

"What does he do all day?"

"He's with me."

"Are you in school?"

"No."

"Ummm. I would think that you do need some help at a mental health center or a therapist. Don't let it slide. Okay?"

"Okay."

"Thanks a lot for calling."

"Thank you."

You know, I never try to practice sex therapy over the radio. I give some advice, some suggestions, some information, and all the people listening are soaking it up. It's a sex education hour, not sex therapy. When someone calls in and I see it's a case, something for a social worker or a therapist, I say that is where the caller should take the problem.

This girl is not thinking before going to bed, but she is wondering. He says he loves her, he hangs around and has sex with her during the empty part of the day, and then he's off with his pals. No job, no money to take her out, and who knows if he'd take her out if he had the money. Maybe she's a girl friend for when he doesn't have a job or money.

In her wondering she is coming near to having a thought, but thoughts don't come too well to her. Sex urges come to her very well!

She knows he's using her, but if she gives him up, what will she have left? That's what you call needing help—more than you can get over the telephone in less than five minutes. You're in trouble when you're hooked on sex with somebody and can't think your way out of it.

BEING FREE TO CHOOSE

This is not a good society for getting into sex very young, before you have your schooling, before you know who you are and have confidence in your own ability to think and steer your own course in life. When you are like that in this society, you are a child, but a child they allow to have sex. No one pays you, no one praises you, you have no self-confidence. A person like that does not choose freely to go into a relationship on an equal basis. She trades sex for the little attention he gives her. I don't blame this over-age child, but I think it's terrible that young people like her go to bed before they can think for themselves.

BRIGHT, MAYBE, BUT NOT THINKING

It isn't only pathetic kids who do bad thinking about sex, of course. People who make good salaries and use their heads all day in business turn their thinking off when it comes to sex. A good deal of this is what is called cultural, by which I don't mean concerts and art museums but the popular culture of the present. Sex has been painted as something wonderful that will keep you happy as a six-year-old with a new balloon as long as you don't get into anything heavy.

A young woman works all day, supports herself, and lives her own life, using her brain in the office and then unplugging it when she unplugs her electric typewriter or calculator. She knows all about Mr. Goodbar, then she picks up a stranger in a bar and takes him home with her. In the daytime she would be afraid to be alone with a stranger in the elevator, but at night she sleeps with one.

One young woman took a man home and had sex with him in her bed for hours, then toward morning asked him to leave. He was furious. Why couldn't he sleep there a couple of hours? She got scared by his rage, and asked, "You aren't going to get violent?" He looked at her, realized what she was thinking, and laughed. He put on his clothes and left. She was lucky.

A swinging bachelor took a young woman to his apartment. Besides making love they talked about one thing or another. She let him tell her all about his collection of scrimshaw—expensive carved whale ivory doodads made by crewmen on the old whaling ships. When he woke in the morning, she was gone, and so was the scrimshaw collection, worth a small fortune.

These people were bright, but they weren't thinking before going to bed.

Perhaps some young woman will read this book and get the unusual idea, from this chapter, of not going to bed with a guy named Fred because she met him in Ulric's Pudding and he said he was into unstructured sharing!

UPBEAT THINKING

I want to leave this on a nice upbeat thought, because as I said in the beginning, thinking about sex isn't just a turn-off. Thinking before going to bed includes learning about sex, about relationships, about setting the scene for good sex, about keeping variety in your sex life, sharing fantasies, and storing up in your mind those little touches your partner likes, that only you can know about.

21
AM I
NORMAL?

All kinds of people worry about being normal.

A man of the most upright character dreams at night of having sex with his boss, who is also his uncle. He has never had anything like a homosexual encounter since he was in the third grade. He wakes up in the dark and wonders if he is, unknown to anyone but himself, abnormal?

Let me get this thing about dreams out of the way. Nothing you dream about makes you abnormal. Nothing you think about makes you abnormal. That is part of the incredible, irrepressible inventiveness of the human mind. The best thing is to be secretly amused.

Very common worries are "Is my penis abnormally small?" and "Am I freakish never to have had an orgasm?" It is hard to deal with these worries alone, but that is how people have tried to deal with them for years, while they've gone about asking the question of people in all sorts of indirect ways.

Abnormal is a statistical concept. In a country with no cheesecake, a cheesecake addict is abnormal.

It is normal to wonder "Am I normal?" It's part of our wanting to conform, which can be helpful or harmful. It's normal but very worrisome!

Here is a letter I read over the air:

"Dear Dr. Ruth: I have been seeing my boyfriend for three years. I want him to know how much he pleases me, but I can't during intercourse. I use contraceptives. We have an absolutely superb sex life, filled with both love and fantasy. But when he asks me to tell him what pleases me or wants to hear how good he makes me feel, I can't talk.

"Is something wrong with me? How can I change? Please, please help me. Kaye."

"Number one, I would say to you, don't be so concerned. If your boyfriend . . . after all, you're seeing him for three years, you're using contraceptives—you know that I'm very pleased about that—and I'm sure that your boyfriend does know how you feel and what a good lover he is. I might have one suggestion. If he would like to hear you talk, what I would like to suggest is that once in a while, forget about your being aroused, and when he is very sexually aroused, when he is really at that premonitory sensation, when he's just about to ejaculate, what I would do is you hold back a little bit and talk.

"Once he does ejaculate, and he has his orgasm, then what you can do is then let him pleasure you until orgasm, just so you don't have that pressure of having to talk at the same time that he is making love to you. What I would suggest is just to take turns.

"Please do let me know if this is helpful."

She can't speak at this ecstatic time because she is so caught up—and she wonders if there is something wrong with her! The truth is she should enjoy this intensity.

"You are on the air."

"Hello, Dr. Ruth. My name is Greg and I'm twenty-five. A little earlier a caller talked to you about her boyfriend's size. I was wondering what kind of advice you could give to those of us who are not as fortunate as her boyfriend."

"Look, first of all, let me tell you something very important. Penis size has nothing to do with sexual pleasure of a woman, because the penis expands, and the more important thing is that the vagina accommodates any size of a man's penis. Now there are

268

some men who are particularly richly endowed and there are some other men who are worried about the size of their penises. If they have a good woman-friend and if they can have a good relationship, people should stop worrying about the size. It has absolutely nothing to do with good sexual functioning. Okay? Thanks for calling.''

"Thank you very much."

"You are on the air."

"Hello, Dr. Ruth. I saw you on the David Letterman show the other day. It was great!''

"Ha ha. Thank you. Did you also see the onion rings?''

"Oh, that was funny! I couldn't stop laughing. That was very good.''

"Yes."

"My name is Mike. I'm from Mahopac.''

"No last names, okay, Mike?''

"Okay. I have this problem. Whenever I engage in sexual intercourse with my girl friend, I ejaculate prematurely. What could I do to prolong my ejaculation?''

"Mike, usually somebody who ejaculates very fast, and let me tell you right away that in our society, and we don't know exactly why, there are many, many men who do ejaculate very fast—you know, before they want to ejaculate. Let me give you a suggestion. And if that works, good, and if not, I would like to suggest to you that you see a sex therapist, because it's a very easily treatable sexual dysfunction. When you do have sex and when you do try to prolong, do you try to think of some problems? Do you try to think of some worries? What do you try to think of?''

"I try to prolong my ejaculation.''

"Okay. What you ought to think of is to think very hard about the sensation in the penis and then try to tell your girl friend to stimulate you to erection—not during intercourse, just before, during foreplay—stimulate you to full erection. But before you ejaculate, when you feel that premonitory sensation, when you feel that you are about to, before you feel that, tell her to stop.* You will lose

*A more complete discussion of the premonitory sensation and the treatment of premature ejaculation is to be found in Dr. Helen Singer Kaplan's authoritative text *The New Sex Therapy,* New York: Brunner/Mazel, 1974.

part of the erection. Tell her to do that again and do that like three, four times in a row, and only on the fourth time, do ejaculate. Do you understand what I mean?''

''Yes.''

''Even when you masturbate, you could do that. Masturbate softly. When you feel that you are about to ejaculate, stop. Then bring your penis to an erection again. Stop again. Do it again, and on the fourth time, do ejaculate. What will happen to you, if that works, is that you will recognize that moment before it's too late. Do you know what I mean?''

''Yes.''

''Try that. And if that doesn't work, then try to find a psycho-sexual therapist. If you can't find one in Mahopac, send me a letter, and I'll send you a name.''

''Okay. Dr. Ruth, I have another question. Is it abnormal to masturbate? My friends think I'm weird because I masturbate.''

''Absolutely not.''

''Oh, thank you.''

''There is nothing wrong with masturbating. And you know what? Most people do it. Even married people do it during their life at one time or another, either when the husband or the partner is not available, or when the wife is not available. There is nothing wrong with masturbating.''

''Thank you so much.''

''You are very welcome. Thank you for calling.''

As I said earlier, Arabs call masturbation *the secret*. But Mike doesn't, all his friends know about it. Well, now he can tell them all what Dr. Ruth said about it!

''You're on the air.''

''Hello, Dr. Ruth. I have a question. I was wondering, my girl friend thinks it's weird that I would go out and buy a magazine and masturbate to it.''

''That's not weird at all. Not only do many men do it, but there are women who do get these magazines and who get sexually aroused and masturbate with them. There's nothing wrong with that. Tell her that it does not mean that you don't love her. Sometimes women are very concerned that if a man picks up a magazine like that, it would mean as if he doesn't love her.''

"I'm not in love with these girls in these magazines. My head is in this relationship."

"So tell her: Your head is in the relationship."

"It's just a fantasy."

"I have an idea. Tell her the head is in the relationship, but your penis is getting aroused by the pictures. All right?''

"Right."

"Thanks a lot for calling.''

The mail that comes to me at WYNY contains many letters seeking reassurance about normality.

Dear Dr. Westheimer:

I've been going steady with my boyfriend for six and a half years. I am twenty-one. He is twenty-four. We are both satisfied when we make love. In fact, our lovemaking is so terrific I can't imagine it any better. I have one question which is beginning to bother me. One thing you must know about me is that I am a very natural person. I think nothing of wandering around naked with him (neither does he). This means anywhere, in the bathroom (we often shower and bathe together), kitchen, when we're upstate camping, etc.

About a year ago he started asking me to wear a garter belt with stockings. I couldn't understand that. I am the type of person who feels that the naked body should be enough to turn somebody on. Anyway, I went along with it, and I wore the garter belt with stockings. At first I hated it. Now I don't really mind as long as I can make him happy. (I'm still not crazy about it.) But I'd rather be my natural self without an outfit.

I really want to know if this is normal. Do most couples do this?

Fredda

Dear Fredda:

Don't be too concerned about your boyfriend's request that you wear stockings and garters. After being together for sever-

al years, people sometimes feel the need for something differ-
ent or spicy, and this is normal.

If you do not feel comfortable with stockings and garters,
however, don't use it. If you can only oblige him once in a
while, then you might save it as a special treat. We can only do
what feels right and comfortable, and should never do some-
thing we don't feel right in doing to satisfy our partners.

Dr. Ruth

Dear Dr. Ruth:

Listening to your radio show has prompted me to write. I
have several questions. First of all, I am a seventeen and
three-quarter year old girl. I am still a virgin. However I want
to prepare myself for when the moment is right and I lose my
virginity. I know I need birth control and I don't think a con-
dom is enough. I am curious as to what you would recommend.
Thus far I have only engaged in manipulation of the male geni-
tals, but have never given a blow job. Is this normal? I have
been stimulated by my boyfriend's fingers and have reached
orgasm in this way. I have tried to stimulate him but really
don't know how. I am too embarrassed to ask him. Can you
help me? Also, does a girl have to follow the lead of a guy
when they are kissing? I think it is sexist to always follow the
guy. Is this right? Thank you.

Pauline

Dear Pauline:

You have asked me very good questions! I hope I can answer
all of them.

I think it's great that you want to prepare for having sexual
intercourse by choosing a birth control method. I suggest that
you do two things. First, buy or borrow the book Our Bodies,
Ourselves. *It explains about the different forms of birth con-*
trol. Then, call Planned Parenthood and make an appointment
to see a birth control counselor. This person will help you
choose the right method for you.

It is perfectly "normal" that you have never given a blow
job. If you would like to try, you can start just kissing the base

of the penis and just do what you feel comfortable doing. You mentioned that you feel funny talking to your boyfriend about stimulating him. Maybe you can bring it up when you're not making love. Tell him that you really want to please him, but you need him to show you how, the next time you make love. Also, there should be no "leader" and "follower" in making love. It should be a mutual event so that sometimes one person takes the lead and sometimes the other. And most important, only do what you feel comfortable doing.

Dr. Ruth

Dear Dr. Ruth:

I'm writing to ask you if it is abnormal to sort of be afraid of sex? I have had many opportunities to have sexual intercourse with many young ladies but I back off because I think that they might not be satisfied with me. I also am aggressive when I drink alcohol but then my partners don't want to. What should I do?

I was told by some of my friends that if you ejaculate before sexual intercourse you would have a longer time before you ejaculate during sex. Also, I was wondering how would I know if my partner had an orgasm or not during sex?

Thank you very much.

Bob

Dear Bob:

You write that you are afraid of having sex. I think this is quite normal. You should have a lot of thought and reflection before you have sex with someone. You said that you are afraid you won't be able to satisfy your partner. Perhaps if you first develop a strong relationship and did a lot of kissing and hugging, then that fear wouldn't be there. Then you would know that she loves you and you love her and you will feel free to pleasure each other (with contraceptives).

You also asked if ejaculating before having intercourse prolongs ejaculating during intercourse. This may happen to some men because it takes them longer to get excited. There is no rule.

Your last question was how can you tell if your partner has an orgasm. The only way to really tell is to ask her and then be aware of the way her body changes when she orgasms. In other words, be sensitive to the messages she's giving you.

Dr. Ruth

Dear Dr. Ruth:

I've gone out with many guys and I've finally found Mr. Right. We've gone out about eight times (but I see a lot of him). Around our fifth date, we started having sex. On our sixth date, I had oral sex with him. (This is the first time I've ever done this.) When I told him I didn't like the idea, he gave me some advice similar to the advice you give to other women who have trouble "going down" on a man. You know how you tell women to imagine that when they are licking the penis, to imagine they're licking an ice cream cone. Well, I love whip cream. And what Paul did was get a tub of "cold" whip cream and told me to smear it all around his penis. Now when I went down on him, we were both satisfied. He was satisfied with me doing this and I was satisfied with the penis tasting like whip cream.

The funny thing though is that I must have had ten orgasms and he had more than ten.

Is it normal to have so many, considering what we did? He says it's normal, but how does he know?

Carla

Dear Carla:

There is absolutely nothing wrong with either of you having ten orgasms or more as long as you both enjoy it and show no ill effects. Go ahead and enjoy.

Dr. Ruth

Dear Dr. Ruth:

I have two problems that concern my boyfriend and myself. We are both in our mid-twenties.

The first problem is concerning my boyfriend. When he has

an erection his penis is not straight. Instead it curves downward. He never has had a physical injury but does masturbate often. We can have intercourse (with a contraceptive) but only in a limited number of positions because of his curvature, and he does ejaculate. Is this unusual? Please tell me where and who he can go to, to further discuss this problem.

The second problem might have something to do with the first problem. My boyfriend and I have oral sex. I can receive great pleasure and orgasms from oral and finger stimulation. Unfortunately, I cannot do the same for my boyfriend. He can get an erection but can't ejaculate. I know it isn't my misdoings because I have had successful results with other young men I've dated. Could his first problem have some connection with this? Please recommend something I can do.

Alice

Dear Alice:

Many men have penises that curve downward or to the side. This is not unusual. If your boyfriend is concerned he should speak with his doctor.

I think your boyfriend's inability to ejaculate when you perform fellatio is also not unusual. Many men have trouble having orgasms like this. You may want to try different techniques on him, but do not worry if he still does not orgasm. I'm sure it is pleasurable to him anyway. You may want to buy The Joy of Sex *to get some ideas.*

Dr. Ruth

Dear Dr. Ruth:

Is it abnormal for a girl's hymen not to pop or bust when she has intercourse for the first time? I also was wondering, do all girls have a discharge of blood, after they have sexual intercourse for the first time? When I did, there was no blood, and a lot of my friends said that they did have a discharge of blood. I sure hope it isn't abnormal.

Angie

Dear Angie:

Thank you very much for listening to Sexually Speaking.

A woman whose hymen does not break when she has inter-course for the first time may have already broken it during some other kind of physical activity. This may also explain the absence of bleeding. It is perfectly normal. If you have a doubt about this, it is wise to be examined by a physician.

Dr. Ruth

22
WOULD YOU MARRY YOU?

Dear Dr. Ruth:

My problem is with my marriage. I have too much invested in it to back out now but I feel like a prisoner in my life as I am leading it now. I am married 14 years and we have two children and I couldn't face the trouble a divorce would cause them. But my husband and I hardly have any contact with each other though we live in the same house. We have sex and say things like "I'm going to the mall after lunch" and "The mayor called. He wants you to call him back." That's about it. My husband can talk a blue streak, he talks to his friends, he talks in court (he's a lawyer) but not to me. I am very hurt because when we were first married I worked and helped put him through law school. . . .

The mood of this woman when writing her letter was very depressed, and from hearing stories like this so many times, I know that she was feeling helpless and inadequate. I advised her to get marriage counseling because she needs to see her problem clearly, look for a way to solve it, and she needs support from *someone*, support that, at the moment, she will not get from her husband and "his" friends. You notice she doesn't mention *her* friends.

She is in a predicament that is very common. As his wife she worked to help him through professional school. That is perfectly reasonable. It would also be reasonable for him to put her through similar training, and I can think of several couples where that was done. But when he became a lawyer, suddenly he had friends, and she was excluded. That seems so outrageously unfair to her, but brooding over the injustice will not improve her situation!

When one partner works to put the other through school, hoping to increase that person's earning power and raise his or her status in the world so they both can have a better life, the wage earner, the one making the sacrifice for the other, should look ahead to the time when the professional one moves among professional people and community leaders. Usually the one who paid the other's tuition was the wife. Besides helping her husband to get ahead, she must keep up with him socially and intellectually. This need not be a totally husband-oriented effort: For her own good she must develop interests of her own, for herself—by taking courses, developing skills, learning to mix with people who talk about community affairs, politics, art—with confidence and with opinions of her own. Or, when the husband is established, after the schooling and the first year or two of professional work, she will find herself unable to keep up socially with her husband's associates.

She doesn't have to find out about things that other attorneys' wives talk about, or that other doctors' wives talk about, but she should be a person on her own, self-confident, with interests of her own that other people will respect and take some interest in. Because it is not so much what other people think of her that counts, but the kind of respect she can command through her own good feelings about herself.

If one partner does not keep up with the other, grow with the other, then there will be a gap between them, which is not always fatal to the relationship, but will always cause some unhappiness.

A happy partner in a marriage does not think only that he or she is lucky, has married a wonderful person, has benefited from this marriage. That is not a good position to hold in the give-and-take of marriage. You have to believe that your partner has benefited, and is still benefiting, by being married to you.

The wife who put her husband through school and then found herself isolated socially excites one's sympathy, and at first you can't help thinking that the husband is an ungrateful fellow, not very admirable. But the husband can't help seeing that she is less interesting than the people he associates with.

In the past it has been the parents who had the experience of educating their children above themselves. But where a parent can be glad to see the child more skilled, more knowledgeable, than the parent, the wife or husband can't really take that kind of pleasure in being left behind!

That's why you should ask yourself, "Would I marry me?" Say that you are married now, but only imagining how it would be if you were unmarried. Would you marry a person like you? I don't suggest doing this so that you can be depressed, but so that you can take some kind of action to help yourself. You should never get into a position where you feel that you are less than an individual, an interested, contributing kind of person. The precise way that you use your energy and make your contribution is not so important—it might be painting, it might be selling insurance part-time—as the fact that you like it, that it makes you feel good about yourself, that it makes you feel that anyone married to you is married to a good partner.

MAKING A LIST

A client of mine, a widower, wanted to get married *so badly*! First he was lonely, and he had grown accustomed to being married and having that constant companion. Then he had the children. Managing them and his job was too much for him to handle. But he felt that no woman of the kind *he* would want would want to marry *him*, in his circumstances.

He went out with women, and friends tried to line him up with women. But the same thing always happened—he would talk about his kids! Boring! What woman wants to hear a man talk about his kids when he should be concentrating on her?

Whether the women really were put off by his parental obsession or not, I don't know. That may have been mostly in his mind. But all these women had come to nothing. And he still wanted and needed a wife. And he really thought his case was hopeless.

Even without children, the self-image of a person who is looking for a second or third spouse is often bad. They feel that they are

279

old, a little run-down and seedy; they are afraid to court or to try having sex with a new person.

My client had some of those doubts, as well as thinking that no one would have him with his mind, and his house full of children.

I asked him to make up a list of his own qualities as a potential husband. This is a method I use quite often, making lists. So he went home and made up his list and showed it to me. He had been very clear-eyed and honest in his self-appraisal, as people usually are when asked to make a list like that. People aren't as self-deceived as you might think. The list that I saw showed a picture of a man with many good qualities. We talked about the list, and then I asked, "Would you marry you?"

He had to admit that he would. He was a decent, hardworking guy, and he himself didn't mind a man having children and thinking about them all the time.

"Well," I said, "don't you suppose there are women who feel the same way about a nice fatherly man, and would want to help him with his problems?"

He went away with that thought in his head, and it grew until his idea of himself as a suitor for some woman's hand became very positive. In a short while he found a woman who had children of her own to worry about. He found what he wanted. But he wouldn't have if he hadn't gone out hunting, in good spirits, showing off his best aspects.

FEAR OF COMMITMENT
Poor self-image keeps people from making a commitment sometimes. A woman came to me who had been living with a man for some time, a man who was fifteen years younger than she. She had been willing to drift along in the relationship as long as it lasted, not expecting too much, pretty certain it would end and he would go off and settle down with someone closer to his age, or maybe younger than himself.

Then one day he proposed to her! He wanted to tie the knot, share the serious commitment of marriage with her. She was upset because she *knew* that such a marriage could not work. As soon as they were married she would begin to look older to him. He would be like the man who bought a house. As soon as the property was legally his, he saw cracks starting in the walls.

She told her lover that she would not marry him and why. He laughed. He said that he wasn't really that much younger. If she was a young forty-seven, he was a very old thirty-two going on sixty. He was a quiet man, liked his life with her, liked her children, didn't feel the need of having any children of his own. So if she wouldn't marry him, he would have to stay single all his life.

He kept up his proposals of marriage, and one day she came to me, because the situation was troubling her. I had her make out a couple of lists. One, of her own qualities as a possible wife. The other, of the things she would want in a man that she would consider marrying.

She realized after making the lists and studying them that she was a good catch for the right man—and her suitor was very much like the man she would consider marrying. So they got married.

She had asked herself if *she* would consider marrying a person like herself, and fifteen years older. On thinking it over, she decided it would be a quite acceptable idea.

LIKING YOURSELF

If *you* don't like you, who will? It is hard to like anyone who has a poor opinion of himself or herself. You have to believe you are worthy of another person's love, that in marrying you your lover is doing a smart thing!

Some mutual esteem exists in most marriages at the beginning. But in marriages where two people join under pressure—say from parents—the thing of prime importance is likely to be overlooked. The question of whether they like, respect, and love each other becomes secondary to things like getting out of the parents' house, away from the nagging and boredom; or marrying into money, to climb up into a more elegant social set.

This kind of marriage is not a thing of the past, I am sorry to say. I hear complaints of having married that way more often from women than from men, but men complain of having made this mistake as well.

There may be real advantages in a marriage besides getting

along together. "Practical considerations," as people used to say. Don't turn anybody down just because he or she has money! But where these "sensible" marriages work there are couples who enjoy each other's company. Being together makes them happy. They just didn't let the other advantages stand in the way.

THAT CERTAIN FEELING

The sight of her brushing her hair sets you a-tingle. It is a sexual excitement that amazes you.

You see him striding along the street, going to an appointment. The way he moves does it for you! It's the basic male appeal. You feel weak and wonderful at the same time.

That is the strong, unexplainable thing that does happen, and it can be a very strong element in a marriage when other good elements are present. This male-female appeal or sexual bond may be the strongest thing in a marriage. But it doesn't have to be in a marriage for the marriage to turn out well.

All the other good reasons for marrying can add up to a good marriage prospect *without* that strong sexual attraction. I say this because there are many good reasons for marrying, and many people want to marry, but they feel cheated of that old Hollywood thrill that they always thought *had* to be there.

When you like a person enough to want to be with him or her most of the time, when you want to go to bed with such a person, the indications are good for marriage. And I have heard it so often— "He began to look better to me with time. You know, I think he is really handsome now." I heard that from one woman whose husband really was handsome! She just hadn't seen it when they first married—not the style she had in mind.

People who also love talking to each other have a stronger reason for marrying than people who are only powerfully attracted to each other sexually. After all, you have to talk together much more than you have to have sex together.

MAKING LISTS OF SEXUAL DESIRES

There is another kind of list I have people make sometimes, when sexual difficulties have come up between them, or when they are considering marrying but with some doubts about the sexual aspect.

I sometimes suggest to people that they make a detailed list of what they want and expect in their marriage. It is important to make the list honestly and realistically. Not to look at the relationship only with the rosy glow of love but also with a hardheaded practicality. Make the list as you might make a list of what you want when considering taking a new job or going to school, or buying a house or a car. It is important to ask yourself honestly what you want, what you don't want, and where you are willing to compromise. The compromising is the important part, because you do have to be flexible.

In a sexual relationship it is important to be willing to go along with the other person's sexual preferences from time to time. Partners should openly discuss their preferences with each other when they are considering marriage. Of course, nothing is carved in stone. Sexual tastes do change. But such sexual discussions and comparisons can be a healthy starting point. Some couples exchange their sexual checklists and then compare them to get an idea of how sexually compatible they really are.

THE ART OF COMPROMISE

When one man made up his sexual checklist, one of the things he listed was that he wanted to have sex every night. Another thing that was important to him was that his wife have an orgasm during every sexual encounter. When he showed his list to his wife, she was surprised and troubled. "What happens if I'm not in the *mood* for sex every night?" she worried. "And what if I *don't* have an orgasm every time?"

Having an orgasm during every sexual encounter was not important to her. She realized there were going to be times when it wouldn't happen. And she explained to him that she didn't mind pleasuring him to orgasm when *he* was in the mood but she wasn't. It would be all right with her if he just lay back and let her pleasure him.

He realized that he was being too rigid in his demands and that his wife's outlook was much more realistic. The compromise they worked out satisfied them both.

If, however, one of the partners is so rigid about sex as to be unable to accept some compromise, there may be difficulties already built into that relationship. If, for example, one of the partners feels that sex is an unpleasant duty that should only be performed once every month, or only in one position, or only in one specific setting, or only at one specific time, there is a problem in the making.

DYSFUNCTIONS, DISABILITIES, AND MARRIAGE

People who have sexual dysfunctions, such as premature ejaculation or vaginismus, should discuss it with their partners *before* marriage.

Since the therapy for many sexual dysfunctions requires that two partners work together over a period of time and with a great deal of understanding and patience, it is only realistic to discuss the problem before getting married. If your potential partner is unwilling to work with you on the problem, it is not a good idea to marry.

But the person with the sexual dysfunction has to *want* to deal with it. For example, if a woman says to a sex therapist, "The reason I'm here is because my husband wants me to learn how to have an orgasm," chances are very slim that she will overcome her problem. She has to want to overcome it for herself. Similarly I sometimes see men who say they want to learn how to overcome their problem of premature ejaculation because their wives want them to. In that case the prognosis is not good, either. *He* has to want to learn how to control his ejaculation.

Someone with a nonsexual disability should discuss that with the potential partner. It is unfair and unrealistic to expect your spouse to find out that you have a waste-disposal bag strapped to your leg only *after* the wedding. Your partner has to be able to adjust to the problem before marriage. You would want a partner to be equally honest with you.

A DIFFERENCE IN SEXUAL APPETITES

The woman was in love with the man, and they had discussed getting married, but she was troubled by the fact that his sexual appetite was much less than her own. During the two years they had known each other she had wanted sex every day, and often several times a day. He was content to have a sexual encounter only once or twice a week. She worried that their marriage might be a big mistake for both of them.

After some counseling, they realized that he could satisfy her even if he himself wasn't sexually aroused, that he could hold her and hug her and kiss her and bring her to orgasm manually or orally without being sexually aroused himself. At first they both thought there was something wrong with one-sided pleasuring. But since they did love each other very much and were suited so perfectly for each other in every other way, they realized there was nothing wrong with dealing with this one mismatch in their tastes in the best way possible.

Again and again people tell me they love each other when there is some persistent sexual difficulty. I believe them, and the more I work in this field the more I believe them. People love each other when there are sexual difficulties. People love each other even when there is no sex between them. Gay men and lesbian women have had long heterosexual marriages with great love and not just to have a "cover." Now, I could talk ponderously about companionship and mutual tastes and ambitions and ideals, but the truth is that love remains a mystery.

And when two people love and want to have mutually satisfying sex, in most cases they can have what they want. This is one of the ways in which "Love will find a way."

The very special and private way that two people "make love" or "have sex" is a strong bond.

AND THEN THERE ARE THE IN-LAWS

It is a fact of life, happy or unhappy, that to some extent you marry not only a person but the person's family. Usually you do have some kind of relationship with your spouse's parents and other relatives. And while how you get along with in-laws may not be a *deciding* factor in whether or not you marry someone, such relationships are a factor. Here is a thing that happens fairly often in this age of frequent divorce.

One woman's childhood had been unpleasant and she admitted that she had married her husband not so much because she liked him as because she liked his warm, loving family and wanted to be a part of it. After a few years they divorced, and she was surprised when his family turned somewhat cold to her. In-laws *are* a factor in marriage, but a factor that should be kept in the proper perspective.

THE IMPORTANCE OF TIMING

To the question "Would you marry you?" should be added the word *now*.

There are times in life when people may not be able to devote time and energy to working at a relationship. And a marriage really needs to be worked at.

It is usually not wise to marry someone who has just recently been divorced and is still somewhat lost and disoriented. A man or woman who is single-mindedly devoted to the struggle to start a business or to advance in their profession or to complete a degree may not be able to give the thought and emotional effort necessary to begin a marital relationship.

If the time does not seem right, but the person does, there is nothing wrong with waiting for a while. Marriage needs to be built upon a good relationship, and good relationships will not be hurt by the passage of a little time.

After all, wouldn't you wait for you?

23
RECIPE FOR A SEXUAL MARRIAGE

"For a *sexual* marriage?" you are probably asking. "What else? What other kind is there?"

Maybe you really don't know! Forgive me for being obvious if you *do* know. Many, many marriages have all the appearance of contentment, of being a good way of living for both partners, a mutually supportive, affectionate pairing. The couple smile and only have those little disagreements you might expect. You see them kiss and get along pleasantly. And this is not just a hollow show for the world, either. They are company for each other in the home they share, better than turning on the radio for a human sound, better than living alone with a few plants or a cat for company. They perform many good services for each other—one drives, the other is good at handling the bills and the income tax. If a party is going to be given, they help each other pretty up the house or apartment and share the shopping. One reminds the other of a dental appointment. One can call the other to pick up clothes at the cleaner or a book at a downtown bookshop. In hundreds of little unlisted ways they do things for each other, and most of all they provide each other with the decent appearance of a marriage that helps each partner maintain self-respect.

Of all your friends, you might say from time to time, they are certainly the likeliest to stick together, as they have the most successful marriage.

You may never learn differently. The big surprise that they are splitting up may never disturb the picture you have. But what you don't know is that although it is a marriage in many sound ways, the sex is missing. Their marriage is an example of the amazing adaptability of human beings to special circumstances, to disappointments and deprivations. Their life together is not as strange as some others that you have seen or heard about. They are not hermits or solitary livers, not sexual adventurers who live essentially by themselves in an unshared world, not perpetual wanderers.

They may not even be truly disturbed by the lack of sex in their lives; they may have swallowed that disappointment and absorbed it. Or they may be living with a certain amount of rankling bitterness between them that is seldom expressed.

Sometimes marriages like that go on to the end. Nowadays it is more common for the sexless marriage to come apart at some time, or to come to some kind of crisis.

Please read this letter from one of my listeners, which I read over the air:

"Dear Dr. Westheimer: I don't know who to go to so I decided to write you about our problem. About two years ago, my husband gradually lost interest in having sexual intercourse with me. The few attempts he did make failed miserably. He refused to go for help. I went for a consultation but the therapist told me that both partners need the treatment and that we shouldn't wait too long or else the problem would get worse. My husband finally told me he went for a physical examination, and the doctor said he didn't have a physical problem. As time has gone on, my husband shows less and less attention to me and very rarely expresses a desire for oral sex.

"Our lovemaking was never all that great to start with, but now I'm feeling neglected, and cool whenever he does attempt to make love. I feel that will lead to more frustration. He once told me that he knows he's not impotent and that it will work out. He feels that after being married for thirteen years this kind of thing isn't so unusual. He tells me he loves me, not often. But he has put this problem on the back burner, so to speak. We do not have children. To all people who know us we seem to be a happily married couple and are except for this problem.

"He has also mentioned that my 'excessive cleanliness' in the house bothers him. I have tried to relax on that issue as much as I can but I feel that there is more to it than these things. I sincerely doubt that he is having an affair or that he is gay. Please tell me what you think we should do. This is on my mind constantly, and I do not want to get to the point that I would look to other men for sex. We are both in our mid-thirties and shouldn't be wasting our precious youth with sex lives like this. Please help me.''

"This is a serious problem," I told this listener over the air, "and I would agree with you not to let it slide, under *no* circumstance. First of all, you are in your thirties, and, even if you were older, I would say that there is something that is probably not physical, since your husband did go for a checkup. It could very well be that when he did have the sexual episode where he failed, that he—when you said he 'failed miserably'—that he feels really miserable about it. And it may be that every single time now that he attempts to have sex, that he is so worried about failing again miserably, that he is just not daring to attempt.

"When he tells you he knows that there is nothing wrong with him, that he's not impotent, it probably means that he knows that he does have erections—maybe sometimes in the morning, maybe not every morning, but sometimes in the morning. And also what it does tell me is that there are some other reasons for it.

"Now, I would certainly agree with you that you can't just make a solution or a discussion by just thinking that he is probably not having an affair, or that probably he is not attracted to men. I would have a *very* calm discussion with him, saying, 'Look, we *both* need to go to a therapist.' There are plenty of psychosexual clinics and psychosexual therapists available to at least have a consultation. And I do agree that you both should go for such a consultation. If you need the address of private therapists, please do write to me at 30 Rockefeller Plaza, New York, N.Y. 10020, and I will send you a list of therapists. Otherwise, New York Hospital–Cornell Medical Center and Mount Sinai and some other hospitals do have human sexuality programs available. Do not think that this is something that will just disappear by itself. I also don't think that the excessive cleanliness alone is a reason for this unhappiness and for this problem.

"In the meantime, I do hope that you do masturbate, that you bring yourself to sexual satisfaction, that you do keep the interest in sex alive. And do insist, because, after all, you seem to have a good relationship—you have been married for thirteen years. It is really a pity to just take the solution of just going out and looking for another man, even if it is just for sex. I really do hope that I will hear from you and that you are not just going to let this slide. Thank you very much for writing."

His complaining about her "excessive cleanliness" is a kind of thing I hear very often. With a problem on his hands as big as his married sex life going dead, he picks on a little thing. Something that is either a minor fault or an excessive virtue, which may be very irritating to him, but not as serious as the sex life that is down to oral sex, few and far between. A house so clean it seems more like a showroom, or a person who jumps up and cleans ashtrays or puts things back in place that you are using, or cleans while you are trying to read, can be very irritating. Perhaps he thinks, I'm impotent, and you're cleaning the house, that's all you care about me. But I have also heard marriage partners complain of having to live in disorder and dust, when the big issue was being avoided.

He may be having an affair. He may be paying a prostitute for something. This, while symptomatic, is not of the first importance; the total lack of sex, or near-total lack of it, with his wife, is the real issue. He may be and probably is having sex with himself, which is less demanding than facing failure in the bedroom.

Therapy may bring this couple back to having a sex life again, if the husband can be talked into wanting to repair the damage that has been done. But if they had been following a recipe for a sexual marriage, a marriage that meets the sexual needs of the partners, things would not have come to this.

What would a recipe like that be?

Everyone who cooks in a home—pardon me, I almost said every housewife!—has recipes that have been adapted to the taste of the cook or the family, and a recipe for a sexually happy marriage would, in use, undergo little changes. But I think this recipe would be of use, with little changes made by the couple, in most marriages where the couple live together, meet every evening, and say good-bye every morning. (Well, a sailor and his wife don't do that, do they? They would have a different set of problems and pleasures!)

• Before marriage, or early in the marriage, establish the custom of discussing sex as a common interest. This can begin by buying a good illustrated how-to sex book and reading it together and discussing it. I would like it if rabbis and clergymen suggested this to couples in those premarriage counseling sessions they have. They could tell couples that this is a serious matter, as serious as managing the family income; that marriages are made and broken in the bedroom, and that every couple should get in the habit early of talking about sex in general and their own sex in particular.

• On their calendar the couple should mark one day in each week for sitting together and going over their common business—bills, budget, errands to be run, appointments, plans for trips or recreation, etc. Now, this is a good thing in itself, but it has a purpose in establishing good regular habits that carry over into their sex life.

• Just as they have a regular night for family business, let them have a regular date for sex discussion, or sex appreciation, or sex self-education. This should be regarded as seriously as the other meeting about bills and such, and if it has to be missed on a Tuesday, then it should be rescheduled for another day. You think I'm kidding? I'm not. Now, it may not be easy to sit down and say "Okay, sex. You say something." So something should be scheduled for that session. A new book or magazine article can be discussed. Or, if that seems a bit too heavy to do every week or every two weeks, try something else: go to a movie that is reviewed as being about a sexual relationship; or go to a museum or art gallery where nudes and love scenes are on display; or shop for pictures that are erotic in nature (they need not be porno, they can be respectable pictures you can hang on the wall and leave there no matter who is coming to dinner). Whatever the couple does to make use of this date should be in the realm of sex discussion, education, appreciation, and fantasy—*not* a workout on the bed or even on the kitchen table! After all, the problem is not that people don't make attempts at sex but that they don't have a habit of talking about it on many levels. They can make the widest, most imaginative use of this sex-talk date—each might write a poem or a short essay on some sex topic, for instance, or they might go for a walk to spot lovers, the way bird-watchers spot birds on their walks. But make an institution and a ceremony of considering sex together.

• The television set must be tamed, kept in its place. Let it sit dark and silent unless there has been a discussion of what is on and what is worth watching. Turn and turn about, of course—let each partner have a night for picking the programs. But don't let the set run all evening on any night. Decide what to watch and set a limit of one or two hours. And don't watch the eleven o'clock news! And have at least two nights a week when you don't turn the set on at all, but sit together reading, listening to music, in an atmosphere in which one may speak to the other if a thought occurs to them. You'd be surprised how much there is to say if the TV isn't on.

• Every day one must send the other a message. Take turns. It can be a phone call, and it must have something in it besides "Okay, this is the call." *Invent.* "Baby, I'm at Forty-second, and I'm looking at my shoes. I had them shined by an old guy in sneakers, and they look great." Or if you miss the phone call, write a note and put it on the refrigerator or the bathroom mirror. "Honey, I became sexually aroused looking at your picture on my desk. Do you think we could do it in the office sometime?" Or just "I passed that fruit stand where we bought the cherries that time when your heel broke, and the fruit stand man is still there and the drop is still on the end of his nose." Man or woman, think of *something* for the daily message. You think I'm kidding about this, don't you? I'm not.

• The one who goes out all day must bring home dessert. Who knows what it will be? It doesn't have to be a serious dessert, maybe it shouldn't be (calories). But the one at home never knows what dessert will be. It's the other person's choice and responsibility. A ceremony, a daily surprise, a little joke or lightness every day. If both go out to work, let the one who isn't going to do the main dinner-fixing bring dessert.

• Bedtime: a time set aside, planned for some love. Big-time sex sometimes, just holding each other and talking sometimes, maybe a little sexual appetizer or dessert without the main course. This is why you skip the news at eleven, so there will be time.

• Massage. Everybody can use a massage. If you don't like it, try it—you'll like it! Get a book and practice back massage, all-over massage, hand and foot massage. This is great for tired or aching bodies and isn't always sexy—it's mutually pleasing physical contact, though.

• Position of the Month. Every month, try a new position. This can get silly. It should. But why should you not be the most versatile lovers in the world? The last day of the month put a secret symbol only you two know on the calendar. That means you tried your new position that month.

• At least once a month, do it out of the bedroom! Take turns deciding how and where. Plan it or make it a surprise, but don't miss this exciting event.

• Buy a little notebook and use it just for keeping track of these monthly encounters. Keep entries in it of places where you had sex and the date. Like this:

5/7/84—At Bill and Sally's while baby-sitting so they could see a show.

8/13/84—In the cove at Ogunquit.

11/11/84—At the Red Lion Inn, Stockbridge, MA.

This is good as a record, because it will show how well you are keeping this up!

• Trade favors once a month. This is doing what the other thinks up. It's her turn, and she says, "I want you to massage my feet and paint my toenails, then when they're dry, turn on an all-music station and go down on me while I read *Cosmopolitan* and eat an apple." It's his turn, and he says, "I'm in a motel with a sleep mask on, and someone, I never see her, comes in, gets me up, and does me."

• Once a month have a Complaints Hour. Very solemnly sit down and tell each other what it is you want and what it is the other is doing wrong—housework, public decorum while you're walking on the street, *sexual behavior*—always include the latter. Now, this is silly, of course, but do it. And if there are no real complaints, clown it up, invent. Because sometime there will be a real complaint, and this will be the established time for registering complaints and neither should be stiff or shy about dealing with this.

• Eat out together twice a month, without anything else on the program—just sharing a meal with no cooking before or dishes after, strolling a little before and after instead.

• Let each partner have an outside activity, together with or apart from the other. A night course, a camera club, a woodworking class, drawing class, community playhouse (where you can always do stagecraft if you can't get a part), church or synagogue, hospital volunteer work, political club work, service organization work.

• Listening training. Married people have a listening problem. One or the other doesn't listen while the other is talking. Learn to listen. Let each partner have the privilege of saying "It's my turn, angel, and your eyes are glazing. Stop thinking about the office." Keep at each other to listen, and give each other little quizzes (in a friendly way) about what has been said now and then. Learn the names of the other one's friends and associates, the people he or she talks about. And practice *listening*.

I have two things to say about listening. I know a man who charms every woman he meets. Simply by taking an interest in what she says, listening when she talks, and asking good questions about what she has said.

The other is, one of the signs of a good actor is that he looks as if he's listening when the other actor is speaking. This makes for reality on the stage. I told an actor I know that he listened well on stage. How did he do it, what was his trick? "I really listen," he said. "It's the best way."

Good listening practice: turn on a talk show, something rather dry and informative, not a junk show, and practice listening. Don't let your mind wander. When the session is over, turn off the set and write down notes of what you have heard as best you can. Just notes, not a text. Just what you *can* recall. Then ball up the sheet of paper and throw it in the wastebasket.

When you talk to people, make a point of listening and then saying something back that shows you have listened, that you have been thinking about this thing that is of interest to the other person.

A trained listener gets to really be interested in what the other person is saying. In a marriage it works wonders to have this ability. You can pick up threads of conversation months later. Your whole life together is a long conversation, interested and interesting.

I need hardly say that this ability to listen will do no harm in your work, whatever it may be. Maybe not sculpting but certainly in any job where you deal with people.

When your love mate is the person you like to talk to, the conversation becomes the marriage. And it is the great problem-solving medium. When you talk together and talk out problems of all sorts, it is much, much easier to deal with sensitive differences that come up between you.

- When talking about sex, always be courteous. You may frolic a bit, but remember that this is a subject about which everyone is sensitive. *Everyone.* That is the safest rule to go by in life! Though you share bed, bathroom, and each other's private parts, when sex is the subject, act as though you were dealing with a customer, a client, someone you can persuade but cannot afford to offend.

- Never demand sex. Ask for it, suggest it, never demand. Flirt, play in the erogenous zones at the back of the neck with fingertips, whatever, but don't demand.

- Always use the tactful way to say things in bed. One woman gets tired of being poked for an hour, gets dry inside, begins to wish he'd stop showing how long he can keep it up. She feels like saying "Come, already!" But she doesn't. She says, "Oh. Oh. Oh! That's so exciting! Come!" There is a tactful way of saying anything.

- Never argue in the bedroom. Make it a rule between you, so one can say "Not in here, darling." What if you live in one room? Then not on the bed—or find some way of separating the place or time sacred to sex from the place and time for a good squabble.

- Have a rule never to go to sleep mad. There must be an apology, an acceptance of the apology, a touch or a kiss before sleep. So that you both *can* sleep. Not lie there losing sleep and burning up.

It's a great thing to have rules to go by, instead of floundering through life, trying to deal with these subtle relationships with no guidelines or landmarks. Settle on a set of rules early in your marriage or relationship, whether it's your first, your second, or your fifth.

And don't worry about seeming pedantic or silly with all the rules and ceremonies. You won't; the most graceful people in the world are following long-practiced rules they have learned and grown used to.

24
YOUR
SEXUAL I.Q.

I think it's always fun to take a test when nobody is going to give you a grade or flunk you, just to see how much you know about something, particularly if it's a test about something you are really interested in—like sex!

There are one hundred questions here, all True–False, not essay questions, so you can take this test sitting in an easy chair or lying back nice and comfy on your sofa or in bed. The answers are given right under the questions, so you can check whether you were right or wrong right away. If you like, you can hold a card over the answer to make sure you don't see the answer, so you don't cheat too much.

After reading this book, you should get a pretty good mark, and after taking the test once and reading the answers, you should get even a better mark next time, if you give yourself the test again—which I doubt. And it can be fun to give the test to a friend.

It wouldn't do to get one hundred right out of one hundred questions, that would be showing off and too boring! And no one would believe you, since you gave yourself the test on the honor system.

So do take the test, and see how sexually literate you are.

1. In this age of sexual equality and liberation, it is the woman's job to use the contraception because, after all, she's the one who might get pregnant.

True
False

Answer: False and rotten! The responsible male is ready to provide the contraception at all times—condoms by choice. Especially in casual sex, where it also helps protect him against herpes and other sexually transmittable diseases.

2. A woman can't get pregnant the first time she goes all the way.

True
False

Answer: False—absolutely. Just like in an old movie, in real life she can get pregnant the first time she has sex. One time is all it takes if a sperm cell and egg cell get together.

3. A woman can't get pregnant if she has sex standing up.

True
False

Answer: False. The spermatozoa, or sperm cells, can travel straight up as well as down, east, west, north, and south, once they get into the vagina.

4. A young man should get hold of a condom and keep it with him so that he's always ready, even if he has to keep it for years.

True
False

Answer: False. Don't count on a condom for more than a three- or four-month pocket life. Rubber deteriorates and springs leaks, and rubbing against your behind in your jeans wears a condom out.

5. A menstruating woman can be impregnated.

True
False

Answer: True.

6. A certain famous carbonated soft drink can prevent pregnancy if used as a douche after sex.

True
False

Answer: False. Not before or *after* sex—only if drunk *instead*. That goes for any other soft drink as well.

7. A woman can get pregnant having sex if she doesn't have an orgasm; even if she has a totally boring time and goes home mad.

True
False

Answer: True. The sperm cells and egg cells don't care whether you have a good time or not.

8. If the man withdraws his penis before he ejaculates, like Onan in the Bible, the woman won't get pregnant.

True
False

Answer: False. Someone had given Onan a bum steer. She can get pregnant and very well may, because at least a drop of semen oozes into the vagina before the man ejaculates.

9. If a boy has pimples, it means he masturbates.

True
False

Answer: False. He could be the one boy in the ninth grade who doesn't masturbate (it's possible) and still have pimples, or he could be the champ masturbator in the school and hardly ever sport a zit.

10. If your goal is to grow hair on your palm and you are a boy, masturbating will not help.

True
False

Answer: True. The same applies if you're a girl, as a matter of fact.

11. It is not true that masturbation causes blindness, baldness, idiocy, and impotence.

True
False

Answer: True. That is all false.

12. Through masturbating women can learn to have orgasms.

True
False

Answer: True. That is a standard sex therapy technique.

13. Male masturbation has been linked to premature ejaculation.

True
False

Answer: True, the theory being that boys acquire the habit of ejaculating as soon as possible to avoid being caught.

14. It is bad for a man's health to let an erection just die down or go away.

True
False

Answer: False. Knowing this allows a man to avoid a sexual encounter that he might regret later.

15. If a man gets an erection in a woman's presence, it means they are meant to have sex together.

True
False

Answer: False. A man has freedom of choice in this. And so does the woman.

16. Frequent erections for no apparent reason are a good sign.

True

False

Answer: True. A sign of sexual vigor.

17. A woman should writhe and buck and act wild during sex to show she is not frigid.

True

False

Answer: False. She may do all that if she is really having a good time, but faking it can lead her mate to think he is satisfying her when he isn't. This can lead to endless frustration for her until she is forced to admit that she was acting—if she ever gets the courage to do so.

18. When a man no longer gets an erection from looking at a centerfold or from thinking up an erotic scene, he can still hope to have good sex for years to come.

True

False

Answer: True. The loss of psychogenic erections is not the end. Physical stimulation can still produce a very strong, serviceable erection.

19. When a couple have a good standard sexual routine, they should stick to it and not try out others.

True

False

Answer: False. It is wise to develop a a varied sexual repertoire to avoid sexual boredom.

20. Swallowing semen is harmful.

True

False

Answer: False. It is a slightly nutritious substance with nothing harmful in it.

21. A woman can get pregnant from swallowing semen.

True

False

Answer: False. The semen will meet up with no egg cells in the woman's stomach or alimentary tract.

22. Cunnilingus (going down on a woman) can be dangerous to the person performing it.

True

False

Answer: True. But you run the same risk when you kiss someone. You could pick up herpes organisms that way, for instance, yet cunnilingus is not of itself dangerous.

23. Since they are harmless, fellatio (going down on a man) and cunnilingus are sexual variations everyone should be willing to take part in.

True

False

Answer: False. "Should" doesn't come into it. These things are harmless if people want to do them; no one "should" do them if they go against the grain.

24. To avoid Kaposi's sarcoma one must avoid all anal intercourse.

True

False

Answer: False. To avoid this disease, avoid anal sex with people who may have it—in short, with strangers or people known to be promiscuous.

25. A considerate man avoids all sex with a pregnant woman.

True
False

Answer: False. If the pregnant woman desires some form of sex during pregnancy and the obstetrician has not forbidden it, it is considerate to *have* sex with her. Lying on top of the mother-to-be and any violent actions should be avoided.

26. Basically, men are repelled by pregnant women.

True
False

Answer: False. Many men are *attracted* to women in this condition. Being repelled by them is far from being a basic male attitude.

27. A couple must work to keep their sexual appetities at the same level.

True
False

Answer: False. This could lead to a great deal of resentment. Different levels of sexual appetite are common in marriages. Couples can accept sexual encounters in which one partner gives pleasure to the other without taking full part—that is, without orgasming.

28. The great ideal for lovers to dream about and yearn for is for both partners to be brought to orgasm at the same moment.

True
False

Answer: False. This cooked-up idea has done a lot of harm, creating totally unreal feelings of inadequacy. It is a pleasure sometimes to come together, when it happens. It is also a pleasure for each lover to observe the other coming to climax at different times.

29. If your partner doesn't have an orgasm during sex and you don't know why, you should be concerned.

True
False

Answer: True, and you should try lovingly to bring the partner to orgasm but not stubbornly or at great length without encouragement. Let the partner guide you in this. And later, away from the bedroom, in a good, intimate mood, discuss this and find out what the partner wants.

30. It is wise to agree that sometimes either partner may bring the other to orgasm without having one him or herself.

True
False

Answer: True. But it should be understood, so that one partner is not unwillingly left unsatisfied and so that neither partner ever feels that his or her loving is undesired or inadequate.

31. In a loving relationship neither partner should ever beg off having sex.

True
False

Answer: False and ridiculous. There *is* such a thing as being really too tired or not in the mood. In a loving relationship either partner can take "No, thanks, not tonight, honey," without fearing the relationship is coming apart.

32. A woman can pretty well tell if a man has orgasmed.

True
False

Answer: True, by his having an erection, rising excitement, orgasmic cries and shudders, and the erection leaving.

33. A man can tell if a woman has orgasmed equally well.

True
False

Answer: False. Since she has no pronounced signs to give, like the penis erect and wilting, the man has to take it on faith that she is really having a climax and not "acting" one. This is one reason why talking about sex away from the bedroom is good, to learn her true feelings about the sex between them.

34. You should *never* have sex just to please your partner.

True
False

Answer: False. Why not? Doing this favor is a way of showing love. But you should reserve the right to beg off if you are really "out of it."

35. Freud said a mature woman would have a clitoral orgasm, an immature woman would have a vaginal orgasm.

True
False

Answer: False. Freud said the exact opposite—the immature woman had clitoral orgasms, the mature woman vaginal orgasms. Tricky, eh?

36. The above was one of Freud's great revelations.

True
False

Answer: False. It was a mistake and has led to some feelings of inadequacy in women, because the vast majority of women have only clitoral orgasms, and the other is either rare or some sort of vague feeling. Recently there have been reports of a G spot in the vagina, a sensitive area that can be excited and produce something like Freud's vaginal orgasm. But we can take the clitoral orgasm as the standard, reliable orgasm for the present.

37. Statistics show that most women have orgasms during intercourse without additional stimulation.

True
False

Answer: False. Thirty percent of women are capable of this and the percentage seems to be rising with more widespread sexual education. A great many women never orgasm without additional stimulation given by their partners or by themselves.

38. Women who seem unable to have orgasms can learn to have them.

True
False

Answer: True, through sex therapy or self-exploration guided by sex books such as *For Yourself* by Lonnie Barbach.

39. A woman who does not have orgasms from intercourse without additional stimulation does not have a real sex life.

True
False

Answer: False. She can give and receive full sexual pleasure by many means, the commonest being a combination of intercourse and stimulation by hand or tongue or other means.

40. After childbirth, a woman's capacity for pleasure from sex is lessened.

True
False

Answer: False. When she is healed, she can have full pleasure again. Many women report having more pleasure after childbirth.

41. It is harder to give a woman pleasure with a small penis than with a large one.

True

False

Answer: False. The size of the penis has nothing to do with it.

42. Older people can expect their sex lives to change after a certain age.

True

False

Answer: True, but after these changes, sex can go on.

43. After a woman passes menopause, her vaginal walls may become thinner and lubrication may lessen or disappear, but she can still have good sex using lubricants.

True

False

Answer: True.

44. When psychogenic erections stop occurring, the aging male can sometimes have more prolonged erections than before.

True

False

Answer: True.

45. People who are getting on in age must expect that the day will come when sex is a dead language.

True

False

Answer: False. There is no known age limit for sex.

46. Homosexual relationships in childhood or youth indicate homosexual tendencies, and people who have had such relationships should accept being homosexual or bisexual.

True

False

Answer: False. A person must not accept being categorized in this way, and should not categorize himself or herself so. Human behavior cannot be forced into such narrow patterns.

47. Adult episodes of a homosexual nature do not mean that those who have them are homosexuals.

True
False

Answer: True.

48. True impotence in men is very rare.

True
False

Answer: True. Inability to function sexually may only be temporary, and no man should accept the idea of his impotence without trying to get help from a doctor first, then a psychotherapist or sex therapist.

49. A man who can hold an erection for long periods may sometimes extend a sexual encounter until it becomes unpleasant or painful for the woman.

True
False

Answer: True. Whether or not she has had an orgasm, the woman may stop lubricating. This can make friction painful.

50. Sexual partners should never, ever indulge in sexual encounters except in a suitable setting with plenty of foreplay and afterplay.

True
False

Answer: False. In a good relationship, where most sexual encounters involve good foreplay and afterplay in a secure place that sets the mood, a rough-and-tumble, playful quickie now and then adds to variety so essential for keeping a sexual relationship fresh and stimulated.

51. After a prostate operation, a man is impotent.

True
False

Answer: False. If sexual desire was there before the operation, it will be there after. The man can perform as before, except that his orgasms will be "dry"—he won't ejaculate into the vagina. His ejaculate will go into his bladder instead. The pleasure is as great as it was before.

52. Hospital patients and disabled people are being recognized now as having the right to ask what sexual activities are possible, and to have such suitable sex in the home or in the hospital, though not in all hospitals.

True
False

Answer: That carefully worded statement is true. Some doctors and some hospitals accept and encourage patients to inquire about and have such sex as they can safely have. Yet not all hospitals and doctors. Patients and their families should assert their rights to answers and to such privileges as are available.

53. Thinking of nonerotic matters while having sex, as a means of prolonging erections and delaying ejaculation, does not work very well.

True
False

Answer: True. What a depressing thing to be doing, thinking about something dull or depressing while making love! And it doesn't even work. Premature ejaculation is one thing that pretty nearly always can be cured, by learning to recognize the premonitory sensation, the feeling that says "You're going to come!" and pausing. It takes practice, but a man can learn to control ejaculation.

54. The premature ejaculator can learn to control ejaculation by masturbating gently and stopping, them continuing after the pre-

monitory sensation has passed, but would do better to learn this technique with a willing partner.

True
False

Answer: True. After all, it is in the exciting activity with a partner that the man wants to learn to exercise control. The couple may need guidance from a sex therapist during this learning period.

55. Vaginismus, or fear of the vagina, is a male problem.

True
False

Answer: False. It is a female problem—or it is better to think of it as a mutual problem of the man and the woman. Vaginismus is an involuntary tightening of the vaginal muscles that won't let the penis or anything else into the vagina. It can be overcome gradually with patient persistence on the part of the woman, on her own, and of the man in gentle attempts on that locked door. A sex therapist can be a great help.

56. One should never accept the idea of defeat in approaching a possible sex partner.

True
False

Answer: False. It is best to take risks, but to prepare oneself in advance for the possibility of rejection. You have the right to ask for a date, or later on for a sign of affection or some sexual activity; the other person has the right to decline.

57. In an established relationship one still approaches the partner for sex, or for new forms of sex, or other mutual activities, as taking a risk rather than as something to be demanded and given.

True
False

Answer: True. One must be ready to accept a "No, thanks" from one's lover.

58. A sex therapist can help you to improve your sex life only if you want this improvement for yourself.

True
False

Answer: True. If the wife or husband only comes to the therapist because the other partner wants this improvement, there is little hope of improvement.

59. Sexual boredom does not set in with a relationship that is good in every other way—money, social life, environment, career fulfillment, etc.

True
False

Answer: False. Some couples go on for years accepting sexual boredom as inevitable (which it is not!) while enjoying many other forms of gratification.

60. When a couple has gone without mutual sex for years, it may or may not be possible to start it up again.

True
False

Answer: True. Remarkable recoveries have been made through patient effort, but sometimes it has been too many years and there are too many long-standing resentments. That is why mutual avoidance of sex should be overcome in the early stages.

61. A woman has a right to expect earth-moving orgasms after prolonged foreplay and good intercourse.

True
False

Answer: False. Every orgasm is not like every other orgasm. They vary in intensity, like sneezes. To expect them all to be earth-moving is to court disappointment.

62. With good information and by approaching the event in a mood of mutual exploration, even a virginal couple can make the first sexual encounter a good one, to be cherished in memory.

True
False

Answer: True.

63. In a courtship where there is no premarital sex, the bride- and groom-to-be will do well to exchange confidences and information about sex and first encounters, using a good book on the subject as a guide.

True
False

Answer: True.

64. The first sexual encounters depicted in novels and movies are often very misinforming, leading young people to expect instant admission into full sexual gratification. On the other hand, the discomfort and disillusion women experience in their first sexual encounters have been much overemphasized.

True
False

Answer: True. Many young women are sure they will feel great pain and disappointment, to such an extent that they cannot possibly take any kind of pleasure in this first try at sexual intercourse. The fact is that the discomfort varies widely, and so does the amount of bleeding, which is sometimes hardly discernible.

65. Women who are breast-feeding should not have sex, as they do not have sexual desire or capacity for orgasm at this time.

True
False

Answer: False. After childbirth and healing, many women have very good sexual urges and feel especially close to their husbands.

66. Men who have trouble obtaining or maintaining an erection should abstain from sex longer between sexual encounters to build up desire.

True
False

Answer: False, although a sex therapist will probably prescribe that the man avoid playing the *active* role in sex with his partner for a period. It is not the absence of intense desire that makes keeping an erection so difficult. It is the presence of worry about erections. And you know how hard it is to take the advice "Just don't worry!" The advice itself makes you worry.

67. The missed orgasm is a sexual difficulty of men who come so fast, they can't discern the orgasm.

True
False

Answer: False. The missed orgasm is a woman's problem; it is having an orgasm without having it register as a pleasure. The cure is in learning to know one's orgasms when one has them.

68. A boy cannot have a true erection under the age of six.

True
False

Answer: False. Newborn boys have been observed to have erections.

69. Vaginal lubrication is unknown before puberty.

True
False

Answer: False. Newborn girls sometimes have lubrication.

70. A great lover can bring a woman to orgasm even though she does not want to take pleasure in the encounter.

True
False

Answer: False. I am almost sorry to say this, but even Casanova could not give a woman this physical pleasure if she didn't want him to. I hate to see a legend like Casanova debunked.

71. When you have had great sex with someone, great mutual enjoyment, it means you are meant for each other.

True
False

Answer: False. One of the great heartbreaks of this era of permissiveness has been that of the male or female swinger who thought a great weekend *had* to be part of a great love affair. Talk about stepping off the moving train! The deluded ones can't believe it's all over.

72. A man should never give up hope of improving his sexual performance, with the goal of having erections at will: anywhere, anytime, with anyone. This is his right as a man.

True
False

Answer: False. Even a healthy, well-functioning man is incapable of such machinelike erections.

73. A disfigurement or physical peculiarity should not hold a person back from wooing; it should simply not be mentioned or revealed except in the full glow of all-embracing, all-forgiving love in the privacy of the bedroom.

True
False

Answer: False. A thing of that sort should be told to one's lover before things have gone that far. The involuntary shock or revulsion

314

such a revelation can cause in the love chamber is rotten for both parties. Physical oddities are things people can get accustomed to if given time, however.

74. A good lover is one who will do whatever his or her partner suggests in the way of sexual activities.

True
False

Answer: False. That is not necessary in a good lover. In sexual relations you can perform well without being prepared for everything in the total catalog of human sexuality.

75. A promiscuous lover is missing something, always.

True
False

Answer: False. Not if he or she doesn't notice it. *You* may see that *you* would not like that life—that's different.

76. A person with a high-volume, rapid turnover love life, with many casual sex partners, can experience sexual boredom.

True
False

Answer: True. I have encountered this often in my private practice. Sometimes I recommend fewer sexual encounters, holding off until someone interests the bored one on another level than the sexual. Or I recommend setting aside time for personal relationships, apart from the swift hello, sexual encounter, and good-bye of the swinger's life.

77. The sexual and relationship problems of homosexuals are wildly different from those of "straights."

True
False

Answer: False. In my practice I find almost all the same sexual and relationship problems among gays as among heterosexuals.

78. In modern psychology homosexuality is considered a sexual preference rather than a neurosis.

True
False

Answer: True.

79. According to late reports, certain strains of the herpes virus appear to be resistant to penicillin.

True
False

Answer: False. *All* strains of herpes virus are resistant to *everything*. There is no cure for herpes at present.

80. Herpes symptoms die down and disappear until the victim is reinfected from a fresh source.

True
False

Answer: False. Herpes becomes dormant in the system, and the symptoms reappear periodically, with sometimes months or years between appearances. But you can be infected with a new strain that you haven't had before.

81. Not all gonorrhea organisms can be killed with penicillin anymore; some strains produce a substance that destroys penicillin.

True
False

Answer: True. The disease must be identified by strain or the victim risks using the wrong drug and going into the later, more damaging stages of the disease.

82. There is no cure for the gonorrhea you get from penicillin-resistant gonococci.

> True
> False

Answer: False. There are antibiotics other than penicillin that are effective against the new strain.

83. When gonorrhea is suspected, a culture should be grown from the smear taken from the victim, rather than just taking a smear to examine for the presence of gonococci.

> True
> False

Answer: True. To detect the penicillin-resistant strain of gonococci, the culture must be grown.

84. One can become infected with herpes simply by kissing an infected person.

> True
> False

Answer: True. The disease can be caught through mouth-to-mouth, mouth-to-genital, or genital-to-genital contact.

85. The missionary position has little to recommend it.

> True
> False

Answer: False. It is a very good position, giving a maximum of skin-to-skin, body-to-body contact and good penetration. It probably became overused *because* it is so fine a position. It is only an unvarying diet of missionary position that produces sexual boredom.

317

86. Some older men can maintain erections longer than they could in their youth.

> True
> False

Answer: True. After psychogenic erections are no longer obtainable, some older men find they can maintain erections much longer.

87. Not everyone can satisfy a sexual partner, but certainly everyone can masturbate without instruction.

> True
> False

Answer: False! Many women have never masturbated. In order to use certain exercises in sex therapy, they have to learn how.

88. If her nipples get hard when her father accidentally brushes them, a young woman can't help feeling guilty.

> True
> False

Answer: False. If she recognizes this as a normal sexual reaction unconnected with the fact that he is her father, she will feel no guilt at all.

89. No one should ever feel guilty about his or her sexual behavior.

> True
> False

Answer: False. A moral person will feel guilt about wrongdoing. There is guilt in some sexual activities just as there is in stealing, killing, and so on. The man who leaves a woman with an unwanted pregnancy should feel guilty; the person who infects others knowingly with herpes should feel guilty; the person who cheats on a trusting lover or spouse should feel guilty. A person can feel guilty without wallowing in his or her own remorse, but without the capacity for accepting guilt, a person is not a moral being.

90. Touching is good in a relationship between lovers. All touching is really a form of foreplay—extended foreplay is the term.

True
False

Answer: False. There are all kinds of touches that convey warmth, comfort, "I like you," "I respect you." These are not all part of the arousal technique. Foreplay can be extended for hours. But not to the day before, when you patted your partner for not forgetting to mail a letter!

91. No one ever feels lonely in a relationship when the sex is good.

True
False

Answer: False. The loneliness of people who get nothing but good sex from their partners is one of the ills I deal with most often. Interest, listening, talking, providing company, fondness, these can all be missing, though the basic sex is "great."

92. There is no such thing as being happy without sex.

True
False

Answer: False. But most people do want sex, and they want good sex, and that is what this book is about and what the sex therapist's work is about.

93. Forty years ago oral sex was considered perverse, nasty, foreign; people who tried it wondered afterward if they were normal. Now people often wonder if they are normal if they don't want it.

True
False

Answer: True. And while I consider oral sex a perfectly wonderful variation and very useful in foreplay, no one should feel abnormal for having a strong personal feeling against it.

94. As the general feeling about oral sex has changed, so a person's individual feeling about it may change.

True
False

Answer: True. And if one partner is urging it, the other can say, "Let's do this other thing for now. Perhaps I'll change my feelings in a while."

95. A person should really try to like all kinds of sex to keep variety in his or her sex life.

True
False

Answer: False. A person should not try to do this or that if it really turns him or her off. One should try to find a variety of things that one does like to do with one's partner.

96. If a person has more intense orgasms masturbating than having sex with a partner, chances of a real relationship are poor.

True
False

Answer: False. The intensity of an orgasm is one thing; the need to have closeness, tenderness, acceptance with another human being, is the glue that holds relationships together. Besides, a couple can masturbate together, or pleasure each other with their hands.

97. A good lover has to be able to slip a condom on his rigid penis in the dark, without losing the erection and without the lady knowing what he's doing.

True
False

Answer: False—of course it's false! How many guys are Houdinis? You don't have to pretend there is no condom, that you are doing it without one, like nymphs and satyrs in the woods. The condom is part of it, like drawing the shades and folding back the bedspread, or taking off the clothing. I say make putting it on part of foreplay; let the lady put it on the gentleman. And he can learn to insert her diaphragm, too.

98. Having intercourse with a condom on is like washing one's feet with socks on.

True
False

Answer: False—the loss of feeling is so slight, it's hardly noticeable. That saying goes back to long ago, when condoms were really thick and discouraging.

99. With so much sex on TV and in the movies, people have learned how to have great sex lives.

True
False

Answer: False. These moving images of sex, which are rehearsed and photographed with great care to produce a beautiful sexual ballet, with gorgeous creatures who never stumble over the rug, or get a little clumsy inserting the penis, or do anything like real life, provide a model that people unfortunately take for reality. I say unfortunately, because, of course, their own sex lives are not like that at all.

100. Fear of herpes, the new sexually transmitted scourge, is likely to send us back into a cheerless era of sexual deprivation and repression.

True
False

Answer: False. It would take a long time and something worse than herpes to put *that* cat back in the bag. But people will be more cautious. There is no harm in that.

RECOMMENDED READING LIST

Barbach, Lonnie, Ph.D. *For Yourself: The Fulfillment of Female Sexuality*. New York: New American Library, 1976.

Calderon, Mary S., M.D., and Eric W. Johnson. *The Family Book About Sexuality*. New York: Harper and Row, 1981.

Comfort, Alex, M.D. *The Joy of Sex*. New York: Crown, 1977.

Friday, Nancy. *Forbidden Flowers: More Women's Sexual Fantasies*. New York: Pocket Books, 1975.

————. *Men in Love*. New York: Delacorte, 1982.

————. *My Secret Garden: Women's Sexual Fantasies*. New York: Trident, 1973.

Kaplan, Helen Singer, M.D., Ph.D. *The New Sex Therapy: Active Treatment of Sexual Dysfunctions*. New York: Brunner/Mazel, 1974.

————. *Disorders of Sexual Desire*. New York: Brunner/Mazel, 1979.

Kinsey, A. C.; W. B. Pomeroy; and C. E. Martin. *Sexual Behavior in the Human Male*. Philadelphia: W. B. Saunders, 1948.

RECOMMENDED READING LIST

Kinsey, A. C.; W. B. Pomeroy; C. E. Martin; and P. H. Gebhard. *Sexual Behavior in the Human Female*. Philadelphia: W. B. Saunders, 1953.

Masters, William H., and Virginia E. Johnson. *Human Sexual Inadequacy*. Boston: Little, Brown, 1970.

Silverstein, Charles, Ph.D. *Man to Man: Gay Couples in America*. New York: William Morrow, 1981.

Silverstein, Charles, Ph.D., and Edmund White. *The Joy of Gay Sex*. New York: Crown, 1977.

Sisley, Emily, and Bertha Harris. *The Joy of Lesbian Sex*. New York: Crown, 1977.

Tripp, C. A., Ph.D. *The Homosexual Matrix*. New York: New American Library, 1976.

Vida, Ginny, Ed. *Our Right to Love: A Lesbian Resource Book*. Englewood Cliffs, N.J.: Prentice-Hall, 1978.

Zilbergeld, Bernie, Ph.D. *Male Sexuality: A Guide to Sexual Fulfillment*. Boston: Little, Brown, 1978.

INDEX

A

Abnormal, 267
Abortion, 160, 166
Adolescence, 224, 225. *See also*
　Teenagers.
Affairs
　boyfriend having, 213–214
　with married man, 212–213
　with relative, 18–19, 138–139,
　　211–212
　with teacher, 245–246
Affection. *See also* Touching.
　of parents toward teenager in
　　public, 51–52
Afterglow. *See* Afterplay.
Afterplay, 94–95
　forms of, 98–99
　and multiorgasmic women, 97
　spoiling, 97–98
　tenderness at, 95–97
Age. *See also* Aging.
　and sexuality, 137
Aggressor, woman as, 76
Aging. *See also* Elderly.
　and ejaculation, 131
　and erections, 33, 125–126, 128,
　　129, 130–131
and psychogenic erections, 33, 128,
　129
and sex life, 125–126
and sexual appetite, 130
and sexual desire, 33
Alcoholism, 235
Anal sex, 154
　and disease, 154, 177–178
Anus, stimulating, 92, 153, 154
Aphrodisiacs, 108–109, 115
Appearance, and self-image, 112
Arguments, in bedroom, 295
Arthritis sufferers, and sex, 195–196
Avoidance, sexual, 113, 115–116

B

Babies. *See also* Children.
　sexuality at birth, 33
　and touching, 48, 49
Barbach, Lonnie, *For Yourself,* 27,
　84, 247
Behind (anatomy), 53–54
Birth control pills, 159
Birthday present, 119
Bisexuals, 187, 188
　women, 14–15, 218

Boredom, sexual, 4, 107, 112–113, 311
  and avoidance, 113, 115–116
  from meaningless relationship, 119–120
  relieving, 4–5, 113–115
Bottom (anatomy), 53–54
Breast-feeding, and sex, 312–313
Broken hearts, 217–218
Brown, Susan, 13

C

Carson, Johnny, 9
Chair, intercourse on, 146
Childbirth, sex after, 205, 206, 306, 312–313
Children. See also Teenagers.
  parents discussing sex with, 38
  and parents' sexual activity, 38–39, 79–80
  and sexuality
    at birth, 33
    masturbation, 34
    orgasm, 34
    three-year-olds, 34–35
    touching genitals, 35–36
  and touching, 48, 49
Chin, David, 13
"Cleanliness, excessive," 289, 290
Clitoral orgasm, 84–85, 305–306
Clitoris, 33
  stimulating in intercourse, 45, 88, 146
  stimulating in oral sex, 153
Clothes, and self-image, 112
Coitus interruptus, 37, 164
Comfort, Alex, The Joy of Sex, 5, 19, 106
Commitment, fear of, 280–281
Communication. See also Talking.
  and intimacy, 74
Complaints, talking about, in marriage, 293–294
Compromise, 283–284
Condom, 159, 161–162
  and erectile difficulties, 162

intercourse with, 161, 321
life of, 298
and premature ejaculation, 162
protection from sexually transmittable disease with, 298
slipping on, 320–321
Contraception
  birth control pills, 159
  and coitus interruptus, 37, 164
  condom, 159, 161–162, 298, 320–321
  diaphragm, 155–156, 159, 160
  importance of, 156, 163, 166
  intrauterine device (IUD), 163
  Knaus system, 164
  in later years of life, 167–168
  overdoing it with, 166–167
  rhythm method, 163
  spermicidal foam, 164
  spermicidal suppositories, 163
  taking turns with, 163
  vasectomy, 164–165
  vinegar douche, 3
  when to use, 158
Conversation, leisurely, 104. See also Talking.
Costume dramas, 118–119
Cunnilingus, 152–153
  dangers of, 302
Cupid's arrow, 109

D

Diaphragm, 155, 159, 160
  gel for, 156
  use of, 160
Dildo, 85, 89, 153
Diseases, sexually transmittable. See Sexually transmittable diseases.
Disfigurement, telling partner about, 314–315
Dog-fashion position, 156, 198
Douche, vinegar, 3
Dressing, and self-image, 112
Dr. Jekyll and Mr. Hyde, 74–75
Drug abuse, 235

E

Egg, 157
Ejaculation
  aging and, 131
  controlling, 309–310
  and oral sex, 150–151
  premature, 162, 269–270, 284, 300
Elderly, 122–137. *See also* Aging.
  and changes in man, 125–126,
    130–131
  and changes in woman, 125–126,
    130
  and erection, 33, 125–126,
    130–131
  at geriatric facilities, 133–134
  health, and sex, 136
  and intercourse positions, 131–132
  loneliness of, 135–136
  and masturbation, 123–124,
    135–136
  sexuality of, 132–133
Erection
  and aging, 33, 125–126, 130–131
  controlling, 29–30
  difficulties with, 162, 313
  exercise for maintaining, 57–58
  psychogenic, 33, 128, 129, 301
  random, 32
Erotic quickies, 141–142
Exercises
  Kegel, 149, 198
  for maintaining erection, 57–58
  sensate focus, 57–58

F

Faking orgasm, 37–38
Fallopian tubes, 175
Fantasies, 5, 106
  exchanging, 114–115, 116
Fear of sex, 273
Fellatio, 143–144, 150–152
Female superior position, 146, 147
Fertilization, 157
Fiddler on the Roof, 224
Films, pornographic, 1, 117–118

First sexual encounter. *See* Sexual
    encounter, first.
Flattery, 110–111
Foreplay
  aging and, 125–126
  initiating, 207–208
  lack of, 71–72
Forest, Dr. Jack, on sexually
    transmittable diseases, 174–178
Freud, Sigmund, 84–85, 305–306

G

Games, sex, 106, 116, 118–119
Garters and stockings, 271–272
Gays
  changing ideas about, 181–182
  compared with heterosexuals, 180,
    181–183
  counseling, 185–186, 191–192
  couples, 185–186
  family problems of, 182
  first experience, 182–183
  having heterosexual relationship,
    183–184
  and Kaposi's sarcoma, 177–178
  myths about, 181–182
  sex life of, 180–181
  sexual attraction between, 181
  sexual problems of, 185–190
  and society, 190–191
Genital herpes. *See* Herpes.
Genitals
  children touching, 35–36
  exploring with mirror, 89, 92–93
Geriatric facilities, 133
Gigolo, 25–26
Gonorrhea, 171, 175–177
  diagnosing, 317
  symptoms of, 175
  treating, 316–317
G spot, 305–306
Guilt feelings
  about having first sexual encounter,
    251
  about sexual behavior, 318
  about sexuality, 41–42

H

Health, and sex, 136, 193–194
Heart attack, and sex, 193
Hepatitis, 176
Herman, Fred, 13
Herpes virus, 172–174, 176
  contracting, 317
  effect of epidemic, 321
  epidemic, 171, 172
  symptoms, 173, 316
  treating, 173, 316
Homosexuals. *See also* Gays.
  and Kaposi's sarcoma, 177–178
  myths about, 181–182
  relationship, and effect on future
    relationships, 307–308
  suspecting girl/boy friend of having
    relationship, 14–15, 186
Human Sexuality Clinic (The New
  York Hospital), 187
Hymen, 275–276

I

Illness, and sex, 193–194
Imagination
  as aphrodisiac, 115
  power of, 69–70
  and sex lives, 114–115, 116,
    118–119
"I'm Gonna Wash That Man Right
  Outa My Hair," 111–112
Impotence, 33, 308
Infidelity. *See* Affairs.
Inflammatory pelvic disease,
  175
In-laws, 285
Institute for Human Identity, 179,
  182, 190
Intercourse. *See also* Sex.
  with condom, 321
  pornographic films and, 1
  pornographic magazines and, 1
  positions. *See* Positions.
  varying place for, 4
  varying time of, 4

Intimacy
  at afterplay, 98
  and talking to partner, 74
  touching and, 56
Intrauterine device (IUD), 163
IUD. *See* Intrauterine device.

J

Jaundice, 176
Jewish Family Service, 236
Jews, Orthodox, 24, 62

K

Kaplan, Dr. Helen Singer, 7, 57, 187
Kaposi's sarcoma, 177–178
  preventing, 302–303
Kegel exercises, 149, 198
Kinsey report, 145
Kinsey three, 187
Knaus system of contraception, 164
K-Y Jelly, 197

L

Leisurely conversation, 104
Lesbians, 14–15. *See also* Gays.
  couples, 185–186
  myths about, 181–182
Letterman, David, 9
Listening, 103, 294–295
Loneliness
  of elderly, 135–136
  in relationships, 319
Lonely hearts, 217–218
Lovemaking. *See also* Intercourse;
  Sex.
  first time. *See* Sexual encounter,
    first.
  recreational, 165–166
  sounds of, 77–79
Lubricating vagina, 197
Lubrication, vaginal, 33, 313

M

Magazines
  masturbating to, 270–271
  stimulation by before intercourse, 1
Marriage, 287–288
  compromise in, 283–284
  inadequate feelings in, 277–279
  sexless, 43–44, 288–290
  sexual, recipe for, 290–296
  sexual compatibility in, 283
  sexual disabilities and, 284
  timing and, 286
Married man, affair with, 212–213
Massage, 293
Masters and Johnson
  Human Sexual Response, 36
  and sensate focus exercise, 57
Masturbation, 36, 300
  children and, 34
  elderly and, 123–124, 135–136
  learning, 318
  learning to have orgasm with, 38,
    89, 300
  and magazines, 270–271
  in marriage, 205, 206
  myths about, 34, 300
  and pimples, 299
  and premature ejaculation, 300
  and virginity, 68–69
  while in bed with partner, 16
Men
  and contraception in later years of life,
    167–168. *See also* Contraception.
  and ejaculation. *See* Ejaculation.
  and erection. *See* Erection.
  fertility of, 167–168
Menopause, 167
  vagina after, 130
Menstruation
  myths about, 36
  and pregnancy before, 245
  and pregnancy during, 299
Mirror, exploring genitals with, 89,
  92–93
Missed orgasm, 84, 87, 313
Missionary position, 145, 317
  origin of, 143
  variations of, 145–146

Mr. (Mrs.) Right, 101
Multiorgasmic women, 97
Multiple orgasms, 97, 274
Music, during lovemaking, 77
Myths
  about homosexuals, 182
  about masturbation, 34, 300
  about menstruation, 36
  about pregnancy, 36–37
  about swallowing semen, 152
  about woman's orgasm, 86–87
  about women not needing orgasm,
    37

N

Normal, 267
  questions about what is, 268–276

O

O'Brien, Steve, 13
Oral sex, 319
  cunnilingus, 152–153
  dangers of, 302
  fellatio, 143–144, 150–152
  to man, 143–144, 150–152
    and ejaculation into mouth,
      150–151
    technique for, 144, 274
  new attitudes about, 153
  to woman, 152–153
Orgasm
  bringing partner to, 304, 314
  children and, 34
  clitoral, 84–85, 305–306
  determining if partner has had, 274,
    304–305
  faking, 37–38
  missed, 84, 87, 313
  multiple, 97, 274
  mutual, 303–304
  myths about for women, 86–87
  myths about women not needing,
    37
  never experienced, 26–27, 306
  recommended book about, 27

Orgasm (Cont.)
  vaginal, 84–85, 305–306
  variations in, 311–312
  for women, 306
    aging and, 130
    clitoral, 84–85, 305–306
    at first sexual encounter, 63
    fulfilling, 93
    how it feels, 83–84
    learning to have, 38, 89–90
    multiorgasmic, 97
    myths about, 37, 86–87
    statistics on, 85–86
    vaginal, 84–85, 305–306
Orthodox Jews, 24, 62
Our Bodies, Ourselves, 240, 272
Ovary, 157
Ovulation, 158

P

Paraplegics, and sex, 195
Parents. *See also* Teenagers.
  and affection toward teenager in
    public, 51–52
  discussing sex with children, 38,
    225–227
  explaining sexual activity to
    children who walk in on, 79–80
  overprotective, 253–255
  sexual activity, and their children,
    38–39, 79–80
  strict, 234–235
  and teenagers, 222–238
    attitudes about, 238
    disapproving of girl/boy friend,
      233–234
    discussing bodily changes with,
      226
    discussing menstruation with, 226
    discussing sex with, 225–227
    fostering independence in,
      229–230
    getting them involved in groups,
      224
    offering guidelines about having
      sexual relationships, 231–233
    respecting privacy of, 227,
      228–229

Peanut butter, and sexual desire, 5–6
Peeping Tom, 209–210
Penicillin, 171–172, 175
Penis, 45–46
  curvature of, 275
  negative attitudes about, 45
  size of, 45, 87–88, 268–269
  small, 87–88
  stimulating with pubococcygeus
    muscle, 148–149
  stimulation by, 45, 88
  technique to arouse, 46
  and urine seeping out during sex,
    46
Physical peculiarity, telling partner
    about, 314–315
Pills, birth control, 159
Pimples, and masturbation, 299
Planned Parenthood, 7, 159, 272
"Pleasure muscle," 148–149
Pornographic films, 1, 117–118
Pornographic magazines, 1, 270–271
Positions
  on a chair, 146
  dog fashion, 146
  and elderly, 131–132
  experimenting with, 5
  female superior, 146, 147
  lying side by side, 146
  missionary, 143, 145–146, 317
  rear entry, 176–177
  trying new, 147–148
  varieties of, 145–148
  when pregnant, 146
Pregnancy
  before menstruation, 245
  during menstruation, 299
  at first sexual encounter, 59
  myths about, 36–37
  and reproduction, 157
  sex during, 303
  teenage, 2, 36, 67, 157
  while having sex standing up, 298
  without orgasm in woman, 299
Premature ejaculation
  discussing with partner, 284
  linked to masturbation, 300
  overcoming, 162, 269–270
  using condoms for, 162

Premonitory sensation, 162, 269
Privacy
    individual, 75
    for teenager, 228–229, 243
Prostate operation, and sexual desire, 309
Psychiatrist, aroused by, 22–23
Psychogenic erections, 33, 128, 129, 301
Psychosexual therapist, 7
Pubic hair, 118
Public affection, of parents toward teenager, 51–52
Pubococcygeus muscle, 148–149

Q

Quickie, 140–142
    erotic, 141–142
    as first sexual encounter, 142

R

Radio shows, Sexually Speaking, 2
    calls, 8–9
    letters to, 4–5
    reactions from callers, 9
    theme, 13
Random erections, 32
Rape victim, 15–16, 199
Rear-entry position and infection, 176–177
Recreational lovemaking, 165–166
Relationships, 201–221
    approaching, 202
    taking risks in, 204, 219–221, 310–311
Relatives
    affair with, 138–139, 211–212
    attraction to sister-in-law, 29–30
Religion, and sexual practices of Orthodox Jews, 23–25, 62
Reproduction, 157, 168
Rhythm method of contraception, 163
Risks, taking in relationships, 204, 219–221, 310–311

Robbins, Harold, Dreams Die First, 36
Rocha el Fuso, La, 13

S

Scrotum, 196
Self-image, 53–54
    and appearance, 112
    and liking self, 281–282
    poor, 53–54, 279, 280, 281
Semen, 128–129
    myths about swallowing, 152
    swallowing, 302
Senior citizens. See Aging; Elderly.
Sensate focus exercise, 57–58
Sensitivity training, 99
Sex. See also Intercourse.
    after childbirth, 205, 206
    anal, 154, 177–178
    bad, avoiding, 257–258
    for disabled, 195, 196
    fear of, 273
    and health, 136, 193–194
    and illness, 193–194
    oral. See Oral sex.
    parents discussing with children, 38, 225–227
    physical problems with, 196–200
    positions. See Positions.
    pressure to have, 65–66, 67, 263
    quickie, 140–142
    saying no to, 17–18, 259–260, 263, 304
    sounds of, 77–79, 81–82
    thinking about before having, 256–257, 266
    unable to speak during, 268
    uncontrollable body movements in, 19–20
    urine leaking during, 44–45, 46
    when to have with new partner, 17
Sex education, 7, 10, 264
Sex fantasies, 106
Sex games, 106, 116, 118–119
Sex life
    aging and, 125–126
    enriching, 4–5

Sex life (Cont.)
excluding children from parents', 38–39
married couples without, 43–44, 288–290
Sex therapist, 7
seeing, 31
Sex therapy, 264
Sexual appetite
aging and, 130
differences in, 100–101, 259–260, 284–285, 303
stimulating, 106–108
with aphrodisiacs, 108–109
flattery for, 110–111
with sex games, 116, 118–119
techniques for, 109–110
thinking positively about, 110
Sexual avoidance, 113, 115–116
Sexual boredom, 4, 107, 112–113, 311
and avoidance, 113, 115–116
from meaningless relationship, 119–120
relieving, 4–5, 113–115
Sexual boundaries, 5
Sexual compatibility, 283
Sexual desire, 31–32
absence of, 44
aging and, 33
and expectations in marriage, 282–283
Sexual disabilities, 284
Sexual dysfunctions, 284
Sexual encounter, first, 312
anxiety in, 60, 63
and bleeding, 275–276
discussing beforehand, 64
fears about, 247
in good relationship, 67–68
with inexperienced lover, 63–64
learning from, 70
pain during, 59, 63
and pregnancy, 59
problems of male during, 60–61
and quickies, 142
right time for, 239–241, 251
unsatisfying, 60, 68, 70

on wedding night, 61–62
wondering about performance in, 65
Sexual fantasies, 5, 106
exchanging, 114–115, 116
Sexual feelings, 32–33
at birth, 32
feeling bad about, 39–40
Sexual impulses, 32
Sexual I.Q. test, 297–321
Sexual marriage, recipe for, 290–296
Sexual partner, selecting, 101
Sexual problems. See specific problem.
Sexual publicity, 40–41
Sexual silence, 78, 80–81
Sexual thoughts, controlling, 42
Sexual urges, healthy, 31–32
Sexuality, 33
age and, 137
of elderly, 132–134
misplaced guilt feelings about, 41–42
surrendering to, 89
Sexually Speaking radio show, 2
calls, 8–9
letters to, 4–5
reactions from callers, 9
theme, 13
Sexually transmittable diseases, 169–178
from anal intercourse, 176–178
gonorrhea, 171, 175–177
hepatitis, 176
herpes, 171, 172–174, 176
Kaposi's sarcoma, 177–178, 302–303
syphilis, 171
telling spouse about contracting, 169–171
"Significant other," 102
Singles, disabled, and sex, 196
Sounds of lovemaking, 77–79, 81–82
Spermatozoa, 157
Sperm cells, 157
Spermicidal foam, 164
Spermicidal suppositories, 163
Stockings and garters, 271–272
Surrendering to own sexuality, 89
Surrogate lover, 185
Syphilis, 171

T

Talking
  about sex, in marriage, 291–292,
    295
  during sex, 268, 295
  and intimacy, 74
  intimately with partner, 99–100,
    102–103
  leading to touching, 75–76
  leisurely, 104
  and listening, 103
  to lover about self, 99–100
Tattoos, 119
Teenagers. *See also* Children.
  concerns, 245–255
  and parents. *See* Parents.
  and parents' affection in public,
    51–52
  and pregnancy, 2, 36, 67, 157
  respecting privacy of, 228–229, 243
  rights of (granted by family),
    242–245
  right time for sex. *See* Sexual
    encounter, first.
  sexual experimentation by, 230–231
Tenderness, and afterplay, 95–97
Tests, sexual I.Q., 297–321
Testicles, 196–197
Theme for radio show, 13
Thinking before having sex, 256–257,
    266
  about person you are with, 257,
    265
  when it is not mutual, 260–262
  when you never say no, 263–264
  when you want to say no, 263
Three-year-olds, and sexuality, 34–35
Timing, and marriage, 286
Touching, 319
  babies and, 48, 49
  children and, 48, 49
  "cost-effective," 52–53
  decrease of in marriages, 50, 52–53
  exercises in, 57–58
  importance of, 47, 50
  and intimacy, 56
  inventive, 55–56
  kinds of, 47
  and learning how, 54–55
  and learning when, 54–55
  as medium of exchange, 52
  need for, 49–50
  and need to be touched, 49–50
  talking leading to, 75–76
  too tired for, 56–57

V

Vagina, 44–45
  after menopause, 130
  lubricating, 197
  negative perceptions of, 44
  noises from, 77–78
  and pubococcygeus muscle,
    148–149
  tightening, 148–149, 198
Vaginal fluids, 129
Vaginal lubrication, 33, 313
Vaginal orgasm, 84–85, 305–306
Vaginismus, 63, 284, 310
Vasectomy, 164–165
Venereal diseases, 2. *See also*
    Sexually transmittable diseases.
  gonorrhea, 171, 175–177
  herpes, 171, 172–174, 176
  syphilis, 171
Vibrator
  for men, 92
  for women, 85, 91–92, 153
Vinegar douche, 3
Virginity. *See also* Sexual encounter,
    first.
  losing, 65–67, 241
  and masturbation, 68–69
  religious feelings about, 24

W

Wedding night, 61–62
Westheimer, Dr. Ruth
  accent, 6, 10
  childhood, 6
  education, 7
  radio show, 2, 8–10
  work experience, 7

Wine, 5, 108
"Withdrawal method," 164
Witkin, Mildred, 57
Women
  as aggressor, 76
  contraception for. *See* Contraception.
  elderly, and masturbation, 123–124
  older, aroused by, 22–23
  and orgasm, 306
    aging and, 130
    clitoral, 84–85, 305–306

faking, 37–38
at first sexual encounter, 63
fulfilling, 93
how it feels, 83–84
learning to have, 38, 89–90
multiorgasmic, 97
myths about, 37, 86–87
statistics on, 85–86
vaginal, 84–85, 305–306
Women's Conference Identity House,
218